NIETZSCHE AND
ASIAN THOUGHT

Nietzsche

AND ASIAN THOUGHT

Edited by Graham Parkes

THE UNIVERSITY OF CHICAGO PRESS

Chicago and London

The University of Chicago Press, Chicago 60637
The University of Chicago Press, Ltd., London
© 1991 by The University of Chicago
All rights reserved. Published 1991
Paperback edition 1996
Printed in the United States of America

00 99 98 97 96   5 4 3 2

Library of Congress Cataloging in Publication Data
Nietzsche and Asian thought / edited by Graham Parkes.
    p.   cm.
    Includes bibliographical references and index.
    Contents: The orientation of the Nietzschean text / Graham Parkes
— The other Nietzsche / Joan Stambaugh — Questioning one's "own"
from the perspective of the foreign / Eberhard Scheiffele ; translated by
Graham Parkes — Nietzsche's early encounters with Asian thought /
Johann Figl ; translated by Graham Parkes — Nietzsche and the
suffering of the Indian ascetic / Michel Hulin ; translated by Graham
Parkes — Nietzsche's trans-European eye / Mervyn Sprung —
Deconstruction and breakthrough in Nāgārjuna and Nietzsche / Glen T.
Martin — Zhuang Zi and Nietzsche / Chen Guying ; translated by
James Sellman — Nietzsche's will to power and Chinese virtuality (De) /
Roger T. Ames — The highest Chinadom / David A. Kelly — The early
reception of Nietzsche's philosophy in Japan / Graham Parkes —
Nietzsche's conception of nature from an East-Asian point of view
Ōkōchi Ryōgi ; translated by Graham Parkes — The problem of the
body in Dōgen and Nietzsche / Arifuku Kōgaku ; translated by Graham
Parkes — The eloquent silence of Zarathustra / Sonoda Muneto ;
translated by Setsuko Aihara and Graham Parkes.
    ISBN 0-226-64683-1 (cloth)
    ISBN 0-226-64685-8 (paperback)
    1. Nietzsche, Friedrich Wilhelm, 1844–1900—Knowledge—
Philosophy, Oriental.   2. Nietzsche, Friedrich, 1844–1900—Influence.
3. Philosophy, Oriental.   4. Philosophy, Modern—19th century.
5. Philosophy, Modern—20th century.   I. Parkes, Graham, 1949–
B3318.075N54   1991
193—dc20   90-24809
                                                                CIP

⊗ The paper used in this publication meets the minimum
requirements of the American National Standard for Information
Sciences—Permanence of Paper for Printed Library Materials,
ANSI Z39.48–1984.

In memory of
Nishitani Keiji (1900–1990)
the major precursor

Contents

Acknowledgments

A grant from the University of Hawaii Research Relations Fund, for which I am most grateful, provided fees for the translations of those essays originally written in Chinese and Japanese.

All but two of the essays were written especially for this volume. Chen Guying's contribution was excerpted with some alterations from his book *Beiju Zhexuejia Nicai* (The Tragic Philosopher Nietzsche), and an earlier, rather longer version of Ōkōchi Ryōgi's essay appeared in German in volume 17 of *Nietzsche-Studien*.

My heartfelt thanks go to Tim Freeman for his unfailingly gracious assistance in preparing the manuscript and index.

Abbreviations

AC	*The Antichrist*
BGE	*Beyond Good and Evil*
BT	*The Birth of Tragedy*
D	*Daybreak*
EH	*Ecce Homo*
GM	*On the Genealogy of Morals*
GS	*The Gay Science*
HA	*Human, All Too Human*
KGB	*Sämtliche Briefe: Kritische Gesamtausgabe*
KSA	*Sämtliche Werke: Kritische Studienausgabe*
NCW	*Nietzsche contra Wagner*
PTAG	*Philosophy in the Tragic Age of the Greeks*
TI	*Twilight of the Idols*
UM	*Untimely Meditations*
WP	*The Will to Power*
Z	*Thus Spoke Zarathustra*

In quoting from Nietzsche's works, the authors/translators have used—where available—the translations by Walter Kaufmann and/or those by R. J. Hollingdale. In most cases they have noted any modifications they have made. References to Nietzsche's works are given by abbreviated title and the section or aphorism number, so that the relevant passages may be easily found in any edition. References to the unpublished Nachlass are to Kaufmann and Hollingdale's translation of *The Will to Power* when the passage is to be found there, and otherwise to the volume and note number of the *Kritische Studienausgabe* of *Friedrich Nietzsche: Sämtliche Werke* (München: dtv, 1980).

In cases where the division of the text is twofold, the Roman numeral refers to the larger division (in *EH* and *Z* the part, in *GM* the essay, in *TI* the chapter, and in *UM* the meditation) and the Arabic numerals to the aphorism or sub-section. In *EH* III the chapters dealing with Nietzsche's earlier texts are referred to by the appropriate abbreviations.

Notes added by the editor or translator are preceded by the abbreviations "EN" and "TN" respectively.

1

OTHERS

1

The Orientation of the Nietzschean Text

Graham Parkes

I imagine future thinkers in whom European-American indefatigability is combined with the hundredfold-inherited contemplativeness of the Asians: such a
combination will bring the riddle of the world to a solution. In the meantime
the reflective free spirits have their mission: they are to remove all barriers
that stand in the way of a coalescence of human beings.

Friedrich Nietzsche, 1876

I

The past decade or so has seen a powerful resurgence of interest in the
thought of Friedrich Nietzsche on a global scale. Yet while this revival
has surged along several fronts in the United States and Europe—in
literary theory, psychology, and social and political theory as much as in
philosophy—it has generally been informed by a peculiar parochialism.
To judge from a perusal of the dozens of books and articles on Nietzsche
that appear each month, one would have no idea that his work has had
a significant impact on the intellectual life of any non-Western culture,
or elicited any worthwhile response from thinkers outside the Continental European or Anglo-American philosophical traditions. Only a handful of commentators in the West has had anything to say about
Nietzsche's references—and they are by no means infrequent—to non-
Western philosophies or religions. It would be worthwhile to reflect on
the implications of these references for our thinking about modernity,
and for appropriate orientations toward what is succeeding the modern.

The "and" linking the name "Nietzsche" to the "Asian Thought" in
the title of the present collection is intended to work both ways, relating

Nietzsche's philosophy back to Asian ideas that may have influenced it (and here it is a case only of the Indian tradition), as well as forward to the influence his ideas have had on Asian thought in the course of the past hundred years (in this respect the focus is on China and Japan, where the response has been most sustained).[1] The figure named "Nietzsche" appears to confront what was then called the Near East while looking forward to the Far East of Asia. The Nietzschean text may thus be oriented both with respect to the ways in which threads from earlier, foreign texts have been incorporated into it and with respect to the strands of Nietzsche's ideas that are being woven in turn into the intellectual fabric of East Asia. A number of Nietzsche's latter-day pronouncements concerning the imminent impact of his ideas upon the world convey an uncanny prescience that his influence would extend far beyond the boundaries of Europe. The history of the subsequent decades suggests that the hyper-global resoundings of his rhetoric did not issue merely from the megalomania of impending insanity.

While Nietzsche was more pleased than surprised that his works were nowhere less appreciated than in his native land, it was not long after his mental collapse that his fame spread rapidly throughout Germany, and from there to the rest of the European continent.[2] Indeed, his madness was to a large extent a catalyst for his immediately ensuing fame, especially as it was exploited by his sister Elizabeth for the promotion of the "Nietzsche Cult."[3] By 1888, a year before Nietzsche's collapse, the Danish scholar Georg Brandes had begun to give public lectures on his philosophy in Copenhagen. The many articles and the book on Nietzsche that Brandes went on to publish over the next several years served to develop an intelligent receptivity to the ideas of the "mad philosopher" throughout northern Europe.

Most ardent of Francophiles as he was, Nietzsche would have been gladdened to see the affirmative response his works were soon to attain in France, engendering an interest there that has been more steadily sustained than anywhere else and that has become especially fecund over the past several decades.[4] In view of his love of the South, the reception of his ideas in Latin countries would also have been heartening. A book on Nietzsche in Spain discusses, among other things, his impact on the two greatest Spanish philosophers of the century: Ortega y Gassett and Miguel de Unamuno.[5] Contributions to a volume of papers from a conference on "Nietzsche in Italy" discuss that country's importance for him and, to a lesser extent, the response his works have evoked there.[6] Nietzsche's reception in Great Britain has been the subject of two lengthy monographs, and more detailed studies concerning particular figures in English literature continue to appear.[7] Apart from a doctoral dissertation, however, no major study has as yet been published chronicling the course of his influence on the American intellectual world. It would surely be an illuminating exercise to document the decades up to the appearance of Walter Kaufmann's *Nietzsche: Philosopher, Psychologist, Antichrist* in 1950. And while Nietzsche took a certain delight in the news that his works had been banned in Russia more or less from the time *The Birth of Tragedy* appeared, he could hardly have guessed at the breadth of his subsequent influence in that vast land.[8]

A perusal of the literature would not, however, suggest that the shock waves of Nietzsche's impact on the intellectual and cultural world spread any farther eastward than into Russia—and hardly as far as to the Far East. The revised and expanded edition of the *International Nietzsche Bibliography* purports to include a large proportion of the serious scholarly articles on Nietzsche and "virtually all of the books and monographs that came to [the editors'] attention."[9] Of the twenty-six different languages under which the citations are listed, however, only two are Asian: in the main body of the book there is one entry in Vietnamese and two in Japanese (though both the authors cited in this latter case are European). There is no reference to any of the work on Nietzsche published in Chinese. With the addition of the Supplement, which covers the years 1960–67, twelve titles by Japanese authors find their way into the lists, bringing the total of Asian entries to thirteen—among a grand total of 4566 works listed.

Essays on Nietzsche began to appear in periodicals in Japan while he was still alive, during the last decade of the nineteenth century. Raphael von Koeber, who taught philosophy at the Imperial University of Tokyo, began to talk about Nietzsche in his lectures there during the mid-eighteen-nineties, and in 1897 the Head of the Philosophy Department there, Inoue Tetsujirō, bought an edition of Nietzsche's complete works in Germany and, on his return to Japan, introduced some of the German philosopher's ideas to his students. In 1898 an article appeared in one of the leading literary journals which presented Nietzsche's ideas as a challenge to stimulate Japanese Buddhism to engage in philosophical reflection upon its foundations. Three years later, in 1901, the "aesthetic life" debate broke out, a controversy among the most famous literary figures of the period which raged for over two years.[10] Hundreds of pages of attacks and counterattacks were published; reputations were defamed, careers ruined; mere anarchy was loosed upon the hitherto orderly intellectual world of Japan. And at the eye of the storm, the figure of a recently deceased thinker who had spent the previous decade benighted by madness, gazing almost wordlessly into the invisible.

This was a time at which many students from China were studying in Japan, and several of the brightest returned home full of enthusiasm for the ideas of the German philosopher who had fired such an unprecedented uproar in Japanese intellectual life. The two most eminent figures here are Wang Guowei, who published a book on Schopenhauer and Nietzsche in 1905, and Lu Xun (Lu Hsün), the first of whose many writings on Nietzsche appeared in 1907.[11] These works sparked an interest in Nietzsche in China that has ranged—and often raged—from enthusiastically *pro* to fanatically *contra* and embraced the political spectrum from Left to Right and back again. In the past several years, significantly, the interest in Nietzsche in Chinese intellectual life has enjoyed a special resurgence.

The tragic irony of Nietzsche's fate—that he sacrificed his mental and physical health for the sake of writing books which hardly anyone read during his career, but which became enormously popular shortly after he lost his sanity (in 1889)—is intensified as one comes to learn the history of the enthusiastic reception his work enjoyed in these two East Asian countries about which he knew next to nothing, a reception that burgeoned a mere decade or so after his mental collapse. The handful of works on this aspect of the response to Nietzsche represents a minuscule portion of the literature in Western languages which chronicles and analyzes the impact of Nietzsche's work on the rest of the world. The present collection is intended as an initial contribution toward redressing this imbalance.

II

Thus it would have to be possible to use [Nietzsche's] teachings in any given orientation.

Georges Bataille

The exclusionary character of the current "Nietzsche renaissance" in the West is highlighted in advance by the content of an aphorism Nietzsche himself penned in 1879 under the title "Where one must travel to":

Direct self-observation is not nearly sufficient for us to know ourselves: we require history, for the past continues to flow within us in a hundred waves; we ourselves are, indeed, nothing but that which at every moment we experience of this continued flowing. . . . To understand history . . . we have to *travel* . . .

to other nations . . . and especially to where human beings have taken off the garb of Europe or have not yet put it on. (*HA* II/1, 223)

While Nietzsche was in actuality a nomad for the greater part of his adult life, his wanderings were confined to Europe, and to a relatively small area bounded by the Swiss Alps, the south of France, northern Italy, and his homeland near Leipzig. But his prescription is explicitly deliteralized as the passage continues:

But there exists a *subtler* art and object of travel which does not always require us to move from place to place. . . . He who, after long practice in this art of travel, has become a hundred-eyed Argos . . . will rediscover the adventurous travels of his ego . . . in Egypt and Greece, Byzantium and Rome, France and Germany . . . in the Renaissance and the Reformation, at home and abroad, indeed in the sea, the forests, in the plants and in the mountains. Thus self-knowledge will become knowledge of everything [*All-Erkenntniss*] with regard to all that is past.[12]

While the primary thrust of this call to travel is metaphorical and archeo-psychological, we shall see that there is no reason to exclude India, China, and Japan from the way-stations just enumerated for the intellectual odyssey Nietzsche is recommending.

In Plato's *Symposium* Diotima rehearses to Socrates the various ways in which "what is mortal shares in immortality" (208b). Superior to the crudely literal procreation of offspring is the method that proceeds by achieving honor and glory. But higher still is a "pregnancy of soul" which, stimulated by intercourse with another, beautiful soul, gives birth to wisdom in the form of poetic discourses and ideas (*logoi*)—such as the quasi-immortal children produced by Homer, Hesiod, and other great poets. Platonic parent that he is, Nietzsche is fond of adopting (and adapting) Plato's psychological metaphors, and even in his most "scientific" work he speaks of immortality in a context similar to that of the *Symposium*. In the context of a discussion of "real immortality" he writes of the happy fate of the author

who as an old man can say that all of life-engendering, strengthening, elevating, enlightening thought and feeling that was in him lives on in his writings, and that he himself is nothing but the grey ashes, while the fire has everywhere been saved and borne forward. (*HA* I, 208)

The next aphorism elaborates the idea of the work of art or of thought as a vehicle for a kind of immortality on the part of its creator:

The thinker, and the artist likewise, who has secreted his better self in his works, feels an almost malicious joy when he sees how his body and his spirit are being slowly broken down and destroyed by time; it is as though he observed from a corner a thief working away at his money-chest, while knowing that the chest is empty and all the treasures saved. (*HA* I, 209)

In the well-known discussion of writing in Plato's *Phaedrus*, Socrates contrasts the written text unfavorably with living speech, denigrating it as a bastard form of discourse consisting of "dead" characters incapable of defending or explaining themselves in the absence of the father who engendered them. From a Nietzschean perspective Socrates would appear to be a pathologically protective parent:

Once a thing is committed to writing it circulates equally among those who understand the subject and those who have no business with it; a writing cannot distinguish between suitable and unsuitable readers. And if it is ill treated or unfairly abused it always needs its parent to come to its rescue. . . . (*Phaedrus*, 275e)

Aphorism 208 of *Human, All Too Human* bears the title "The Book Almost Become a Human Being," and its author shows himself to be a relatively relaxed progenitor of vital works:

Every writer is surprised anew how, once a book has detached itself from him, it goes on to live a life of its own; . . . it seeks out its readers, enkindles life, makes happy, terrifies, engenders new works, becomes the soul of new designs and undertakings. . . .

It is instructive to reflect on the changes that such an "almost human" being undergoes when it travels to foreign lands. Rather than move us to complain that the Nietzschean text is inevitably distorted and misunderstood when it is interpreted in an alien cultural context, that readers from a different tradition read too many of their own assumptions into the author's "own" text, the responses of foreign interpreters may serve to open us to hitherto concealed aspects of the corpus. It is interesting enough to contemplate the mutations and adaptations of a strain of plant or species of animal in response to the different conditions of a new environment; how much more can be learned when the creature in question is possessed of an "almost human" intelligence.

III

A growing number of collections of essays on Nietzsche has been appearing recently—a happy circumstance, for the most part, in view of the anthology's being such an appropriate genre for secondary literature on a primarily literary thinker. Nietzsche is above all a writer in many voices, and one problem with books written about his work is that they have been mainly "monological," with the author speaking in only one voice. There is a far greater chance that justice will be done to the polyphony of Nietzsche's thought and the diversity of his styles in an anthology, where an actual multiplicity of different voices is invited to discourse on his texts. The present collection improves the odds still further by bringing a number of voices from East Asia as well as from Europe into the dialogue. The expectation is that such an anthology (the term originally refers to a collection of the flowers of poetry) may lend new bloom and fresh perspectives to our picture of the thinker Nietzsche.

Joan Stambaugh opens the conversation by invoking a figure who has been largely neglected in the scholarly literature: Nietzsche the mystical poet and "poetic mystic." She closes by suggesting an affinity between Nietzsche and the thinkers of classical Daoism, though in the context of a disavowal of explicit comparisons in what has just gone before. Her essay is richly allusive, its initial discussion of Zarathustra's paean to the heaven sounding a chord that evokes immediate and lasting resonances with the idea of "Heaven" (*tian*) in Daoism. Stambaugh suggests, on the basis of a consideration of some of the more mystical episodes in *Thus Spoke Zarathustra*, that an important aspect of *das Fremde* (the foreign, the Other) for Nietzsche may well have been the realm of mystical experience. In this context she adduces some passages from Meister Eckhart and the thirteenth-century Japanese Zen thinker Dōgen which appear, in spite of their very different contexts, to be describing similar realms of experience to those explored by Zarathustra.[13]

In his hermeneutically oriented essay, Eberhard Scheiffele surveys the spectrum of Nietzsche's discussions of "the foreign," which—from the perspective of his "own" German culture—range from France, Italy, and Poland, through Greece and the Near East, to India and China. He argues that Nietzsche's primary concern with other cultures distant in space and time grew out of the hermeneutic enterprise of attaining a better understanding of the contemporary European cultural situation. For that, according to Nietzsche, it is necessary to gain some distance, to exit the familiar and transpose oneself into the realm of the foreign. Scheiffele suggests that Nietzsche's excursions to Asia are less in the interests of an understanding of alien cultures and ways of thinking in themselves than in the service of attaining different and enlightening perspectives on the traveler's home environs.

With respect to the influence of Asian ideas on the development of Nietzsche's thought, the only candidates come from India, a country whose culture he was most fond of invoking. Johann Figl begins at the beginning, with a consideration of Nietzsche's first introduction to Asian thought while a student at the famous boarding school at Pforta. From a meticulous study of the archival materials pertaining to that period, Figl carefully delineates the range of texts and ideas to which the young Nietzsche appears to have been exposed.

Moving to a consideration of some of Nietzsche's published works, Michel Hulin examines the rather complex attitude of their author to the topic of asceticism, with particular reference to the ascetic tradition in India. The illumination provided by an Indologist points up the limitations of some of Nietzsche's views of Indian culture, highlighting his tendency to make broad generalizations on the basis of insufficient knowledge. But at the same time this essay prompts an appreciation for the intuitiveness of some of his insights into a culture so foreign to his own. Personally an ascetic character himself, Nietzsche's reflections on asceticism in an alien context serve to fill out his picture of the phenomenon as it manifested itself closer to him, in the Christian tradition in which he grew up.

Mervyn Sprung presents the results of his research into the archives concerning an aspect of Nietzsche's adult life. A complementary examination of correspondence and biographical documentation by Nietzsche's friends leads the author to what may be for many a surprising conclusion concerning the extent of the mature thinker's acquaintance with and interest in Indian culture and philosophy. However intrigued the young Nietzsche may have been by the subject, the evidence presented here militates against an abiding interest in Indian thought per se—and may be seen as supporting Scheiffele's claim that Nietzsche's primary concern with "the foreign" is as a moment in a hermeneutic strategy of distancing for the purpose of better self-understanding.

Leaving the question of influence behind, Glen Martin undertakes a comparison of Nietzsche's methods and ideas with those of a major figure in the Mahayana Buddhist tradition (with whom Nietzsche was presumably not acquainted), Nagarjuna. There have been about as many arguments in the literature concerning the true nature of Nagarjuna's aims and methods as there have been (in a different literature) concerning Nietzsche's, and Martin's intelligent juxtaposition of the two thinkers in this context may well serve to settle some of them. In the concluding section of the paper he broaches the topic of nihilism in Nietzsche, relating it to a recent extension of Mahayana Buddhist thought in the work of the contemporary Japanese philosopher Nishitani Keiji.

The initial reception of Nietzsche's works in foreign countries was almost always on the part of literary figures rather than philosophers, who have in general been slow to apppreciate the full depth to his ideas. The case of China is no exception to this rule, as a recent essay by Yue Daiyun demonstrates in some detail.[14] Many of the writers associated with the May Fourth Movement of 1919 were great Nietzsche enthusiasts, seeing his ideas as tools with which to build a "new China." No less enthusiastic were the right-wing intellectuals aligned with the Guomindang in the early forties, but they had to highlight quite different aspects of Nietzsche's thought in order to use it for opposite ideological purposes. This salient feature of Nietzsche receptions in many places—that enthusiasm may run equally high at opposite ends of the ideological spectrum—is especially interesting in the case of China and Japan, where his putative "individualism" exploded with the force of a fragmentation bomb, igniting blazing controversies on either side of a variety of ideological fences.[15]

Chen Guying looks back to some of the earliest texts of the Chinese canon, to a thinker whose texts resonate more sympathetically with Nietzsche's than those of any other from that tradition: the classical Daoist thinker Zhuang Zi (Chuang Tzu). Chen's discussion, which is exemplary of modern Chinese scholarship on Nietzsche, articulates a number of similarities between the two philosophies—in spite of their stemming from totally disparate social and cultural circumstances.[16] The author also delineates the major areas of difference, concluding with some criticisms of both for being unnecessarily antisocial in their thinking.

Roger Ames keeps the discussion extended across the same span of time in his comparison of the Daoist idea of *de* ("power," "virtuality") with Nietzsche's notion of *Wille zur Macht*. Both ideas are notoriously difficult to understand, but in this case suspicions of explanations of *obscurum per obscurius* are dispelled as the bifocal scrutiny begins to shed light on both poles of the comparison. By elaborating an idea from the Daoist tradition of a cosmology that is significantly different from the traditional Western conception, Ames aims to highlight some unconventionally cosmological aspects of Nietzsche's thought. Not only does the essay constitute an invitation to students of Nietzsche to look at some of the texts of classical Daoism, but it also provides readers from the East Asian tradition with an avenue of approach to one of Nietzsche's most difficult ideas by way of something implicitly familiar.

David Kelly contributes an essay on the reception of Nietzsche in China in the more recent past, ranging from the responses to Nietzsche's work on the part of such figures as Lu Xun and Li Shicen in the early decades of the century, to the "Nietzsche cult" of the eighties as exemplified in the work of the contemporary writer Liu Xiaobo. Again, the ambivalent tone of the response to Nietzsche's works is strikingly evident, as a variety of hyperbolic misunderstandings and vulgarizations are exposed. Kelly's first-hand account of the contemporary intellectual world in Beijing just prior to the Tiananmen Square massacre poses a number of intriguing questions concerning the possible roles Nietzsche's ideas might play in the Chinese context—whether or not they are allowed free expression—in the years to come.

The history of Nietzsche's reception in Japan provides equally rich material for reflection, and some of the salient events are discussed by Graham Parkes. The treatment is, however, relatively "straight," leaving for the most part musing on reasons and motives, as well as pondering of implications and interpretations, up to the reader who may be so inclined.

Nietzsche's views of nature constitute an important—though generally neglected—aspect of his philosophy, and they are articulated in the contribution of Ōkōchi Ryōgi from the perspective of several East Asian conceptions of the natural world. The essay brings together a number of important passages from Nietzsche's *Nachlass* in order to articulate his understanding of nature against the background of some corresponding ideas from the Daoism of Lao Zi (Lao Tzu), from the medieval Japanese Buddhism of Shinran, and from modern Japanese philosophy as represented by Nishida Kitarō and Nishitani Keiji.

Arifuku Kōgaku undertakes a fruitful comparison of Nietzsche's ideas about the body with those of the thirteenth-century Zen master Dōgen. His treatment has the virtue of pulling together a number of strands of Nietzsche's ideas from a range of texts into a coherent theme, while his presentation of Dōgen serves to introduce the idea—central to Zen Buddhism—of the precedence of "somatic" over "spiritual practice." In the course of his comparison Arifuku argues for a correspondence between the moves from the ego-self and individual body to the "great self" of the body of the natural world in both Dōgen and Nietzsche.

Sonoda Muneto considers Nietzsche's ideas on the role of language in the communication of certain kinds of truths against the background of some corresponding ideas from the Buddhist tradition. The center-piece of the essay is a reading of *Thus Spoke Zarathustra* in which So-noda examines the place of silence in the protagonist's attempts to give voice to the thought of the eternal recurrence of the same. He draws an illuminating parallel between the rhetorical situations of Zarathustra and the authors of the Buddhist sutras, suggesting a deeper function to language than that of communication. The essay ends with a richly al-lusive discussion of the well-known central episode in the *Vimalakīrtinir-deśa Sutra*.

IV

It was not in his nihilistic view of Buddhism but in such ideas as *amor fati* and the Dionysian as the overcoming of nihilism that Nietzsche came closest to Buddhism, and especially to Mahayana.

Nishitani Keiji

Nietzsche studies continue to be pursued with enthusiasm and rigor in Japan today. One indication of the contemporary importance of Nietzsche there is the fact that the entirety of the Colli and Montinari critical edition of the published works has been available in Japanese for some time, while the project to translate this edition into English is only now getting under way. Indeed, a significant absence from the present collection of essays is a contribution from the foremost living Nietzsche scholar in Japan, Nishitani Keiji (whose work is nevertheless referred to by several of the contributors). Professor Nishitani is a major precursor in the discipline of comparative philosophy in general, and in the com-parative approach to Nietzsche's work in particular. Considerations of time and space have not permitted the translation into English, as orig-inally planned, of a seminal essay by Nishitani on Nietzsche's *Zarathus-tra* and Meister Eckhart, written in the late thirties shortly after his return from studying with Heidegger in Freiburg;[17] but an extensive discussion of Nietzsche's work may be found in a 1949 text of Nishitani's recently translated as *The Self-Overcoming of Nihilism*.[18] The author acknowledges Nietzsche as a major mentor, expressing admiration for his affirmative stance (or dance) in the face of nihilism, and offers a rewarding reading of his works from a standpoint informed by Zen Bud-dhist ideas.

The relations between Nietzsche's work and Buddhist thinking in general form one of the potentially most fertile fields for future com-parative research. His acquaintance with Buddhism appears to have come primarily through Schopenhauer, with little evidence of his having done much independent study. His understanding is thus restricted to early, Hinayana forms of Buddhism, and with respect to the philosophical ideas he found there he was quite ambivalent.[19] This ambivalence is summed up in a passage from *The Antichrist* in which Nietzsche on the one hand ranks Buddhism with Christianity as a "*décadence* religion," and on the other praises it for having transcended the "self-deception of moral concepts" to attain a stance "*beyond* good and evil" (*AC* 20).

A major ground for this ambivalence is surely to be found in Nietzsche's eventual repudiation of his early mentors Schopenhauer and Wagner. The former's championship of Buddhism is better known, perhaps, than Wagner's espousal, the latter having received the major impetus to study Buddhism from his reading of Schopenhauer, who soon replaced Feuerbach as his favorite philosopher.[20] Wagner was writing enthusiastically about Buddhism as early as the mid-eighteen-fifties, and Schopenhauerian and Buddhist ideas together exerted a strong influence on the rest of his career—on his music dramas as well as his theoretical writings.[21] If Nietzsche criticizes Buddhism as often as he praises it, his criticisms usually have an anti-Schopenhauerian or anti-Wagnerian tone to them. In *The Gay Science*, for instance, he writes: "Wagner is Schopenhauerian in his attempts to understand Christianity as a seed of Buddhism carried far by the wind, and to prepare a Buddhist epoch in Europe, with an occasional *rapprochement* with Catholic-Christian formulas and sentiments" (*GS* 99). Accordingly, Nietzsche later reproaches Wagner for rewriting the end of *Siegfried* to give it a Schopenhauer-inspired finale of redemption: "So he translated the *Ring* into Schopenhauerian. . . . *nothingness*, the Indian Circe, beckons" (*The Case of Wagner* 4). In a letter to Peter Gast just before this late text was to go to press, Nietzsche seeks to confirm the basis for his criticism by asking for the volume and page reference to "a variant of Brünnhilde's last song that is entirely Buddhistic."[22]

Nietzsche's acquaintance with Buddhist ideas did not extend to the later, Mahayana schools which spread from India to China and from there to Korea and Japan. In China the confluence with the Daoist tradition led to the emergence of Chan Buddhism, which on being transplanted to the shores of Japan assumed the form of Buddhism that is perhaps closest to Nietzsche—namely, Zen.[23] Given the deep resonances between Nietzsche's and Buddhist ideas, there are good grounds for supposing that his revulsion against certain aspects of Schopenhauer's and Wagner's thinking discouraged him from studying Buddhism more seriously—and that if he had had access to the world of later Buddhist

thought he would have found the atmosphere there philosophically brac-
ing and the ideas much to his own taste. (A reader familiar with comparative studies of Nietzsche and the Daoists would have a similarly
justified expectation with respect to Daoism.)

With his characteristic lack of modesty—so off-putting to his detractors
and endearing to his admirers—Nietzsche claimed to have looked into
the most life-denying forms of pessimism "with an Asiatic and trans-
Asiatic eye" (*BGE* 56). Taken together with his suggestion that his freedom from prejudices has to do with his "trans-European eye," we are
faced with a claim to an unusually synoptic and global perspective. Considerable support for the validity of this claim is provided by a number
of the essays that follow.

Asian-comparative studies of Nietzsche bear upon the issue of his
status as a global thinker also with respect to the debate—initiated by
Heidegger and furthered more recently by thinkers such as Gadamer
and Derrida—concerning the "end" of the Western metaphysical tradition. The contention that Nietzsche managed to extricate himself from
the tradition of Western metaphysics is lent greater force if his thought
can be shown to be congruent in important respects with two radically
unmetaphysical ways of thinking (Daoism and Zen Buddhism) stemming from totally alien traditions with which he was quite unfamiliar.

Nietzsche's fantasy concerning a synthesis of Western and Asian
thought (expressed in the epigraph to this now concluding introduction)
was penned in the summer of 1876—a time at which he first started
talking about becoming a "good European" and issuing impassioned dia-
tribes against nationalism of any kind.[24] It was also a period during
which he was trying to discern his task in life, to determine what he
himself would be able to accomplish in the brief span of time allotted to
him, and what he would have to leave to succeeding generations of
thinkers. He saw it as one of the major shortcomings of modernity that
it discouraged people from striving for truly long-term goals—ones that
would take generations to achieve. One may therefore be justified in
imputing to Nietzsche an aim—that of effecting a synthesis between
Eastern and Western thinking—which he had no illusions about being
able to achieve within his lifetime. He saw himself as sowing the seeds
of such a synthesis, in the full realization that the tending and harvest-
ing would come only later, and from hands other than his own. To borrow an image from a work of the same period: he was concerned to
"plant a tree that would demand constant tending for a century and is
intended to provide shade for long successions of generations" (*HA* I,

22). Playing on the root meaning of the term just a little, one could say that the present anthology is intended to cultivate a few scions from such a tree, saplings whose branches might eventually overshadow at least some of the borderland between orient and occident.

Notes

1. Nietzsche's impact in India appears to have been less widespread than in China and Japan. The major Indian figure in this context is the Islamic thinker and poet Mohammad Iqbal, who in his thirties spent several years in Europe (1905–08) and began to publish works influenced by Nietzsche in 1915. See Subhash C. Kashyap, *The Unknown Nietzsche* (Delhi, 1970), and R. A. Nicholson's Introduction to his translation of Iqbal's first Nietzschean work *Secrets of the Self* (Lahore, 1944).

2. The most comprehensive study of Nietzsche's influence on German (and to some extent European) letters is the monumental two-volume work by Richard Frank Krummel, *Nietzsche und der deutsche Geist* (Berlin and New York, 1974 and 1983). Volume I covers the years 1867–1900 and Volume II 1901–1918.

3. A detailed account (with magnificent illustrations) of the impact of the figure of Nietzsche on the visual arts in Europe around the turn of the century is Jürgen Krause, *"Märtyrer" und "Prophet": Studien zum Nietzsche-Kult in der bildenden Kunst der Jahrhundertwende* (Berlin and New York, 1984).

4. The classic work on Nietzsche's influence in France is Geneviève Bianquis, *Nietzsche en France: L'influence de Nietzsche sur la pensée française* (Paris, 1929). See also her *Nietzsche devant ses contemporains* (Monaco, 1959), and Pierre Boudot, *Nietzsche et les écrivains français 1930–1960* (Paris, 1970). Few countries have fielded as formidable a team of Nietzsche interpreters in recent years as France: Maurice Blanchot, Eric Blondel, Gilles Deleuze, Jacques Derrida, Jean Granier, Luce Irigaray, Pierre Klossowski, Sarah Kofman, Philippe Lacoue-Labarthe, Bernard Pautrat—to name some of the better known.

5. Gonzalo Sobejano, *Nietzsche en España* (Madrid, 1967).

6. Thomas Harrison, ed., *Nietzsche in Italy* (Saratoga, 1988). This collection contains a number of interesting papers that look at Nietzsche from a variety of literary, musical, filmic, and even equine perspectives.

7. David S. Thatcher, *Nietzsche in England 1890–1914: The Growth of a Reputation* (Toronto, 1970) offers a detailed account of the early British reception of Nietzsche, and especially of his impact on such men of letters as George Bernard Shaw, William Butler Yeats, Havelock Ellis, A. R. Orage, and John Davidson. His chapter on the early English translations of Nietzsche's works is of particular interest. Patrick Bridgwater's *Nietzsche in Anglosaxony: A Study of Nietzsche's Impact on English and American Literature* (Leicester, 1972) appears to have been written independently since it covers many of the same authors, but it also has interesting chapters on Herbert Read and D. H. Lawrence. The last five chapters discuss the effect Nietzsche exerted on several figures in Amer-

ican literature, notably, Jack London, Eugene O'Neill, and Wallace Stevens. John Burt Foster's *Heirs to Dionysus: A Nietzschean Current in Literary Modernism* (Princeton, 1981) traces Nietzschean influences on the novels of D. H. Lawrence, André Malraux, and Thomas Mann, with some discussion of his impact on Gide, Yeats, and the Russian novelist Andrei Bely. Among the studies to have appeared more recently are: Colin Milton, *Lawrence and Nietzsche: A Study in Influence* (Aberdeen, 1987), Frances Oppel, *Mask and Tragedy: Yeats and Nietzsche* (Charlottesville, 1987), and Keith May, *Nietzsche and Modern Literature: Themes in Yeats, Rilke, Mann & Lawrence* (Basingstoke, 1988).

8. See Bernice Glatzer Rosenthal, ed., *Nietzsche in Russia* (Princeton, 1986), and also Edith W. Clowes, *The Revolution of Moral Consciousness: Nietzsche in Russian Literature 1890–1914* (DeKalb, 1988), especially chapter 3: "Nietzsche's Early Reception."

9. Herbert W. Reichert and Karl Schlechta, eds., *International Nietzsche Bibliography* (Chapel Hill, 1968).

10. An account of the debate may be found in chapter 11 of the present volume.

11. The pioneering work in this field (which is as small in Western languages as that concerning the Japanese reception) is Marián Gálick, "Nietzsche in China (1918–1925)," *Nachrichten der Gesellschaft für Natur- und Völkerkunde Ostasiens* 110 (Hamburg, 1974). This essay, published in English by an author from Czechoslovakia, is informative, though on the side of Nietzsche it relies rather heavily on secondary sources. A more recent treatment is Raoul David Findeisen, "Die Last der Kultur: Vier Fallstudien zur chinesischen Nietzsche-Rezeption," *minima sinica* (1989):1–41 and (1990):1–40, which focuses on the four most important figures: Mao Dun, Guo Moruo, Yu Dafu, and Lu Xun. On more particular themes, see David A. Kelly, "Nietzsche in China: Influence and Affinity," *Papers on Far Eastern History* 27 (Canberra, 1983), Mabel Lee, "From Chuang-tzu to Nietzsche: On the Individualism of Lu Hsün," *Journal of the Oriental Society of Australia* 17 (1985), and also Cheung Chiuyee, "Lu Hsün and Nietzsche: Influence and Affinity after 1927," *Journal of the Oriental Society of Australia* 18 & 19 (1986–87).

12. HA II/1, 223. I have modified Hollingdale's translation here and in several subsequent passages from this work.

13. A comparison of the "mystical" aspects of *Thus Spoke Zarathustra* with some ideas in Zen, inspired in part by Joan Stambaugh's studies of time in Nietzsche, can be found in Graham Parkes, "Nietzsche and Nishitani on the Self through Time," *The Eastern Buddhist* 17/2 (1984). See also my more general essay "Nietzsche and East-Asian Thought: Influences, Impacts, and Resonances," in Kathleen Higgins and Bernd Magnus, eds., *The Cambridge Companion to Nietzsche* (Cambridge, 1995), pp. 356–83.

14. Yue Daiyun, "Nietzsche in China," trans. Cathy Poon, *Journal of the Oriental Society of Australia* 20 and 21 (1990).

15. Such internal antitheses in the reaction to Nietzsche's ideas were nowhere more pronounced than in Germany itself, where his earliest proponents were socialists, anarchists, and feminists, while it took some time for the nationalists,

racists, and imperialists to extract and deploy their ideological ammunition from his works. An interesting study is R. Hinton Thomas, *Nietzsche in German Politics and Society 1890–1918* (Manchester, 1983; LaSalle, 1986).

16. For a somewhat different reading of both Nietzsche and Zhuang Zi which draws attention to the stylistic similarities as much as to the ideas themselves, see Graham Parkes, "The Wandering Dance: Chuang-Tzu and Zarathustra," *Philosophy East and West 29* (1983), and also "Human/Nature in Nietzsche and Taoism," in J. Baird Callicott and Roger T. Ames, eds., *Nature in Asian Traditions of Thought: Essays in Environmental Philosophy* (Albany, 1989). A more extensive treatment will be found in *Nietzsche, Heidegger, Nishitani.*

17. "Niche no Tsaratsustora to Maisutah Ekkuharuto," first published in Nishitani Keiji, *Shūkyō to bunka* (Tokyo, 1940).

18. Nishitani Keiji, *The Self-Overcoming of Nihilism*, trans. Graham Parkes with Setsuko Aihara (Albany, 1990), especially chapters 3, 4, 5.

19. For a comprehensive account which documents the sources of Nietzsche's acquaintance with Buddhist thought, distinguishes his references to Buddhism based on genuine understanding from those based on misunderstanding, and draws a number of interesting parallels, see Freny Mistry, *Nietzsche and Buddhism* (Berlin and New York, 1981).

20. The relevant facts are adduced in Guy Richard Welbon, *The Buddhist Nirvāṇa and its Western Interpreters* (Chicago, 1968), ch. 5, "Interlude: Schopenhauer, Wagner, and Nietzsche on Nirvāṇa."

21. In a letter to Franz Liszt of 7 June 1855, Wagner writes, "The deep longing [for the extinction of one's individual existence] is expressed more purely and more significantly in the most sacred and oldest religion of the human race, the doctrine of the Brahmins, and especially in its final transfiguration and highest perfection, Buddhism" (Albert Goldman and Evert Sprinchorn, eds., *Wagner on Music and Drama* [New York, 1964], p. 277).

22. Letter of 17 July 1888, a translation of which appears in *The Birth of Tragedy* and *The Case of Wagner*, trans. Walter Kaufmann (New York, 1967), p. 193. A meticulous and insightful account of the mutual philosophical and artistic influences between Wagner and Nietzsche is Roger Hollinrake, *Nietzsche, Wagner and the Philosophy of Pessimism* (London, 1982).

23. For a comparison of Nietzsche's ideas concerning the *Affekte* and *Leidenschaften* with those of the Zen thinkers Rinzai and Hakuin, see Graham Parkes, "The Transformation of Emotion in Rinzai Zen and Nietzsche," *The Eastern Buddhist* 23/1 (1990). *Pace* Freny Mistry, there is reason to suppose that investigation of the parallels between Nietzsche's thought and later Buddhist ideas will be bilaterally far more enlightening than comparisons adducing early Buddhism. A careful study of the similarities between the idea of the *Übermensch* and the "bodhisattva ideal" of the Mahayana tradition could prove most illuminating, all the more so since it would require clarifying the relations between the Buddhist idea of compassion and Nietzsche's conception of love in contrast to pity. The Vajrayana tradition, as it evolved in Tibetan Buddhism, offers another potentially fruitful field for comparison, especially on the topic of the

optimal disposition of the emotions and passions in the greater economy of the psyche.

24. That early note was not simply a temporary aberration. A note from 1884 reads: "I must learn to think *more orientally* [*orientalischer*] about philosophy and knowledge. An oriental [*morgenländischer*] overview of Europe" (*KSA* 11, 26 [317]). Part of what Nietzsche means by "oriental" here is discussed by Eberhard Scheiffele in chapter 3 below; more would have to be gleaned from a reading of the many passages in Nietzsche where the relevant terms occur.

2

The Other Nietzsche

Joan Stambaugh

I

Everyone seems to have his own Nietzsche. There are various versions of Nietzsche belonging to literary criticism and also to musicologists. There is the Nietzsche distortion perpetrated by the Nazis. There was a lot of pre-Kaufmann nonsense about the Nietzsche who was mad from the outset and produced nothing but the ravings of a madman. More recently and more philosophically, the two main continental interpretations have been expressed by the French, neo-Freudian and Derridian line, and by the German, Heideggerian line, which sees in Nietzsche the completion of the history of metaphysics. These two interpretations are valid in varying degrees. What I should like to explore in this paper is a Nietzsche relatively untouched by all of these interpretations. It is not the whole of Nietzsche by any means; but it is there. To bring out the connection with Eastern thought, which is the topic of this volume, I shall call it the other Nietzsche: Nietzsche the poetic mystic.

A word about the terms "poetic" and "mystic." Justifying the exclusion of poetry from the well-ordered state, Plato had said that there was an ancient quarrel between poetry and philosophy. Poetry and the arts in general appealed to and strengthened the irrational side of man, nourishing the feelings and impairing the reason. Well, it seems that philosophy has pretty much won that quarrel. Few philosophers turn to poetry to find "truth." And yet Plato himself was a poet, as was Nietzsche. There have always been a few thinkers willing and able to listen to the inspiration of the poets. Surely there is a great deal of truth and insight into human nature in, for example, the works of Shakespeare. So much for the term "poetic."

The word "mystic" has fared even worse. Not only are we dealing with a harmless bard enchanted with beauty as was the case with the poet; we are now faced with someone utterly devoid of reason *and* sense and who, to compound the chaos, is unable to state coherently anything about what he has supposedly experienced. To quote William James:

The words "mysticism" and "mystical" are often used as terms of mere reproach, to throw at any opinion which we regard as vague and vast and sentimental, and without a base in either facts or logic.[1]

But as Paul Tillich pointed out, "mysticism" and "mystery" are derived from the Greek verb *muein*, which means "closing the eyes" or "closing the mouth." This means that a mystical experience is an experience that transcends the subject-object structure of seeing and that therefore cannot be adequately expressed in ordinary language belonging to that structure.

Apropos of Tillich and the term "mystic," the theologian Langdon Gilkey once related an amusing anecdote. Tillich, who liked to call himself a nature mystic, was visiting at a conference. Wishing to please him with lots of nature, his hosts drove him to a large, beautiful garden. Much to everyone's surprise, Tillich, refusing to get out of the car, inquired anxiously: "Are there any serpents in this garden?"

But enough of this general discussion. The label "poetic mystic," like all labels, is not even important. I just wanted to give some indication of the direction in which I am going and also to establish a tie to the East which, after all, has never made such a clear-cut distinction between philosophy and poetry and which abounds with so-called "mysticism."

For my texts I shall restrict myself to four sections of *Thus Spoke Zarathustra*. The first is entitled "Before Sunrise" (III, 4). The Prologue to *Zarathustra* began with Zarathustra rising at dawn and addressing the sun. Since in the course of the text he also addresses the moon and the stars, we might call him a kind of cosmic figure. In "Before Sunrise" he speaks to the heaven. Here he is speaking not to something *in* the heaven such as the sun, moon, or stars, but to the heaven itself, which he calls an "abyss of light."

This section is replete with paradoxes, contradictions, with *coincidentia oppositorum*. To begin with, the heaven is addressed as an abyss of light. Abysses are not customarily *above* one, as is the heaven; nor are they full of light. Abysses are traditionally beneath one, and they are dark. An abyss of light is an extraordinary phenomenon indeed.

Zarathustra compares the heaven with gods and the godlike by saying "Gods are shrouded by their beauty; thus you conceal your stars." Furthermore, he describes the heaven as "a dance floor for divine accidents . . . a divine table for divine dice and dice players." And when Zarathustra sees the heaven, he trembles with godlike desires. This puts not only the heaven out of the domain of the ordinary and the naturalistic, but also Zarathustra himself. When the heaven, the abyss of light is about him, he is transformed into a figure of affirmation; in a sense difficult to articulate he himself becomes a kind of heaven, protecting and blessing things:

> But I am one who can bless and say Yes, if only you are about me, pure and light, you abyss of light; then I carry the blessings of my Yes into all abysses.
> I have become one who blesses and says Yes; and I fought long for that and was a fighter that I might one day get my hands free to bless.
> But this is my blessing: to stand over every single thing as its own heaven, as its round roof, its azure bell, and eternal security; and blessed is he who blesses thus.
> For all things have been baptized in the well of eternity. . . .

The azure bell is an important image that recurs frequently in *Thus Spoke Zarathustra*, as we shall see. To mention a few more cases of the coincidence of opposites, Zarathustra longs to throw himself into the heaven's height, for that is *his* depth. To hide in the heaven's purity, that is *his* innocence. Ordinarily, innocence does not need to hide at all, let alone in the heaven's purity. What Zarathustra wants with all his will is "to *fly*, to fly up into *you.*"

The rest of this section is concerned with getting beyond good and evil, compulsion, goals, and guilt. The purity of the heaven consists in the fact that things are freed from their bondage under purpose and reason:

Over all things stands the heaven Accident, the heaven Innocence, the heaven Chance, the heaven high spirits (*Übermut*). . . .
> This freedom and heavenly cheer I have placed over all things like an azure bell when I taught that over them and through them no "eternal will" wills.

These are ideas that occur consistently throughout all of Nietzsche's writings. What is dictinctive about this section is the strange kinship, affinity, and would-be identity between Zarathustra and the abyss of light, the heaven. Both are described as the azure bell standing over all things.

II

My next section is the one entitled "On the Great Longing" (III, 14). It follows immediately upon the crucially important section entitled "The

Convalescent" where Zarathustra finally conjures up his most abysmal thought of eternal recurrence and, overcome with unexpected nausea, collapses and stays unconscious for seven days. His animals try to interpret for him what has happened to him and who he is. But Zarathustra does not really listen to them, and we are told that he was lying still with his eyes closed, "Like one sleeping, although he was not asleep; for he was conversing with his soul."

We learn that after the confrontation with his most abysmal thought his soul has in a way become all things, but in a way that goes beyond Aristotle's similar sounding statement. His soul is beyond all disparateness of time and space, beyond all clouds (good and evil) and sin:

> O my soul, I taught you to say "today" and "one day" and "formerly" and to dance away over all Here and There and Yonder. . . .
> With the storm that is called "spirit" I blew over your wavy sea; I blew all clouds away; I even strangled the strangler that is called "sin". . . .
> O my soul, now there is not a soul anywhere that would be more loving and comprehensive and encompassing. Where could future and past dwell closer together than in you?

This soul, which is nothing "eternal" and unchangeable, Zarathustra has shaped and set free from old values, and he is now ready to baptize it with new names:

> O my soul, I took from you all obeying, knee-bending, and "Lord"-saying; I myself gave you the name "turning of need" and "destiny."
> O my soul, I gave you new names and colorful toys; I called you "destiny" and "circumference of circumferences" and "umbilical cord of time" and "azure bell."

We have basically four new names for Zarathustra's soul. *The azure bell*, which in the section previously discussed characterized the heaven, now names Zarathustra's soul and explicitly indicates the close affinity, if not identity, between his soul and the heaven.

The *circumference of circumferences* has the exact same imagery as in the previous quote from this section, comprehensive and encompassing. The soul reaches out and around to embrace all things, not just symbolically, but quite "literally."

The umbilical cord of time is a new image characterizing time thus transmuted (future and past dwelling closest together in Zarathustra's soul) as a nourishing link to the source of life. Instead of being a principle of impermanence and finitude, this transformed time gathers all things together at the source.

Finally, Zarathustra's soul is called *destiny* and *turning* of need. Destiny is a key concept in Nietzsche's thinking that gets its fullest expression in the recurrent phrase *amor fati*, love of fate, which intentionally echoes Spinoza's *amor dei*, love of God.[2] Turning of need (*Wende der Not*), which Kaufmann mistranslates as *cessation* of need, is a play on the word for necessity (*Notwendigkeit*) that distances necessity from any kind of determinism and freshly reinterprets it as turning a need (*Not*) around to work for you. It is a conception of fate, destiny, and necessity not as something outside or above us to which we are subject, but as something *within* us, as our innermost being.

III

The third section to be discussed is entitled "At Noon" (IV, 10). In general, the seasons of the year and also the times of the day or night play an important role for Nietzsche. In the section entitled "On Involuntary Bliss" Zarathustra speaks repeatedly of the "afternoon of his life," the hour when all light grows quieter. The section "Before Sunrise" has already been discussed. And an entire book is named by the time of day: *Dawn of Morning*, or *Daybreak*. Probably the two most important times for Nietzsche are noon and midnight. Midnight will be discussed in the last section of *Zarathustra* to be considered here.

Nietzsche's *Nachlass* is replete with sketches and plans for future works. Many of these sketches have the recurring phrase "noon and eternity." There is a sense in which noon is not really a time of day at all, but rather out of time, timelessness, eternity. Timelessness is precisely what Zarathustra experiences in the section "At Noon." He decides to lie down beside an old crooked and knotty tree that is embraced by a grapevine from which hang yellow grapes in abundance. The colors yellow and especially gold are linked with eternity; the grapes remind us of Dionysos. Zarathustra falls asleep, but when he speaks to his heart we are told that sleep left his eyes open and his soul awake. Apart from Zarathustra's description of his state, we know that it is one in which no time elapses, since when he gets up again the sun still stands straight over his head, at exactly the place where it was when he lay down. With characteristic levity, Nietzsche defuses the pathos of this experience of timelessness by quipping: "But from this one might justly conclude that Zarathustra had not slept long." The fact that Zarathustra gets up from his resting place at the tree as from a strange drunkenness again evokes the Dionysian. The German word for "strange" here, *fremd*, indicates that Zarathustra has been in a state completely foreign and other to his normal way of experiencing.

Zarathustra begins speaking to his heart during this state by saying:

Still! Still! Did not the world become perfect just now? What is happening to me? . . . O happiness! O happiness! Would you sing, O my soul? You are lying in the grass. But this is the secret solemn hour when no shepherd plays his pipe. Refrain! Hot noon sleeps in the meadows. Do not sing! Still! The world is perfect.

Many of the sections of *Thus Spoke Zarathustra* end with the phrase: Thus spoke Zarathustra. The three song sections, The Night Song, The Dancing Song, and The Tomb Song, end with the phrase: Thus sang Zarathustra. For Nietzsche, singing is a higher expression than speaking; music is more profound than words. But in the passage just quoted the experience goes even beyond singing. His soul wants to sing, but Zarathustra restrains it. The world has become perfect. The only appropriate response to this "perfection" is utter stillness. Nietzsche's use of the word "perfection" echoes that of an earlier thinker with whom he felt considerable affinity: Spinoza. The important thing to note here is that by perfection neither Spinoza nor Nietzsche understand an *ideal* type or *model*. We are accustomed to think, for example, of a perfect human body as an ideal type which we then use as a criterion to judge actual individual bodies. Spinoza explicitly argues against this usage, stating that it boils down to making perfection and imperfection "really only modes of thought, that is to say, notions which we are in the habit of forming from the comparison with one another of individuals of the same species or genus."[3] Quite to the contrary, for Spinoza, as for Nietzsche, "By reality and perfection I understand the same thing."[4]

I do not wish to pursue this issue further, since that would entail a discussion of Spinoza's adamant rejection of teleology, a stance, moreover, which he also shares with Nietzsche. Suffice it to say that when Nietzsche says the world has become perfect, he means it has become totally *real*. What does that mean? We must try to interpret the rest of this section to see if some clarity can be gained as to what Nietzsche meant when he said the world had become perfect, i.e., completely real:

What happened to me? Listen! Did time perhaps fly away? Do I not fall? Did I not fall—listen!—into the well of eternity? What is happening to me? Still! I have been stung, alas—in the heart? In the heart! Oh break, break, heart, after such happiness, after such a sting. How? Did not the world become perfect just now? . . . Leave me alone! Still! Did not the world become perfect just now?

Zarathustra has fallen out of time into the well of eternity. When he says "Do I not fall? Did I not fall?" he has left behind the distinction of past and present. Whereas previously he had wanted to *fly* up into the *abyss* of light (the heaven), now he *falls* into the *well* of eternity. Both flying and falling entail a shift of dimension, an abrupt transition to another level or realm. The abruptness is expressed in Zarathustra's words: I have been stung in the heart! A sudden sting may be linked with the image of the lightning flash (*Blitz*) which occurs repeatedly in *Thus Spoke Zarathustra* and in the *Nachlass* sketches and plans for future works. A sudden sting or lightning flash stings or strikes all at once, vehemently transforming the person struck. The image of the lightning flash is also to be found in Meister Eckhart:

If this birth [of the son in me] has really happened, then all creatures cannot hinder you; rather, they all direct you to God and to this birth, for which we have an image in the lightning flash: whatever the lightning flash hits when it strikes, be it a tree or an animal or a human being, it turns around toward itself on the spot; and if a man had turned his back, in the same instant it would hurl him around to face it.[5]

Zarathustra tries to get up, falls asleep again, and finally succeeds in waking up. At the conclusion of this whole experience he again speaks to his soul:

"Who are you? O my soul!" (At this point he was startled, for a sunbeam fell from the sky onto his face.)
"O heaven over me!" he said, sighing, and sat up. "You are looking on? You are listening to my strange soul?
When will you drink this drop of dew which has fallen upon all earthly things? When will you drink this strange soul?
When, well of eternity? Cheerful, dreadful abyss of noon! When will you drink my soul back into yourself?"

Here Zarathustra is forced to ask who his soul is, even though in previous sections he has had extensive conversations with it. His soul seems to be utterly unfathomable. Again, we find kindred sentiments in Meister Eckhart:

A master who spoke of the soul best of all says that the whole of human knowledge never penetrates to know what the soul is in its ground. (To comprehend) what the soul is requires supernatural knowledge. After all, we know nothing about how the energies go out from the soul into works; perhaps we know a little about it, but that is little. No one knows anything about what the soul is in its ground.[6]

What we all assume we know and are is totally unknown. Zarathustra is abruptly startled as a sunbeam falls from the heaven onto his face. He has quite literally been touched by the heaven whom he now addresses. The heaven is the well of eternity, the abyss of noon (the abyss of light). In a situation like this Nietzsche's philosophy of the will and the will to power simply has no place. The will, which is the great liberator from bondage and all obstacles, can do nothing here. It is not so much the case that the will is *unable* to do anything; rather, *there is nothing for it to do*. To give a feeble analogy that echoes the Zarathustra section (and, strictly speaking, there are no analogies to this kind of situation; it is always unique), when there is a beautiful sunrise, "willing" is inappropriate. There is nothing to will. One can perhaps only hope to be allowed to participate in it, to be a part of it. This has nothing to do with Schopenhauer's will-less contemplation. It is more a matter of learning all things:

To learn the Buddha Way is to learn one's self. To learn one's self is to forget one's self. To forget one's self is to be confirmed by all dharmas [all things]. To be confirmed by all dharmas is to effect the casting off of one's own body and mind and the bodies and minds of others as well. All traces of enlightenment (then) disappear, and this traceless enlightenment is continued on and on endlessly.[7]

IV

The last section to be discussed is "The Drunken Song" (IV, 19). It is now midnight, presumably the dead opposite of noon. Midnight is more mysterious than noon; above all, it is more explicitly Dionysian. This Dionysian quality makes it impossible to simply say that noon and midnight are opposites. Otherwise one would have to try to assert that noon was Apollinian in character, going back to Nietzsche's initial primordial vision that informed and inspired all of his later works in varying degrees. Noon and midnight are neither opposites nor are they identical. Perhaps one could venture to say that they form a *coincidentia oppositorum*, a coincidence of opposites, a *falling together* of opposites, which is the literal and pregnant meaning of the word "coincidence."

At the beginning of the episode we are told that "Zarathustra stood there like a drunkard." This whole experience that now begins is one of *hearing* and of *smell*. The customary, overwhelmingly prevalent mode of experiencing, that of seeing, is conspicuously absent. Nothing is seen. The dualistic subject-object structure of experiencing involved in seeing falls away. There is no object involved in the experience of hearing. We hear sounds, not objects. We smell odors, not objects.

Zarathustra seems to be hearing something. Everything becomes quiet and secret around him. The German word for secret, *heimlich*, literally means "home-like," further strengthening and intensifying the nondualistic quality of what is to come:

Then it grew still more quiet and secret, and everything listened, even the ass and Zarathustra's animals of honor, the eagle and the serpent, as well as Zarathustra's cave and the big cool moon and the night itself.

Everything is listening, even the moon and the night itself. What do they hear? From the depth comes the sound of a bell, the midnight bell "which has experienced more than any man." Now we are not only out of the dualistic subject-object structure of experiencing; we are also outside of all anthropomorphic preconceptions. The midnight bell goes beyond ordinary human experience.

The paragraphs that follow are each punctuated by a line of the song that had already appeared in Part Three at the end of the section entitled "The Other Dancing Song" and that appears again at the end of this section in its entirety, bearing the name "once more" and "into all eternity":

> O man, take care!
> What does the deep midnight declare?
> From a deep dream I woke:
> The world is deep,
> Deeper than day had thought,
> Deep is its pain—
> Joy—deeper yet than the heart's suffering:
> Pain speaks: Pass away!
> But all joy wants eternity—
> Wants deep, deep eternity!

Now there begins what for lack of more specific and concrete terms one might call a Dionysian experience of eternity:

Where is time gone? Have I not sunk into deep wells? The world sleeps. Alas! Alas! The dog howls, the moon shines. Sooner would I die, die rather than tell you what my midnight heart thinks now. Now I have died. It is gone. Spider, what do you spin around me?

Zarathustra has sunk into the deep wells of eternity. The use of wells as plural may indicate that "well" is some kind of metaphor not to be taken too literally and not to be "localized" and objectified. The howling dog, the shining moon, and the spider all occurred together in Part Three in the crucial section entitled "On the Vision and the Enigma." Perhaps in this section the enigma is trying to become pure vision, to the extent that this is at all possible.

A turning point is indicated with the lines: "Now I have died. It is gone." What is gone and in what sense has Zarathustra died? We learn what is gone further on in the section: "Gone! Gone! O youth! O noon! O afternoon! Now evening has come and night and midnight." In what sense has Zarathustra died? What has died is his extreme, almost inexplicable hesitation to experience midnight.

Zarathustra hears the sounds of the midnight old bell and sweet lyre. Now the sense of smell comes upon the scene, "a smell is secretly welling up, a fragrance and smell of eternity." The sense of smell is perhaps the most *intimate* sense. I must *breathe* in the odor, it has to become a part of me. The sense of smell seems to be somehow suited to transpose us directly out of ordinary time. Proust pointed out the fact that a cetain odor can immediately and most vividly bring the past back to us, not as a "memory" but as a direct experience. Here Zarathustra is transposed, not into the past, but into eternity itself.

Zarathustra asks the higher men, who do not seem able to understand much of what is going on, who he is:

Am I a soothsayer, a dreamer, a drunkard? An interpreter of dreams? A midnight bell? A drop of dew? A haze and fragrance of eternity? Do you not hear it? Do you not smell it? Just now my world became perfect; midnight too is noon.

How can Zarathustra now say that midnight too is noon? This is the last question to be touched upon in this essay. Again, one could be tempted to hear in the opposition of noon to midnight echoes of Nietzsche's fundamental vision of Apollo and Dionysos. Noon is the time of the brightest day, consciousness and individuality. There are no shadows; everything is separate and distinct. Midnight is the time of primordial oneness and unity; nothing is separate and distinct. But this will not work. The experience of noon is not an Apollinian experience; it, too, is Dionysian. At noon the world also became perfect. The abyss of noon was also the well of eternity. The section "Noon" concluded with Zarathustra asking when the abyss of noon, the well of eternity, would drink his soul back into itself.

Noon and midnight are opposites. Now we are told that they are the same. But this "sameness" is not just a dead, flat, static identity. Opposites coincide (*coincidentia oppositorum*). Midnight too is noon. Both are experiences of the well of eternity. But in the noon experience Zarathustra retains something of his own separate individuality and identity, something ego-like. The experience is somewhat incomplete in that it is at the same time an anticipation, a taste of what is to come. Zarathustra asks when the well of eternity *will* drink his soul back into itself. In the midnight experience Zarathustra *becomes*, in the present moment, "a drunken sweet lyre, a ominous bell-frog that nobody understands but that *must* speak, before the deaf." It is out of this experience that he then speaks of woe, which wants heirs, and joy, which is deeper than woe and wants itself. In other words, speaking out of the present experience of eternity, he tries to interpret eternity, to say what it means and what follows from it. We learn that joy wants *every thing*, woe included, back. This is Zarathustra's (and Nietzsche's) statement of the ultimate affirmation of life.

Apart from the reference to Dōgen, this essay has not made an explicit comparison of Nietzsche with Eastern thought. It has attempted to select some strains of Nietzsche's thought that are most consonant with an Eastern temper of experience and to let the reader reach his own conclusions about parallels and affinities. The fact that Nietzsche's own understanding of Eastern thought was pretty well mutilated by the influence of Schopenhauer does not facilitate seeing or understanding these affinities. In particular, Buddhism gets lumped together with Christianity and both pronounced "religions of exhaustion." Temperamentally, Nietzsche was perhaps closest to Lao Zi and Zhuang Zi with his rejection of metaphysical backworlds and his understanding of the world as play.

Notes

1. William James, *The Varieties of Religious Experience* (New York, 1958), p. 292.

2. Spinoza, *Ethics*, V.

3. Ibid., IV, Preface.

4. Ibid., II, Def. VI.

5. Meister Eckhart, *Deutsche Predigten und Traktate* (München, 1955), p. 437.

6. Ibid., p. 190.

7. Dōgen, *Shōbōgenzō Genjōkōan*, trans. Norman Waddell and Masao Abe, *The Eastern Buddhist* 5/2 (1972): 134–35.

3

Questioning One's "Own" from the Perspective of the Foreign

Eberhard Scheiffele, *translated by Graham Parkes*

I

Since the publication of Nietzsche's complete *Nachlass* in a form that is free of editorial manipulation (aside from the chronological ordering of the texts),[1] Nietzsche's work is for the first time surveyable in all its variety and abundance. It is already possible to appreciate what a liberating influence the appearance of the complete Critical Edition has had on Nietzsche scholarship. The figment of *The Will to Power* has finally, it seems, been exploded. There are also fewer attempts to divide the corpus biographically, according to the schema, for instance, of the "three transformations of the spirit" in *Thus Spoke Zarathustra*; and in fact French structuralism even "separates the signifier 'Nietzsche' from the living person."[2] "And"-titles, such as "Karl Marx and Friedrich Nietzsche," "Nietzsche and Critical Theory," ". . . Nietzsche and the Birth of Sociology . . . ," "Nietzsche and Philosophical Hermeneutics . . . ," "Nietzsche, Freud and . . . ,"[3] in which this radical outsider to his own time is brought into association with intellectual currents of our time, are evidence of the intention to view the actual fullness of Nietzsche's thought under particular aspects and in definite perspectives, rather than to extract something like a system from it. According to Mazzino Montinari, who was one of the editors of the *Kritische Gesamtausgabe*: "we are . . . experiencing a strange and highly important—but at the same time problematic—'come-back' of Nietzsche within the enormous cultural syncretism [of today]."[4]

This "come-back" would indeed be "problematic" if it were due to the opinion that Nietzsche had said "everything as well as the opposite of everything"[5] and thus anything at all could be connected to him. Even if one renounces the search for a system in or behind his thinking, one must not overlook what Karl Schlechta rather condescendingly referred to as "a remarkable monotony in the totality [of what Nietzsche said],"[6] and what would be better characterized as an unceasing circling around the same basic questions. Precisely when one takes seriously not only Nietzsche's thoughts about perspectivism but also his distinctively perspectival *way* of thinking, it becomes clear that in his texts—which are at the same time voluminous and condensed, terse and diverse—the form of thinking cannot be separated from the content, so that their "connectability" is severely restricted. Whether one comes across irreconcilable contradictions in his perspectivism, or finds in him a definitive "theory of knowledge," or sees his perspectivism in the context of formerly new world-perspectives (Copernicus, Kant, Hegel), or interprets his perspectivism as a philosophical hermeneutics,[7] it comes down to a restricted number of basic types of thinking, to which all these various approaches eventually lead.

While the treatments of Müller-Lauter, Grimm, Kaulbach, and Figl refer to it, there is no substantial discussion of a primary feature of Nietzsche's perspectivism: namely, *the "estranging" of what is one's own by questioning it from behind (hinterfragen), from the perspective of the foreign.*[8] Perhaps they have not considered this feature because it is so pervasive in Nietzsche's works as a whole that it does not seem to require special treatment. It seems to me, however, that a discussion of this topic is called for, since it promises to set into clearer relief the distinctive nature of Nietzsche's hermeneutical enterprise.

As is well known, Nietzsche's early idea that the *"plastic power* of a man, a people, a culture" manifests itself in the extent to which they are capable of "transforming and incorporating what is past and foreign" (*UM* II, 1) reappeared later under the directive of his major idea of "will to power." Eventually he sees in this "transforming" and "incorporating" the basic drive of organic nature as a whole, and even of inorganic nature (*KSA* 11, 36[20–22]): *"positing* as equal" is said to be in fact a *"making* equal," and all "thinking, judging, perceiving as *comparing* . . . [to be] the same as the incorporation of appropriated material in the amoeba" (*KSA* 12, 5[65]; *WP* 501). At the same time, however, Nietzsche undertook again and again to take what is "old, familiar, seen but overlooked by everyone" (*HA* I/1, 200) and *make it foreign* by envisaging it critically from counterpositions remote from it.[9] In the for-

mer case the appropriation of the foreign is "interpretation [as] a means
. . . of becoming master of something [*Herr über etwas zu werden*]";
in the latter it is one's own that is interpreted, and interpreted from a
foreign standpoint that has precisely *not* been incorporated or assimilated. It is for Nietzsche less a case of "doing justice to" what is foreign
than of seeing one's own *anew* from a different perspective, of questioning what is familiar so as to "get behind" it[10] and letting what is "obvious" appear as something *strange*.[11]

Nietzsche's procedure of "questioning behind" is informed, at least
according to his own claims, by the hermeneutical intention of "understanding the text better [than the author himself understood it]." This
may itself seem strange, the idea of a hermeneutics that aims to "get
behind" the "tradition" [*Überlieferungsgeschehen*] rather than to preserve and extend it, and to reverse perspectives rather than to effect a
"fusion of horizons" [*Horizontverschmelzung*].[12]

We shall begin by trying to show *how* Nietzsche proceeds to employ
foreign perspectives to render strange what is his own: his country, his
faith, his religion, and finally his "own" in the sense of the whole of
European culture. The examples of this are so numerous that it would
be easier to point to those passages that are exceptional in this respect.[13]
Nevertheless, it will be instructive to examine some representative examples in order to get a clearer picture of this technique of Nietzsche's.
I shall then attempt to show, by looking at the "logic" of his imagery,
that the process of interpreting by "questioning from behind" is constitutive of Nietzsche's philosophical hermeneutics as a whole.

II

Nietzsche's early renunciation of "Imperial German" culture, his warning to the effect that the error in supposing that the victory of Germany
over France in the war of 1870 was a victory of German culture, too,
would "turn our victory into a defeat: *into the defeat, if not the extir-
pation, of the German spirit for the benefit of the 'German Reich'*," is
intended primarily as a critique of the contemporary.[14] This judgment is
made from the standpoint of what Nietzsche considers the alienation of
true German culture from its two "Reformations" at the hands of Luther and then subsequently of Goethe and Schiller, whose "lofty spirit"
the Germans "forfeited totally" (*KSA* 8, 17[4]). And in the final paragraph of his "Admonitory Appeal to the Germans" ["Mahnruf an die
Deutschen," 1873] he exhorts his contemporaries to strive in the spirit
of Wagner to regain "a genuinely German art" (*KSA* 1, 897). In the

light of the affinity between the Greek and German spirits which is asserted in *The Birth of Tragedy*, there is a summons to strive for a renewal of "classical culture," to be achieved by thinking back to "our classical scholars" and the Greek culture which they mediate.[15] It is in this that Nietzsche sees the practical task of the philologist, of the philologist informed by Greek culture rather than the "gossipers and triflers" and "philistines" with whom Nietzsche contrasts him.[16]

As is well known, Nietzsche very soon lost the hopes he had placed in the Germans. He no longer compares contemporary Germany with an earlier, better country, but now measures German culture as a whole against a European standard. This change of view has as a consequence a reevaluation of the Reformation, which was so important for the history of Germany. Whereas Heine and Marx saw the Reformation as an epoch of progress, for Nietzsche it came to represent the kind of German backwardness and obsolescence that was to prove disastrous for Europe.[17] As was the custom in his time, Nietzsche traced particular manifestations of culture back to particular characteristics of the people in question, as with the formerly prized "German profundity" which came from "instinctive uncleanliness in relation to oneself": "one does not *want*," he goes on, "to gain clarity about oneself."[18] What still remains valid is pre-Reformation Germany (*KSA* 11, 34[104]), as well as "Germans of the strong race, *extinct* Germans, like Heinrich Schütz, Bach, and Händel" (*EH* II, 7). What still appeals to Nietzsche about the Germans is their "Mephistopheles-nature" (*KSA* 11, 34[97]). Nor is his admiration for Goethe diminished: "Goethe—not a German event, but a European one" (*TI* IX, 49).

Particularly striking is the way in which, beginning with *Human, All Too Human*, Nietzsche commends Germans who with the help of what he regards as higher culture have "degermanized" themselves (*HA* II/1, 323), such as the Hohenstaufen Emperor Frederick II and Frederick the Great of Prussia. The former, whom Nietzsche comes to count as "most closely related" to him (*EH* III, "Z" 4), is said to have desired "Moorish-oriental enlightenment," while the latter yearned for France (*KSA* 11, 35[66]; also 34 [97]). Wagner is said really to belong to Paris, and Nietzsche claims to have respected him "as a foreign country." Nietzsche himself emphasizes his own (imagined) Polishness (*EH* II, 5, 7). To be a "good" German means precisely "to overcome one's German qualities."[19] Here one's own is "good" only as something that has become alien.

This transnational-European perspective also changes his view of the Protestantism that was praised in *The Birth of Tragedy* (sec. 23). This he understands almost exclusively as "Lutheranism," which, conceived as specifically "German," is then attacked with far more vehemence than the more transnational Catholicism.[20] While Luther may still by the time of *Daybreak* count as "the great benefactor" (*D* 88) on the grounds that he awakened "mistrust . . . for the Christian *vita contemplativa*," and in *The Gay Science* is the guarantor for the Germans' becoming "the *un-Christian* nation in Europe" in that he taught them "to be un-Roman" (*GS* 146), it is finally precisely Luther who is made responsible for the Germans' having "cheated Europe out of the last great cultural harvest . . . that of the *Renaissance*," out of its "*revaluation of Christian values*" (*AC* 61). Even if "Catholic" and "un-German" are meant pejoratively in *Beyond Good and Evil*—Nietzsche was aiming at *Parsifal* with this (*BGE* 256)—and Catholicism is basically rejected as being a Christian creed, in the later work the confession that is "alien" to the pastor's son is nevertheless handled far more considerately than Protestantism, and above all Lutheranism, and that from the point of view of *taste* rather than of morals (*GM* III, 22).

These examples show that Nietzsche generally values the foreign, by which he measures what is one's own, more highly than the latter. This is especially striking when he compares Germany and German culture with other European countries. Roughly speaking, a country appears to hold a higher rank for him the more sharply he thinks he can distinguish it from his own. The English fare the worst in this respect (*BGE* 253), and the French the best. Between these two there fall the Poles, the Italians, and the Jews. It is in his attitudes toward France that Nietzsche's technique of reversing perspectives can be most clearly seen. He answers the question "What is German?" for example, as follows: "the uncertain symbolism, the pleasure in sloppy thinking, the false 'sense for the profound', capriciousness, the lack of fire, wit, and grace, the incapability for the *great line*, for what is necessary in—."[21] One can find the absolute opposite of each of these features in Nietzsche's countless remarks about France and the French.[22] His admiration for French civilization is not, however, indiscriminate. While he values the classical period of the seventeenth century, Voltaire, and the Napoleonic era for their independence from corrosive moralities, he dismisses Rousseau as being too "German," and the French Revolution as working counter to the spirit of enlightenment (!) and being besotted with sentimentality (*AC* 6; *HA* I, 463; *HA* II/2, 221). From the perspective of morals, Romanticism and "the modern" are dismissed as *décadent*, while from the standpoint of taste the French are even forgiven their *décadence* (*EH* II, 3–5). France, "the highest school of taste," is said to possess "a masterly adroitness in transforming even the most fateful crises of its spirit into something charming and seductive . . ." (*NCW* "Where Wagner Belongs"; *BGE* 208).

In the case of Nietzsche's relationship to France and things French it becomes especially clear that one's own and the foreign are not simply two entities put into relationship to one another, but are related *always in a particular respect*. The judgment of a particular thing will often change according to which aspect of it is chosen. It has often been remarked that a self-contradiction obtains between many of Nietzsche's utterances, and this can certainly be explained in many cases with reference to his delight in playful and bizarre formulations. The same is true of his aphoristic style, which is often deliberately intended to cause the reader consternation. But often the "self-contradiction" derives simply from the fact that different *aspects* are being considered.

Similarly, it would be a major misunderstanding to take Nietzsche's talk of "intellectual nomadism" [*geistiges Nomadenthum*] as an arbitrary fondness for change of place (*HA* II/1, 211). Just as the nomad adapts himself to changing weather conditions, skilfully follows certain routes rather than simply setting off in any direction, favors certain areas while passing others by, so Nietzsche—when he moves into or abandons, avoids or attacks certain "positions"—orients himself according to "routes" that are opened up by certain perspectives or come to light with the reversal of other ones. Many "places" are given preference: he became such an established settler in "his" France, for example, that his name and thought have even been invoked by French nationalists. If his changes of place had been undertaken simply on whim, the Nietzsche-interpretation of the Nazis could have spared itself the grotesque effort of twisting the Francophile into a "profound" German whose fondness for France was simply incidental, as well as making the declared enemy of anti-Semitism (in spite of some undeniably anti-Semitic remarks) into a hater of Jews and Germanophile, in the face of his contempt for so much that today still—or rather since 1933 again—counts as typically German.

III

From a higher standpoint and a correspondingly broader perspective Nietzsche undertakes a critique of his own religion. In this case the "own" is Christian Europe, and to some extent also Judaism as a religion, while the foreign is now represented by non-European cultures, philosophies, and religions. What was formerly esteemed within the

European perspective about countries such as France and Italy is now in the broader perspective relativized, insofar as they participate in Christianity. This gives rise to the mutual intersection of a number of perspectives. In some respects Nietzsche is able to reconcile his distaste for Christianity with his love for France, as when he emphasizes that he *"loves"* Pascal (*EH* II, 3). Italy is commended, in spite of the Church and the papacy, for having produced a new antiquity in the form of the Renaissance. From the trans-European perspective the Germans again come off looking the worst, insofar as they proved to be the most compliant tools of Christianity (*AC* 60–61).

The foreign against which Christianity is measured is, above all, Hellenism. One of Nietzsche's most radical breaks with tradition is the idea, expressed in the title of one of his aphorisms, of "The Hellenic as Quite Foreign to Us" (*D* 169). The Greeks are said to be more foreign to "us" [free spirits] than "oriental or modern, Asiatic or European." Nietzsche is breaking here with the dominant opinion of the blossoming of bourgeois culture that the unity of European culture is founded upon Greek antiquity and Christianity in the same way.

In view of the voluminous literature on Nietzsche's critique of Christianity, we may restrict ourselves to those aspects of it which are connected with our theme. Just as the deficiencies and weaknesses that he ascribes to the Germans are mirrored by the merits and strengths he finds in the French, so the grounds on which Nietzsche attacks Christianity are reflected against the positive qualities he ascribes to the ancient Greeks. With the former we have "the sacrifice of all freedom, all pride, all self-confidence of the spirit; at the same time enslavement and self-mockery, self-mutilation" (*BGE* 46), while the Greeks "took the all-too-human to be inescapable and, instead of reviling it, preferred to accord it a kind of right of the second rank through regulating it within the usages of society and religion: indeed everything that has *power* within the human being they called Divine and inscribed on the walls of their Heaven" (*HA* II/1, 220). Here, with Christianity, we have "interiorization," there the Greeks have "superficiality . . . *out of profundity*"; here there is *ressentiment*, that "subterranean desire for revenge" on the part of "failures," and there "the moral free-mindedness of antiquity."[23] Nietzsche goes on to sharpen the terms of the contrast even further: here, "contradiction of life," sickness, *décadence,* and there "the outer limits of *affirmation,*" and the greatest health.[24] The final word is *"Dionysos versus the Crucified"* (*EH* IV, 9).

Nietzsche's rejection of Christianity based on "earlier" Hellenism applies also to Judaism insofar as he sees it as the *religion* from which

Christianity grew (*AC* 25, *KSA* 12, 10[72]). Here again the contrast
with the Greeks is emphasized: "The entire morality of Europe is *Jewish*—a deep foreignness still separates us from the Greeks" (*KSA* 9,
15[66]). On the other hand he continually expresses his admiration,
especially in the later work, for the Jews as a *people*. He sees in the Jews
a commendably "cleanly type . . . with a consummate habit of hardness
and frankness with themselves"—all of which Nietzsche, looking back
on his own, finds lacking in most Germans, and especially in "our dear
anti-Semites" (*KSA* 13, 21[8]). He remarks on how much Europe owes
to the Jews, and suggests that they are to play an important role in the
future shaping of the subcontinent (*BGE* 250, 251). What is otherwise,
under the religious aspect, so sharply contrasted (*KSA* 9, 7[175]) is here
brought together: "If Christianity has done everything to orientalize
the occident, Judaism has always played an essential part in occidental-
izing it again: which in a certain sense means making of Europe's mission and history a *continuation of the Greek*" (*HA* I, 475).

As early as his time in Basel Nietzsche despaired of the possibility of
a renewal of culture through a direct reaching back to the ancient tradition: "Only analogous, quasi Greek phenomena of *our* world can help
us now," he notes in 1873 (*KSA* 7, 25[1]). If he was at that time still in
accord with the new humanism of Goethe and Schiller, his opinion soon
changed radically—presumably under the influence of Burckhardt's
History of Greek Culture (*KSA* 14, 561; 8, 5[62–65]). In *Daybreak* he
characterizes "what used to be German culture," which "boasted of its
Greek ancestry," as a "soft, good-natured, silver-glistening idealism" (*D*
190). If Nietzsche confronted his contemporaries more and more with
the foreignness of the Greeks, to whom cultured classicists nevertheless
still felt so closely related, he at the same time suggestively projected a
kind of "healthy counter-world" to the decadent world of modernity. In
short, the foreign is invoked as something genuinely worth striving
after.

None of this is to say that in Nietzsche's denigration of Christianity
he *always* adduced the Greeks for comparison. He often criticizes the
former without any relation to a positive counter-image, frequently
measuring the reality of Christianity against its professed ideals. Thus
in an era of imperialistic colonialism he observes cynically that the
Christian God, "the God of love and cruelty," must be "a very clever
person, untrammeled by moral prejudices: the perfect God for Europeans wishing to dominate the earth" (*KSA* 10, 3[1] 75). Or else he un-
masks Christian bourgeois morality as the expression of a hypocritical
drive for power, by juxtaposing the self-deceived ideal with the reality
in an alienating matter-of-factness: "Marriage as the permitted form of

sexual satisfaction. War as the permitted form of murdering one's neighbor. School as the permitted form of education. Justice as the permitted form of revenge. Religion as the permitted form of the drive for knowledge" (*KSA* 10, 1[34]).

IV

It is significant that Nietzsche, as a critic of culture at a time when the major European powers were subjecting large parts of the world to their domination in the name of civilization, Christianity, and humanism, strove to put into question his own tradition from the perspective of non-European cultures. Even the Greeks, whom he so much admired, are not granted any "autochthonous" culture of their own; he argues rather that they "incorporated the living culture of other peoples" (*PTAG*, sec. 1). He goes so far as to say: "The genuinely *scientific* [*wissenschaftliche*] people, the people of literature, are the Egyptians and not the Greeks. . . . Alexandrine culture is a fusion of Hellenic and Egyptian . . ." (*KSA* 8, 5[122]). In opposition to contemporary aesthetic views which stemmed from Weimar classicism, Nietzsche denies that "the ancients immediately felt their sole sense of comfort within the delightful confines of the world of beauty," as Goethe maintained. He considers it quintessentially Greek "not to create forms, but to borrow them from abroad and transform them into the fairest appearance of beauty" (*HA* II/1, 221).

At a time when people lauded the victory of the ancient Greeks over the Persians as the saving of Europe from an "Asiatic" onslaught,[25] Nietzsche praises the honesty and integrity of the Persians (*KSA* 7, 32[82], 34[9]). Nor is it irrelevant that his major poetic work is named after a Persian (Zarathustra). He also writes of how "the wonderful Moorish cultural world of Spain [is] more closely related to us [free spirits], speaking more directly to our senses and taste, than Greece and Rome . . ." (*AC* 60). Christianity is said to have trampled this culture underfoot for precisely the reasons Nietzsche feels related to it: "because it was noble, because it owed its origin to manly instincts, because it said Yes to life even in the rare and exquisite treasures of Moorish life!" Here the foreign is valued far more highly than what is one's own, because one's own culture is either stuck in barbarism (as many of Nietzsche's remarks about the Germans suggest) or else because it experienced sublimation merely as *décadence*. Refinement *together with* affirmation of life—that is no less enthusiastically ascribed to Moorish and Arab culture than to Greek.[26]

The assertion that the oriental and Asiatic are less foreign to "us" than the Greek loses some of its strangeness when we see that Nietzsche calls "Egyptians, Hebrews, and Persians" "nations of the Orient" (*KSA* 8, 3[7]), as peoples who played a decisive part in the great mixing of cultures that was Hellenism or Alexandrinism; also that when he uses the term "Asiatic" in a cultural-historical sense he generally means the "Near and Middle East" (including India). The Greeks are thus for him "Asia's best heirs and pupils" (*BGE* 238), while Dionysus is an "Asian" deity who totally transformed "Apollinian Hellenism" (*KSA* 1, 591).

Seeing Asia as the continent, the geographical Europe appears to him as its "small peninsula," in contrast to the "cultural concept of Europe." This latter would then include "only those nations and ethnic minorities who possess a common past in Greece, Rome, Judaism, and Christianity" (*HA* II/2, 215). While Nietzsche's observations concerning India and the *Laws of Manu*, which he ranks far above the New Testament (*TI* VII, 3), allow one to infer at least some kind of a position with respect to Indian Buddhism from which he criticizes European culture, the rest of what he says about the cultures of Asia does not amount to a univocal "counter-image." It is true that he calls the Chinese "a well-endowed type" with "more stamina" than the European, and also sees them—along with the Hindus and the Jews—as being "beyond the despicable and wretched nonsense of [belief in] a personal survival of the individual . . ."(*KSA* 13, 15[8], 11[255]). But then there are also pejorative remarks about the Chinese, as in a note from the time of *Thus Spoke Zarathustra* which reads: "the last man: a kind of Chinese" (*KSA* 10, 4[204]).

We have been looking into Nietzsche's style and mode of thinking so far without regard to the validity of its content. The latter is of particular interest in the case of what he says about Buddhism, about which he appears to have possessed a rather limited understanding, and which he adduces when he needs to into the context of his own thinking. In condemning Christianity, Nietzsche expresses the desire "not to have wronged [this] kindred religion . . . [even though] they belong together as nihilistic religions" (*AC* 20; also *KSA* 12, 9[82]; 13, 11[373]). In spite of what they have in common, which he ascertains and rejects from the position of his "pessimism of strength" (*KSA* 13, 11[367]), he ranks Buddhism far above Christianity. Here we come upon another surprising reversal of perspectives. Although he is elsewhere generally critical of the "logicizing of the world" and "dominance of *rationality*" that have come to hold sway since Plato, what he praises about Buddhism is precisely its "philosophical clarity" and "high degree of intellectual spirituality"—above all because it achieves this without recourse to a "two worlds" doctrine.[27] At any rate he strikes a blow against occidental arrogance when he emphasizes that there have been "more thoughtful times, and times more distracted by analytic thinking, than ours," and not in Europe at all and long before the birth of Christianity: namely, at the time of the Buddha (*KSA* 11, 25[16]). Again it is above all the aesthetic aspect that lets Buddhism appear to him in a far more favorable light than Christianity (*GS* 132, 142; *KSA* 7, 13[3]). Further features of Buddhism that are apparently much closer to Nietzsche's way of thinking than the doctrines and commandments of his own religion, against which he fought on moral and aesthetic grounds, are: the absence of a concept of a personal God, "positivism," "phenomenalism," a stance "beyond good and evil," no "compulsion," no "attacks on those who think otherwise," a doctrine that "counters the feeling of *ressentiment*," a healthy way of life, and the rejection of the concepts of the individual soul and the ego.[28]

V

We have encountered in Nietzsche's technique of "estranging one's own by means of the foreign" the following modes:
1. One's own condition is confronted by earlier circumstances that are valued more highly and have by now become foreign.
2. One's own situation is measured by the standard of a more comprehensive and thereby superior paradigm ("European culture"), and thus appears as both restricting and restricted.
3. What is supposed to be one's own but is actually foreign (the Greeks, for example) is set up in opposition, directly as a positive "counter-image" and mediately as a prototype.
4. One's own is taken as a form of culture ("European culture") and is shown in its strangeness from the perspective of other forms of culture (Islam and Buddhism as cultures).

In the majority of these cases what is one's own comes off badly in comparison with the foreign. From the perspective of the latter one's own situation turns out to have deficiencies and weaknesses that are simply not seen within one's own horizon, or else are actually taken to be advantages. What Nietzsche calls the "tiresome gravity" of the Germans, for example, as seen from the Jewish perspective, is esteemed as "profundity" in Germany itself (*KSA* 12, 10[56]). One need hardly add that Nietzsche adopted the position of an extreme outsider not only as an individual but above all as a contemporary of an avowedly nationalistic—or, at best, Eurocentric—epoch. And it is important to understand that he did not value alien cultures because of their close ties with nature, their "primordiality," or because they were morally unspoiled, in the way that eighteenth-century Europe had admired the "noble savage," but precisely because of their intellectual, artistic, and practical *superiority*.

We saw further that Nietzsche's reversals of perspectives do not proceed in an arbitrary way, but rather in accordance with quite definite principles of his philosophical thought. It is therefore no coincidence that most of the positive or negative judgments fall under the aspects of what serves life ("affirmation of life") and of "good taste" or "classical taste" (*GM* III, 19; *KSA* 13, 11[95]). These in turn correspond to two of the major themes in his philosophy as a whole: will to power, and the intrinsic value of "appearance" (*Schein—BGE* 2).

Although Nietzsche usually ranks the foreign higher, his concern lies for the most part with his "own" *as criticized from the perspective of the foreign*. We hardly ever come across observations of a foreign culture in Nietzsche without their being related back in this way. It has been said that Buddhism serves as a "backdrop" against which he sets into relief the features of Christianity which he condemns. This image seems not quite appropriate, insofar as it suggests that one is standing in front of or behind the other, and that both are being seen in the same direction. But in fact Nietzsche is in such cases mostly looking *back at his own from the respective counterpositions*. This reflexivity is captured in a striking image from an aphorism entitled "Estranged from the Present": from out on the ocean upon which one has dared to embark we look back at the coast, and "command a view, no doubt for the first time, of its total configuration, and when we approach it again we have the advantage of understanding it better as a whole than those who have never left it" (*HA* I, 616). This is the sense in which "the genuinely original heads" are not those who see something "new" for the first time, but who see "anew" those features of their own situation that are "obvious" and thus "overlooked" (*HA* II/1, 200). And with this Nietzsche gives expression to a basic problem of philosophical *hermeneutics*.

VI

It is not possible here to examine the whole of Nietzsche's work in order to make his "implicit hermeneutics" explicit.[29] But I think that we can at least determine his hermeneutical stance, or position, by considering the *metaphor-system* that informs much of his thinking. To look at the "optics" of the imagery in which Nietzsche's perspectivism is elaborated is by no means to abandon philosophy in favor of literary poetics. There can be no question that his perspective-metaphorics has a conceptual character too, and is thus no mere rhetorical ornamentation. On the basis of the idea that all philosophical concepts have in any case a metaphorical origin,[30] in his employment of imagery Nietzsche is doing *consciously* what others have previously done without being aware of it. A consideration of the rigor of Nietzsche's "image-concepts" shows in addition that his perspectivism can by no means be equated with relativism.[31]

Optical metaphors are, of course, strikingly frequent in Nietzsche's perspectivism, especially since one of his aims is to "see through" habitual practices that have become incorporated [*eingefleischt*] to the point of being our "flesh and blood" (*BGE* 24). This can be done only if one *distances* oneself from what is one's own, which is otherwise considered "natural" and therefore valid. "*Not* to see many things, not to be impartial in anything, to be party through and through, to have a strict and necessary perspective [*Optik*] in all values," is what characterizes the "weak-willed" and the "believer" (*AC* 54). What Nietzsche earlier (in the essay on history) saw as the basic condition of healthy life is now denigrated precisely in the name of will to power, the mark of which is the "overcoming of narrower perspectives" (*KSA* 12, 2[108]; *WP* 616). Now the unconditional attachment to a *single* view is seen as the "pathological determination" of an "optics" of fanaticism (*AC* 54); and the greater the "strength of spiritual sight and insight," the more "the distance and space around the human being expands" (*BGE* 57). For a "reversal of habitual evaluations and valued habits" what is needed is a "different way of seeing" [*Verschiedenheit des Blicks*] (*HA* I, Preface 1), and this would require an *external* standpoint at a greater distance (ocean metaphors) and height (mountain metaphors—*GS* 15). For only from afar can the *proportions* of what is one's own become visible (*GS* 380), only from a distance can one see it "as a whole" and indeed "for the first time . . . in its total configuration" (*HA* I, 616). "Distance" is more than merely intervening space, but involves for Nietzsche a feeling of superiority, what he calls the "*pathos of distance*" (*AC* 43).

The elements within the metaphorical matrix of perspectives, remoteness, view from the outside, and distance are all conditioned by Nietzsche's image of *Hinterfragen*, "questioning behind" (*D* 523). This term, which apparently first came into use in the 1870s,[32] was chosen by Nietzsche to characterize not just an attitude toward other people (as in the aphorism from *Daybreak*) but also his own subversive activities of "tunneling, mining, and undermining" (Preface 1). The direction implied in the image is clear: what is one's own is not simply examined "frontally." One's view is in addition directed *back*, to the aspect(s) that remain hidden for those who "have never left" it. But since it is after all one's own, it is seen from the front as well. It is in this sense that I would understand Nietzsche's term *Doppelblick*, "double vision."[33] In hermeneutical terms, then, he is encouraging the interpreter to step out *consciously* from his own tradition, so that the double vision of the "unavoidable psychologist and reader of souls" (*BGE* 269) may let his own situation be "devaluated" for the sake of an eventual revaluation.

VII

Let me conclude by summing up some primary features of Nietzsche's hermeneutics which can be extracted from the logic of his imagery:
1. The aspects of one's own situation that become visible from a distance are not discernible from within one's own horizons, having been unconsciously or deliberately covered over.
2. Only when one steps out of the horizon of one's own situation and looks back at it from a distance can one see its overall structure.
3. Because one remains "aboriginally" bound to one's own even after having distanced oneself from it, one is capable of a "double vision": how one's own shows itself and what it conceals come into view simultaneously.
4. This "simultaneous seeing" makes it possible to "evaluate" one's own: what it shows "from itself" can be questioned from the perspective of what it conceals.
5. This kind of *Hinterfragen* presupposes not only the farness of distance (the ocean metaphor) but also the greater height of the newly achieved position (mountain metaphor), which makes the image of "perspective" more important than that of "horizon"—which is a primary concept in Gadamer's hermeneutics.
6. The "logic" of Nietzsche's imagery makes it clear why his primary interest does not lie with *the foreign itself*, in which he adopts a standpoint: his purpose is to look *back* at his own situation from the perspective of the foreign.

The idea has been to show the significance of the place of "the foreign" in Nietzsche's hermeneutic perspectivism. Given the depth of today's universal doubts concerning the nature of human being, it is not surprising that so much attention is being paid to Nietzsche's method of "questioning behind," and that the related ideas in his work are being invoked by representatives of critical theory, postmodernism, and deconstruction.[34] Like Marx's *Kapital* and Freud's *Traumdeutung*, Nietzsche's *On the Genealogy of Morals* "makes us ill and hits us personally."[35] One wonders whether with Nietzsche's significant "come-back" a *getting behind in his sense*—in which one's own is scrutinized far more critically than the foreign—might be at work in our contemporary "syncretism." If this were so, the prospects for the cohabitation of peoples and the side-by-side development of cultures would presumably be much improved.

Notes

1. Nietzsche, *Werke, Kritische Gesamtausgabe*, Giorgio Colli and Mazzino Montinari, eds. (Berlin, 1967ff.).

2. Eric Blondel, "Vom Nutzen und Nachteil des Sprache für das Verständnis Nietzsches: Nietzsche und der französische Strukturalismus," *Nietzsche-Studien* 10/11 (1981/82):518–37, at 527.

3. Reinhold Grimm and Jost Hermand, eds., *Karl Marx und Friedrich Nietzsche* (Madison, 1978); Reinhart Maurer, "Nietzsche und die Kritische Theorie," *Nietzsche-Studien* 10/11 (1981/82):34–58; Horst Baier, "Die Gesellschaft—ein langer Schatten des toten Gottes. Friedrich Nietzsche und die Entstehung der Soziologie aus dem Geist der décadence," ibid., 6–22; Johann Figl, "Nietzsche und die philosophische Hermeneutik des 20. Jahrhunderts," ibid., 408–30; Kurt Rudolf Fischer, "Nietzsche, Freud und die humanistische Psychologie," ibid., 482–99.

4. Mazzino Montinari, *Nietzsche lesen* (Berlin and New York, 1982), p. 1.

5. Giorgio Colli, *Nach Nietzsche* (Frankfurt, 1980), p. 209.

6. Karl Schlechta, ed., *Friedrich Nietzsche, Werke in drei Bänden* (Munich, 1956), vol. 3, p. 1435.

7. Wolfgang Müller-Lauter, *Nietzsche, seine Philosophie der Gegensätze und die Gegensätze seiner Philosophie* (Berlin and New York, 1971); Ruediger H. Grimm, *Nietzsche's Theory of Knowledge* (Berlin and New York, 1977); Friedrich Kaulbach, *Nietzsches Idee einer Experimentalphilosophie* (Cologne and Vienna, 1980); Johann Figl, *Interpretation als philosophisches Prinzip: Friedrich Nietzsches universale Theorie der Auslegung im späten Nachlass* (Berlin and New York, 1982); idem, *Dialektik der Gewalt: Nietzsches hermeneutische Religionsphilosophie mit Berücksichtigung unveröffentlichter Manuskripte* (Düsseldorf, 1984).

8. EN—"*das 'hinterfragende' Fremdmachen des Eigenen vom Fremden her.*" The author remarks on the infelicity of the term *Fremdmachen*, here translated no less infelicitously as "estranging," noting that the more appropriate *verfremden* ("alienate") has already been terminologically "reserved" since Bertolt Brecht.

9. "*Counter*-positions" means here positions from which what is envisaged is seen as a positive or negative "counter-image."

10. EN—*hinterfragen*: literally, "questioning behind." The author refers here to aphorism 523 of *Daybreak*, the title of which is *Hinterfragen*. Hollingdale translates this title "Subsequent questions," but Professor Scheiffele is surely right to take the *fragen* as the infinitive of the verb, in view of the content of the aphorism which follows:

Whenever a person reveals something, one can ask: what is it supposed to conceal? From what is it supposed to divert the eyes? What prejudice is it supposed to arouse? And additionally: how far does the subtlety of this dissimulation go? And in what way has it failed?

11. EN—"etwas *Befremdliches*": this term means "strange, odd, disconcerting, off-putting," and has at its root the word *fremd*, meaning "foreign, alien."

12. See Hans-Georg Gadamer, *Truth and Method*, (New York, 1975), pp. 261f. and 273f.; Nietzsche, *Ecce Homo* I, 1: "Now I know how, have the know-how, to *reverse perspectives*: the first reason why a 'revaluation of values' is perhaps possible for me alone."

13. As, for example, in a passage from the *Nachlass* of the autumn of 1885, where Nietzsche discusses German music, "Baroque style," and philosophy.

14. *UM* I, 1. This idea is developed also in *The Birth of Tragedy* and the lectures *On the Future of Our Educational Institutions* (1872–73).

15. *On the Future of Our Educational Institutions*, lecture 2 (*KSA* 1, 686).

16. *KSA* 8, 5[59]; compare *KSA* 8, 7[7]: "The philologist must, if he wants to prove his innocence, understand three things: antiquity, the present, and himself."

17. See *The Antichrist* 61. Nietzsche sees Luther's Reformation as "disastrous" because without it Christianity, owing to a further secularization of the papacy and thereby the Roman Catholic Church, would have been destroyed.

18. *EH* III, "The Case of Wagner," 3; see also *KSA* 12, 10[56].

19. *HA* II/1, 323; see also 302, where Nietzsche invokes the example of Goethe to show that "a German has to *be more* than a German if he wants to be useful, indeed even endurable, to other nations. . . ."

20. A similar equation of the German and the Lutheran is still to be found in Thomas Mann's novel *Doktor Faustus*.

21. *KSA* 13, 11[322]; the "*great line*" refers to the adoption of a distant perspective in order to see things clearly in their context.

22. One example among many: in contrast to German prose style which is distinguished, in Nietzsche's view, by its "obscurity, exaggeration, and occasional thinness and dryness," would be the "clarity and delicate precision" of the French stylists (*HA* II/2, 214).

23. *GM* II, 16; *GS* Preface 4; *EH* III, "The Birth of Tragedy" 2; *KSA* 12, 8[4]; *HA* II/1, 220.

24. *KSA* 13, 17[4]; *AC* 24; *EH* III, "BT" 1; *The Birth of Tragedy*, "Attempt at a Self-Criticism."

25. Jacob Burckhardt was a significant exception to this tendency. He emphasized that the Greeks had even called the "highly civilized Asians" barbarians,

"whose culture was much older and more complete in technology and ancient wisdom" (*Kulturgeschichte Griechenlands* [Olten, 1934], p. 191).

26. *KSA* 13, 14[180–2], *GS* Preface 4; see also *HA* I, 259, *D* 170, *TI* IX, 47.

27. *The Birth of Tragedy*, "Attempt at a Self-Criticism" 4; *KSA* 13, 11[367]. A further reason for this differential evaluation is probably that Nietzsche sees Socratism and Christianity as having effected a *moralization* of the intellectual, while Buddhism is said to have "left the self-deception of moral concepts behind it" (*AC* 20).

28. "Positivism" means in this context "realism," while "phenomenalism" refers to the refusal to abandon the world of appearances in favor of a "world beyond." See, on this theme, Freny Mistry, *Nietzsche and Buddhism* (Berlin and New York, 1981), p. 53f.

29. EN—The original version of Professor Scheiffele's essay for this volume did in fact contain an extensive and illuminating discussion of Nietzsche's methodology in relation to the German hermeneutical tradition, with a special emphasis on Gadamer; but for reasons of space it had to be omitted.

30. See, especially, the essay from 1873, "On Truth and Lie in the Extra-Moral Sense"; also *KSA* 7, 19[39].

31. On the theme of concept and metaphor in Nietzsche, see Alan Schrift, "Between Perspectivism and Philology: Genealogy as Hermeneutic," *Nietzsche-Studien* 16 (1987): 91–111, at 97f.; Günter Abel, "Logik und Ästhetik," *Nietzsche-Studien* 16 (1987):112–48, at 124; Slobodan Žunjić, "Begrifflichkeit und Metapher: Einige Bemerkungen zu Nietzsches Kritik der philosophischen Sprache," *Nietzsche-Studien* 16 (1987):149–63.

32. Heinz Küpper, *Illustriertes Wörterbuch der deutschen Umgangssprache* (Stuttgart, 1983), vol. 4, p. 1289.

33. EN—The author refers here to a passage in *Ecce Homo* where Nietzsche writes of a proposition of his friend Paul Rée's as possessing "that *double vision* of the world which all great insights share" (*EH* III, "*HA*" 6). Nietzsche is himself citing a passage (without giving the reference) from aphorism 37 of *Human, All Too Human* I. Both Kaufmann (*EH*) and Hollingdale (*HA*) translate *Doppelblick* as "Janus-face," but "double vision" is both more faithful and also nicely evocative of William Blake's desire to be saved from "single vision and Newton's sleep."

34. See, for example, Jürgen Habermas, *Theory of Communicative Action*, vol. 1 (Boston, 1981); Jean-François Lyotard, *The Postmodern Condition: A Report on Knowledge* (Minneapolis, 1979). An excellent comparison of Jacques Derrida's deconstructive thinking and Nietzsche's critical methods can be found in Ernst Behler, *Derrida-Nietzsche/Nietzsche-Derrida* (Munich, 1988).

35. Behler, p. 89 (paraphrasing Michel Foucault).

II

INDIA

4

Nietzsche's Early Encounters with Asian Thought

Johann Figl, *translated by Graham Parkes*

Much of Nietzsche's beginnings lies in the dark. It is true that we have information—more than in the case of almost any other thinker—about countless details concerning his childhood and youth; a glance at the writings and letters of this earliest period easily convinces one of the richness of detailed information that lies at our disposal.[1] Nevertheless, Nietzsche research soon runs up against barriers imposed by Nietzsche's extant notes, either because there is very little or else nothing available on a particular theme, or because potentially relevant notes have not been included in the editions of works from his youth that have been published so far. In the first case it is necessary to adduce further sources lying beyond Nietzsche's own notes, in order to attain at least indirect acquaintance with his position on a specific theme; in the second, one is obliged to go beyond what has already been published and take into account the unpublished materials in the Nietzsche holdings of the Goethe-Schiller Archive in Weimar.[2]

In order to treat the question of Nietzsche's early encounters with Asian thought it is necessary to proceed along both of the ways mentioned above: one has to go back to unpublished materials in the archives, and also ascertain the intellectual "atmosphere" within which it was possible for Nietzsche to learn of Asian ideas. The central orientation must be provided by Nietzsche's writings themselves, insofar as any portrayal of the intellectual background of his thinking should take his texts as its point of departure; and it is toward those writings that any investigations into the broader literature must lead, in order to do justice to the task of documenting the nature and extent of Nietzsche's encounters with Asian thought.

The present essay is concerned exclusively with an early phase of these encounters: the primary focus is on Nietzsche's "high school" years at Pforta (1858–64), while the second part of the essay discusses some unpublished lectures notes from his year as a student at the University of Bonn (1864–65). We are thus concerned with the period of Nietzsche's youthful writings, years before his first publications, which was for that reason perhaps of decisive importance for his later acquaintance with the Asian intellectual and spiritual tradition.

I

Nietzsche's interest in the religion and myth of an Asian culture is evidenced by a request for a book on his seventeenth birthday (1861). In a "request for presents" he mentions—in addition to Feuerbach's *The Essence of Christianity* and *Thoughts on Death and Immortality*—"Wollheim, *Altindische Mythologie*." [3]

Nietzsche's explicit knowledge of Asian—and, more precisely, Indian—ideas during his high school years is documented by two remarks he made at the age of seventeen or eighteen, which will serve as the point of departure for the reflections that follow. In a note from April 1862 bearing the title "Freedom of the Will and Fate," he wrote:

The Hindu says: Fate is nothing other than actions performed during an earlier phase of our existence. (*BAW* 2, 61)

These words embody an acquaintance with the doctrines of karma and rebirth. The remark occurs in the context of an engagement with the Christian belief in the immortality of the soul, in which Nietzsche says to all those who believe in immortality that they must also "believe in the pre-existence of the soul," if they do not want "to have something immortal develop out of something mortal." It is clear that already in high school Nietzsche was contemplating oriental religiosity as a critical alternative to Christianity. This was the time during which Nietzsche was parting company with the Christian faith, as many documents from the period show. [4]

Again in the context of the question of fate Nietzsche comes to speak of two basic documents of Indian literature and religion, the *Mahābhārata* and the *Rāmāyana*. These two epics are mentioned in a draft Nietzsche made of an essay for school dated December 8, 1862 (*BAW* 2, 445 *Nachbericht*), which took as its theme "the characterization of

Kriemhild in the Nibelungen Song."[5] The delineation of the character is here set in the context of a fate-ordained entanglement in guilt. At the beginning of the essay we find the statement that even in situations in which people "think they are swept away by the rolling wheels of an eternal fate," there will always be moments "in which the human being catches sight of the gods in serene and eternal greatness, sitting on their chairs and themselves chained to their guilt and lacerated by remorse" (*BAW* 2, 129). There then follows an allusion to the great epics of the world's literatures:

Such a profound conception of fate shines out—even if visible to only the sharper of sight—from those folk poems in which the spiritual and emotional world of a whole nation comes to light in primordial magnificence and purity, in the Iliad and Odyssey, the Ramayana and Mahabharata, in the Nibelungen and Gudrun. (*BAW* 2, 445 *Nachbericht*)

Having cited these two statements of Nietzsche's about Indian religion and literature, we must pose the question concerning the sources of his modest acquaintance with the Indian tradition. This question can best be answered by considering the teachers and classes, as well as the materials used in class, at Schulpforta. We shall do this with the understanding that it will not be a case of demonstrating direct connections, but rather of characterizing the intellectual atmosphere within which Nietzsche's knowledge of Asian ideas was acquired, and which in principle, at least, made possible an indirect encounter with the Orient during his school years.

With respect to the place of Oriental Studies in the intellectual atmosphere of Schulpforta, we must begin by saying that Asian thought was certainly not of primary interest in the curriculum there. The major emphasis was unequivocally on classical Western languages, as Nietzsche himself remarks in a biographical essay he wrote on the occasion of his call to the professorship at Basel.[6] In assessing the importance of Nietzsche's knowledge of Asia while at Pforta, one is right to surmise that it bears relatively little significance, insofar as non-European cultures were considered only incidentally, being mentioned only in the broader contexts of the subjects taught. The search for sources will therefore turn primarily to the syllabi and course materials,[7] as well as to the publications of Nietzsche's teachers, in order to find things relevant to Asia.

An important source for information that Nietzsche will have encountered in his classes at Pforta are the yearly reports of the programs

of study there.[8] On the occasion of the annual celebration of the found-
ing of the Imperial school there would appear a report from the rector
of the institution, together with a scholarly essay by one of the school's
teachers. This report would contain a list of the contents of the various
grades and subjects at the school, the themes of the free compositions
in Latin and German, the school rules and a chronicle of the events of
the previous year, a list of the pupils with statistical data, and an overview of all instructional materials including a list of books donated to
the school library.

While a survey of syllabi and essay topics gives no indication of a
concern with Asian thought, the catalogues of books do provide some
material that is relevant to our inquiry. These catalogues show that the
contemporary scholarship on Asia, and on India in particular, was taken
account of at Pforta.[9] Evidence that an interest in oriental languages and
cultures was awakened in a number of the pupils comes from the case of
Paul Deussen, the famous colleague and friend of Nietzsche's, who went
on to study Sanskrit at the University of Bonn.[10]

One can assume, moreover, that Nietzsche's teachers at Pforta also
communicated in their classes something of the research embodied in
their professional publications, and that some connections with Asian
cultures were made in this way.

One of the teachers at Pforta who was acquainted with Indian philosophy was August Steinhart (1801–72), who was Professor of Greek and
Hebrew there from 1831 until 1871. Steinhart distinguished himself in
his scholarly research in Neoplatonic and then, later, Platonic philosophy.[11] In 1829 he published a treatise on the dialectic of Plotinus, and in
1840 a work entitled *Meletemata Plotiniana*, both of which appeared
with the annual report at Pforta. Nietzsche took Latin (texts by Cicero)
from Steinhart while in the upper second form, and Greek in the upper
first, when Plato's *Phaedo* was one of the texts studied.[12] Steinhart was
also Nietzsche's Hebrew teacher.[13]

In his publications Steinhart discusses the influence of Asia at the
time of the Plotinian dialectic, saying of the Gnostics that they "confused the Christian truth with their empty phantasms drawn from obscure Asiatic sources." In the *Meletemata Plotiniana* he gives a more
positive estimation of Eastern thought, saying that "the philosophy of
the Asiatic peoples, and above all of the Indians, is not to be neglected,"
if one wants to understand the philosophy of the Platonists properly.[14]
Steinhart's work exemplifies an open reception of the currents of Indian
thought that had been introduced in Europe primarily through H.T.
Colebrooke's work *On the Philosophy of the Hindus* (1824). Proof that

Nietzsche was introduced by Steinhart to Indian philosophy is not to be found in the *Historisch-kritische Gesamtausgabe (BAW)*; to settle that question one has to consult the unpublished notes from Nietzsche's school days.

There is reason to suppose, however, that some acquaintance with Oriental culture came to Nietzsche by way of another of his instructors at Pforta, the German teacher Karl August Koberstein. The significance of this famous literary historian for the school was that he fought to have German taught on the same high level as the classical languages, with the result that this subject came to rank with the highest at this elite school.[15]

As mentioned earlier, Nietzsche had referred to the *Mahābhārata* and the *Rāmāyana* in a German essay, in a comparison with the *Nibelungen*. This connection points directly to one of the major features of the instruction in German that Nietzsche received from Koberstein. The *Nibelungen* was usually on the syllabus for Koberstein's upper second class, and when Nietzsche took it (in the winter semester 1862–63) the title was "An Explication of some Passages in the *Song of the Nibelungen*"; and when he was in the upper first, the course was "A Survey of Older German National Literature." In both classes Nietzsche chose a theme from the *Nibelungen* as the topic for his free composition.[16]

Nevertheless, it remains an open question whether Nietzsche in fact became acquainted with the *Mahābhārata* and the *Rāmāyana* in his German class or through another source. At any rate the juxtaposition of these epic poems from various cultures was to be found in the contemporary literature—as, for example, in a work by Valentin Rose that appeared in 1854, from which Nietzsche transcribed some excerpts three years after leaving Pforta.[17] The important thing is that Nietzsche did compare the Indian epics with the *Nibelungen*; that such a comparison should be not only conceivable but also probable in the context of Koberstein's instruction and publications will now be demonstrated.

Koberstein conducted intensive research on the *Nibelungenlied*. Karl Bartsch, the editor after Koberstein's death of the fifth edition of his survey (*Geschichte der deutschen Nationalliteratur*), writes in the Foreword that he found in the manuscripts left behind by Koberstein "an excerpt of 53 closely written quarto pages on the *Nibelungenlied*."[18] An important place is accorded to the discussion of the *Nibelungenlied* in the editions of his *History* that Koberstein published himself. In the Introduction to the entire work he emphasizes the great age of the epic, and also mentions the theory that "it possibly came from the Orient with migrating German tribes."

Koberstein comes to say more about the Orient when he inquires into the influences on "German national literature." In suggesting that as early as the Middle Ages and even more so in the modern period "foreign elements exerted an influence" on German literature, he again mentions the Orient: "in part directly, but at least indirectly the [literatures] of the Orient have helped at various times to determine, to a greater or lesser extent, the literary life of the Germans with respect to materials, form, and content."

Koberstein points to two such epochs of Asiatic influence: transmission by way of the Crusades, and the Romantic period. With respect to the knights who returned from the Orient he writes: "What is Oriental about many of the German poems of this period, in those concerning the Grail especially, comes as much from the Spanish Arabs by way of the French and the Provencales as directly from Asia." At the beginning of the nineteenth century he maintains, with a rather critical attitude, that there prevailed "a juxtaposition and confusion of conflicting directions, a colorful chaos of modelings and imitations of older indigenous and foreign poems from all countries and epochs," and adduces an abundance of translations from Oriental languages and from Indian poetry which proved decisive for historical scholarship.[19] Koberstein had a detailed knowledge of the manifold influences of Oriental poetry, and one can assume that these relationships were at least mentioned in his lectures.

The relation of Europe to Asia can, however, be established at a more fundamental level: namely, on the basis of the theory of the "Indo-German family of languages," which for Koberstein had been "indubitably established by contemporary scholarship."[20] At the beginning of his *Geschichte* he proceeds from the Asiatic origin of the Germans, having just mentioned the undeniable basic similarity between Occidental and some Oriental languages.

Koberstein took the basic assumptions of early "Indo-Germanistik" as academically certified data, and presumably communicated them as such in the classes Nietzsche attended. The earliest this could have happened was when Nietzsche was in the lower second, for which the syllabus in German reads: "Basic outlines of the etymological part of German grammar, with a survey of the major epochs in the developmental history of our language."[21]

In the context of the linguistic and cultural-historical assumption of an Indo-German family of peoples, Koberstein was also interested in a motif that supposedly demonstrated the connection between European and Asian poetries—namely, a certain "kind of transmigration of the soul" as he expressed it in the title of his essay "Über die in Sage und Dichtung gangbare Vorstellung von dem Fortleben abgeschiedener menschlicher Seelen in der Pflanzenwelt" ("On the Idea in Saga and Poem of the Survival of Departed Human Souls in the Plant-World").[22] It is possible that Nietzsche's acquaintance with the related idea of a preexistence of the soul, which he referred to as Hinduistic, stemmed from his encounters with his teacher's reflections along these lines.

The evidence adduced so far will have shown that at Pforta, in spite of the school's definite classical-philological orientation, Asian thought was by no means excluded but was allowed to come into consideration, at least occasionally, in the context of other topics and issues. Koberstein in particular, who was reputed to be "at home in foreign literatures," was able to build a bridge to the realm of Eastern thought.[23] He was in Nietzsche's estimation "one of the most outstanding teachers of philology" at Pforta, contact with whom Nietzsche regarded as "most fortunate."[24]

The comprehensive erudition of the teachers at Pforta was therefore not only the best preparation for the study of philology, but it also communicated to Nietzsche some sense of Eastern ideas, with the result that he was not totally unprepared for the encounter with Asian thought, to the extent that this took place at the University. He presumably gathered further information there about Asian religions and cultures, as can be seen from unpublished notes he made while a university student at Bonn.

II

Insufficient research has been done so far on the importance of Nietzsche's student days for his subsequent philosophical development. This is shown by the fact that the notes he made while a university student have not yet been published. These can provide information concerning the important influences of his student years, and they often document his first encounters with theologians and philosophers both historical and contemporary.[25] The notes Nietzsche made of the lectures he attended, which are to be found in the Goethe-Schiller Archive in Weimar, can also provide information concerning his encounters with Asian thought and with non-European cultures in general.

One must bear in mind that Nietzsche began by studying theology at Bonn in the autumn of 1864, and then switched to philology and was registered in the philosophical faculty in the following spring. In the summer semester of 1865 he attended a seminal lecture course by Carl

Schaarschmidt entitled "Allgemeine Geschichte der Philosophie" ("General History of Philosophy"),[26] which is the basis for the reflections that follow. After his year at Bonn, Nietzsche went to the University of Leipzig where he continued his studies in philology. Only a small portion of the notes from his time as a university student are from lectures on theology, philosophy, and intellectual history, most of them being from philology lectures (*BAW* 1, LV s.), which will not be considered here. With respect to the notes concerning the history of philosophy, the focus will remain on the theme of the relationship to Asia, since the structure of the notes in general and of the special question of Buddhism have already been treated in detail elsewhere.[27]

Schaarschmidt's lecture course begins with an introduction discussing the general concept of philosophy and the history of philosophy, as well as talking about sources, texts and methodology. Then follows a presentation of "ancient philosophy" (pp. 8–32), "modern philosophy," with emphasis on Spinoza, Locke, Berkeley, and Hume (pp. 44–51), and then "most recent philosophy" (p. 56), which includes a listing and partial discussion of the works of Kant (p. 61f), and, on a separate page (p. 59), an excerpt from the appendix to Schopenhauer's *The World as Will and Representation* under the heading "Kritik der Kantische[n] Philosophie von A. Schopenhauer."[28]

Asian thought is not considered in the contents of the lecture *per se*; in fact it is consciously excluded. After the heading "Ancient Philosophy" it is explicitly stated: "We shall simply exclude Oriental [philosophy]" (p. 8). On Schaarschmidt's view, then, Asian thought is not included in the history of philosophy. He is apparently following here the model that was current in the latter half of the nineteenth century, which excluded Eastern philosophies from the historical narrative, as demonstrated by Wilhelm Halbfass in the case of India.[29]

In spite of this pronouncement, Far Eastern thought is mentioned three times in Nietzsche's notes: in the Introduction, in the discussion of Neoplatonism, and in the excerpt from Schopenhauer.

In Schaarschmidt's introductory remarks, the statement that "philosophy begins with wonder," is followed by the proposition that "the Indo-German and Semitic branches are the bearers of philosophical development" (p. 5). The assumption of Indo-German as basic organically forms a bridge to Asian thought:

The Indo-German branch extends from southwest Asia through Europe, India, Persia. . . . The Indian nation, then the Greek and the German peoples are the bearers of philosophical significance. (p. 5)

To this relationship from the history of ideas based on a putative eth-
nological connection there corresponds the assertion of an economic
basis:

Earlier trading relations between Asia Minor, India, and Greece let us suppose
that ideas, too, were transported. (p. 6)

In both passages there is explicit mention of Asia, but the focus on
"southwest Asia" or "Asia Minor" shows that the Far East, China, and
Japan are not under consideration. Indian philosophy, by contrast, is accorded special consideration and its content cursorily sketched.

First the "Brahmanic system of religion" is presented as "an ossifi-
cation of an originally pure and noble nature-religion," and philosophy
is then said to appear in connection with this system. Sāmkya philosophy is introduced as a discipline that shows "independence from orthodox views." (p. 6)

After a listing of the "three main topics: 1) divine things, God and
creation, 2) the soul and the ascetic compulsion, 3) logical doctrines,"
there follows a kind of summing up:

Basic pantheistic character, the world is an emanation of God, as is the human
soul. Admittedly this is not logically proven. Rather an assertion according to
the Vedas, the popular system. The goal of asceticism is to abolish the bounds
of earthly imperfection. Transmigration of the soul is the consequence. . . .
(p. 6)

Then, after a mention of "The Laws of Manu," there follows a remark
about Buddhism:

In Buddhism there is an even deeper submersion into pantheistic nihilism. Nirvana is the goal "annihilation." (p. 6)

With this Nietzsche would seem to have gained some further acquaintance with Indian thought, or at least a sense of its main currents and
major concepts.

The next reference comes in the context of a presentation of Neoplatonism:

There is an Oriental influence here. Gnosticism. 1) *Parsism* (dualism) 2) *Buddhism* (bells and rosaries) 3) *Judaism* . . . (p. 28)

Finally, in one of the last pages of the manuscript, there is an indirect
reference to Asian philosophy in a discussion of Schopenhauer's major

work. There is an excerpt from the passage in which Schopenhauer compares the achievement of Kant with Indian thought.[30] Nietzsche's notes read as follows:

This is at the same time the primary view of Plato as well as of the Vedas and Puranas. (Allegory of the Cave in the *Republic.* —The veil of Maya) (p. 59)

This concludes the present inquiry, which ought to be developed further in the direction of an intensive historical examination of the communication of Oriental wisdom in Nietzsche's intellectual milieu. Such an inquiry would begin from the chronological limit set here, namely, from the end of Nietzsche's first year of study at Bonn.

III

Nietzsche's earliest encounters with Asian thought took place on several levels and in various thematic areas. The heterogeneity of the influences derives from the circumstance that they took for the most part an indirect form, having been mediated primarily by his teachers at Schulpforta. In particular, it was in Nietzsche's German classes that he was prompted to undertake the comparison between the Indian epics, the *Mahābhārata* and the *Rāmāyana*, and Greek and German epic poems. Then in his first year as a student at the University of Bonn, he became further acquainted with Asian thought through the lectures of Carl Schaarschmidt.

Consideration of the unpublished manuscripts of Nietzsche's lecture notes on the history of philosophy shows that he was exposed at this early stage to Indian thought in a fairly comprehensive manner. This is all the more surprising when one considers that in the notes from this period that have been published so far in the "Historical-Critical Edition" of Nietzsche's works there is practically no mention of such a general acquaintance with the great cultures of Asia. This gives us grounds for supposing that many other notes from Nietzsche's youth that have not yet been published could be relevant to the question of his acquaintance with Asian thought. A comprehensive answer to this question can be given only when the entire *Nachlass* from Nietzsche's youth is made available in a critical edition. This may well show that Nietzsche's knowledge of non-European cultures—as well as his acquaintance with the history of European philosophy and culture—was more fundamental than can be demonstrated on the basis of the extant editions of his early writings.

Notes

1. Since Nietzsche's juvenalia have not yet appeared in the *Kritische Gesamtausgabe* edited by Colli and Montinari, references will be given to the *Historisch-kritische Ausgabe* (abbreviated "*BAW*"), 5 vols., edited by H. J. Mette et al. (Leipzig, 1933–40). The letters will be cited from the *Kritische Gesamtausgabe: Briefe* ("*KGB*") edited by Colli and Montinari (Berlin and New York, 1975ff).

2. My special thanks are due to the directors of the *Nationale Forschungs- und Gedenkstätten der klassischen deutschen Literatur* in Weimar, the Goethe-Schiller Archive, for granting access to the unpublished manuscripts of Nietzsche that are used here: NFG/GSA 71/41 (C II 1); see note 26, below.

3. A. E. Wollheim da Fonseca, *Mythologie des alten Indien* (Berlin, 1856).

4. See Johann Figl, *Dialektik der Gewalt: Nietzsches hermeneutische Religionsphilosophie, mit Berücksichtigung unveröffentlicher Manuskripte* (Düsseldorf, 1984), especially p. 51ff.; also A. Kremer-Marietti, "La pensée de Nietzsche adolescent," *Études Germaniques* 24 (1969):223–33.

5. See R. Bohley, "Über die Landesschule zur Pforte: Materialien aus der Schulzeit Nietzsches," *Nietzsche-Studien* 5 (1976):298–320, at 312; see also *BAW* 2, 129ff.

6. See the letter in *KGB* I 2, p. 366f.

7. On this topic see the pioneering work of R. Bohley, *Die Christlichkeit einer Schule: Schulpforta zur Schulzeit Nietzsches,* 2 vols. (Naumburg, 1975), and the excerpts reprinted in the *Nietzsche-Studien* article cited in note 5, above.

8. The focus here will be on the reports from 1853 to 1860.

9. It is significant in this context that the *Zeitschrift der Deutschen morgenländischen Gesellschaft* is mentioned with some regularity, as well as the *Zeitschrift für vergleichende Sprachforschung*. Other works mentioned are the famous volume by Lassen entitled *Indische Alterthumskunde* (Berlin, 1852), and Weber's *Verzeichniss der Sanscrithandschriften* (Berlin, 1853), *Ueber den Zusammenhang Indischer Fabeln mit Griechischen* (Berlin, 1855), and *Eine Legende des Catapartha-Brahmana* (1855).

10. See *KGB* I 3, p. 75: Deussen's letter to Nietzsche of February 2, 1866, and also Paul Deussen, *Erinnerung an Friedrich Nietzsche* (Leipzig, 1901), p. 21.

11. See the article on Steinhart by R. Hocke in *Allgemeine Deutsche Biographie*, vol. 42, p. 711f.

12. See Bohley, "Über die Landesschule zur Pforte," p. 309; see also Nietzsche's engagement with the speeches in Plato's *Symposium* in August 1864 (*BAW* 2, 420–44).

13. See Figl, *Dialektik der Gewalt*, p. 42.

14. K. H. A. Steinhart, *Quaestionum de dialectica Plotini reationae* (Naumburg, 1829), fasc. I., p. 13; *Meletemata Plotiniana* (Naumberg, 1840), p. 1.

15. See R. Bohley, *Die Christlichkeit einer Schule*, p. 154; also B. Rogge, *Pförtnerleben: Nach eigenen Erinnerungen geschildert* (Leipzig, 1893), p. 53.

Koberstein (1797–1870) was Professor of German at Pforta from 1820 until shortly before his death. See the article on Koberstein by E. Schmidt in *Allgemeine Deutsche Biographie*, vol. 16, p. 360f.

16. See *BAW* 2, 39–42; also Bohley, "Über die Landesschule zur Pforte," p. 312. It was in the essay for the upper first that Nietzsche discussed the characterization of Kriemhild and mentioned the two Indian epics.

17. V. Rose, *De Aristotelis librorum ordine et auctoritate commentatio* (Berlin, 1854); see the passages excerpted by Nietzsche in *BAW* 4, 562: "Thus the Mahabharata and Ramayana were composed after Christ. The same with the Nibelungenlied." Rose's comparison conduces to an argument that will not be pursued further here, to the effect that "such great poems were written down, not orally transmitted." On the pages excerpted by Nietzsche Rose also mentions the *Iliad* and *Odyssey*.

18. See Koberstein, *Geschichte der deutschen Nationalliteratur*, 5th ed. revised by K. Bartsch (Leipzig, 1872). This work, first published in 1827, was what established Koberstein's academic reputation. According to a letter written by Nietzsche in 1865, Anton Springer, the historian of art at Bonn, considered Koberstein to be "by far the most important literary historian of our time" (*KGB* II, 55).

19. Koberstein, *Geschichte*, 2d ed., pp. 44ff., 32, 164f., and 4th ed., vol. 1, pp. 230ff., 15, 3, 220, 183.

20. See Koberstein, *Vermischte Aufsätze zur Literaturgeschichte und Aesthetik* (Leipzig, 1858), p. 56.

21. See Bohley, "Über die Landesschule zur Pforte," p. 309.

22. Koberstein, *Vermischte Aufsätze*, pp. 31–62, especially p. 58.

23. See E. Schmidt in *Allgemeine Deutsche Biographie*, vol. 16, p. 360.

24. See Nietzsche's letter to Wilhelm Vischer of January 2, 1869 (*KGB* II 1, 367).

25. See Johann Figl, *Dialektik der Gewalt*, p. 39ff.

26. The Goethe-Schiller Archive manuscript of Nietzsche's notes named NFG/GSA 71/41; the page numbers after the quotations in the rest of the present essay refer to this manuscript. Carl Schaarschmidt (1822–1909) was himself an alumnus of Schulpforta. Nietzsche came into contact with him at the beginning of his studies at Bonn, having been given a recommendation to him by Karl Steinhart, the ancient philologian from Pforta. Schaarschmidt invited both Nietzsche and Deussen to his home many times in the course of their first semester there, as documented in a number of Nietzsche's letters from that period.

27. See Johann Figl, "Nietzsches frühe Begegnung mit dem Denken Indiens: Auf der Grundlage seiner unveröffentlichten Kollegnachschrift aus Philosophiegeschichte (1865)," *Nietzsche-Studien* 18 (1989):455–71, and "Die Buddhismus-Kenntnis des jungen Nietzsche: Unter Heranziehung einer unveröffentlichten Vorlesungnachschrift der Philosophiegeschichte," in *Das Gold im Wachs*, ed. E. Gössmann and G. Zobel (Munich, 1988). Several brief passages from this latter essay will be excerpted in what follows here.

28. Schopenhauer, *The World as Will and Representation*, trans. E. F. J. Payne (New York, 1966) vol. 1, Appendix. See Johann Figl, "Nietzsches Begegnung mit Schopenhauers Hauptwerk: Unter Heranziehung eines unveröffentlichten Exzerptes," *Schopenhauer-Studien* 3 (1990).

29. Wilhelm Halbfass, *Indien und Europa: Perspektiven ihrer geistigen Begegnung* (Basel and Stuttgart, 1981), p. 165f.; also "Indien und die Geschichtsschreibung der Philosophie," *Philosophische Rundschau* 23 (1976):104f.

30. *The World as Will and Representation*, vol. 1, Appendix, pp. 419–20.

5

Nietzsche and the Suffering of
the Indian Ascetic

Michel Hulin, *translated by Graham Parkes*

Nietzsche's works—both those published during his lifetime and also the posthumously published notes—contain numerous reflections on asceticism in general, and on Indian asceticism in particular. The manner in which these reflections are presented makes it clear that it is not simply a matter of superficial curiosity: their style is at once passionate and distanced, with a singular combination of yes and no, of enthusiasm and violent rejection. Nietzsche was himself conscious of these tensions, and he strove to resolve them by means of all kinds of "synthetic" formulas, never totally satisfactory, which he advanced successively over the course of the years. I shall try in what follows to evaluate this ambivalence in its various aspects, while suggesting a hypothesis with respect to its origins: Indian asceticism will serve as a mirror, at once magnifying and distorting, in which to reflect all the ambiguities of Nietzschean nihilism. Nietzsche himself denounces nihilism, on the one hand, as the decay of the highest values of the culture—or lack of it— of the period, and on the other he proposes it as an enterprise to be undertaken, a path of thorns that must be climbed all the way to the end if the transvaluation of values is to have any chance of coming about.

Although Nietzsche often talks of "Indian" practices and doctrines in general, without further specification, it is desirable to separate out his views on Buddhism from those concerning what he termed "Brahmanism." And this for three reasons: (1) Nietzsche appears to have, at first, more familiarity with Buddhism. In addition to the influence of Schopenhauer, there is the reading he did in the 1870s (C. F. Koeppen's *Die*

Religion des Buddha, for example), whereas he does not appear to develop his acquaintance with Brahmanism until around 1880 or so. (2) Generally, Nietzsche knows Buddhism as a religion but hardly at all as a philosophy. In the case of Brahmanism the situation appears to be more balanced, thanks to the contribution of Paul Deussen (*Das System des Vedanta,* 1883; *Die Sutras des Vedanta,* 1887). (3) While Nietzsche sees Brahmanism as ascetic through and through, he tends to see in Buddhism an antiascetic doctrine as well.

There is perhaps no text more characteristic of the Nietzschean approach to the phenomenon of asceticism than aphorism 113 of *Daybreak,* which bears the title "The Striving for Distinction." There, in a vertiginous encapsulation, he traces the circular and dialectical path that leads from the barbarian to the martyr and from the martyr to the ascetic:

Torment, then blows, then terror, then fearful astonishment, then wonderment, then envy, then admiration, then elevation, then joy, then cheerfulness, then laughter, then derision, then mockery, then ridicule, then giving blows, then imposing torment.

At the beginning, the barbarian tortures innocently, so to speak, discovering with delight the access of vital energy brought on by exercising cruelty on someone else. But the victim may at any time discover in turn hidden reserves of strength in the depths of his very impotence: in accepting the suffering inflicted upon him from the outside, he exalts himself with a feeling of superiority over his tormentor who is incapable of making him yield. The victim may then be tempted to play both roles at once, contriving to torture himself in order to enjoy all the more his own capacity for overcoming suffering. Asceticism would then consist not in the extinction of will to power, but rather in its extreme intensification, thanks to the fusion in one and the same person of the torturer and his victim: "Indeed, happiness, conceived of as the liveliest feeling of power, has perhaps been nowhere greater on earth than in the souls of superstitious ascetics" (*D* 113).

That in all of this Nietzsche has in mind primarily the case of Indian asceticism becomes evident in the continuation of the text, where he adduces the episode of the ascetic King Vishvamitra, who through the practice of penances accumulated sufficient energies to enable him to create a new universe.[1] With astonishing perspicacity (in view of the fact that the relevant materials were imperfectly known at the time) Nietzsche then suggests that even the process of the creation of the world might have been imagined "by some Indian dreamer" on the model of a fierce asceticism imposed by a god upon himself. In so doing he restores the content of the notion of *tapas*, or "ascetic ardor," the importance of which in Vedic and Puranic cosmologies is today incontestable. And it is in perfect consonance with the spirit of the Shaivite *Tantras* that he adds: "Perhaps the god wanted to banish himself into active and moving nature as into an instrument of torture, in order thereby to feel his bliss and power doubled!"

However, in spite of this hyper-lucidity, the Nietzschean interpretation as a whole is unable to maintain itself at such a level. In order to appreciate the range of its validity, one must take into account a number of negative factors which act as so many dead weights and put a brake on its speculative *élan*. Nietzsche was ultimately a victim of the lacunae in his information concerning Indological matters, and a prisoner of a certain stereotypical image of India carried by the culture of his time.

First of all, he regularly exaggerates, as did the Romantics, the antiquity of Indian civilization, representing it as having flourished four thousand years ago or more. In comparison with such great antiquity, comparable to that of a Pharaonic Egypt imagined to have survived up until our era, we (nineteenth-century Europeans) are still "incompetent novices groping after the solution of riddles" (*D*, 113).

Another leitmotiv is the exaggeratedly hot and humid—and thus debilitating—climate, to which the Aryan invaders who populated prehistoric India and molded Indian civilization were never able to adapt (*GM* III, 17). Nietzsche further wants to be a "physiologist," and as such he ascribes particular importance to peoples' diets, in the belief that these condition their way of feeling, acting, and thinking. From this arises his condemnation of rice, and of vegetarianism in general: such a diet would give rise to a certain indolence, induce a certain mental torpidity, and above all lead to an extreme faint-heartedness with respect to suffering in all its forms. This last trait would, in turn, explain the frequent recourse to opium on the part of the Indians, and of Orientals in general.[2]

In addition, Nietzsche never tires of promoting—without further explanation—the aristocratic character of the ideal Indian religions (even while Buddhism and Brahmanism are otherwise both considered "nihilistic" religions for the consolation of the afflicted). All of these traits combined produce something like an Indian "national character" dominated by an extreme excitability or irritability (the German *Reizbarkeit* signifies both). It also includes distinction, refinement, hedonism, and hyper-intellectualism, but also a phobia of exertion and suffering,[3] nostalgia for darkness, coolness, sleep, and annihilation. In this way a new point of reference is established—anticipating in a sense Freud's "Nirvana principle"—as the absolute antithesis to *tapas*, that fiery energy released by the penances of Vishvamitra. Nietzsche's various reflections on Indian asceticism, and on asceticism in general, may then be interpreted as so many attempts to reconcile these opposing views. One will notice, moreover, that this works by virtue of a double slippage of meaning which goes generally unnoticed because it is surreptitious. On the one hand, Nietzsche admits a certain similarity between the Indian mode of life in general and the practices of its "fakirs"; that is, he sees the Indians as the ascetic people *par excellence*. On the other hand, he implies that it is in Indian asceticism that the very essence of asceticism is most clearly revealed, thus authorizing all kinds of generalizations from that case.[4]

As far as Brahmanic asceticism in particular is concerned, it is clear that for Nietzsche it represents above all an aspiration to the complete elimination of suffering. The long development of aphorism III, 17 of *On the Genealogy of Morals*, whose primary inspiration is the work of Deussen, takes as its point of departure the celebrated passage from the *Bṛhadāraṇyaka Upaniṣad* (IV, 3, 9–32) which exalts the states of the dream and profound sleep to the point of seeming to identify them with the supreme liberation (*mokṣa*) itself.[5] Whence Nietzsche's definition of liberation as "total hypnotization and repose at last achieved." The theme of auto-hypnosis as the true goal of ascetic practices—by the repetition of the mystic syllable *Oṃ*, for example—is correspondingly frequent in the posthumously published notes as well.[6]

If it were limited to this, the Nietzschean position would not possess anything very original. The theory of auto-hypnotization, for example, coincides in its essentials with the interpretation of yogic techniques proposed as early as 1826 by Hegel, in a review of Wilhelm von Humboldt's study of the *Bhagavad Gītā*.[7] But other themes surface here and there which give the lie to this kind of coherent yet oversimplified conception. Nietzsche never loses sight of the implications of the notion of *tapas* in particular. This allows him to engage the most ancient Upanishadic idea on a very specific theme: asceticism as an accumulation of energy which allows its possessor to escape from the destiny of the so-called will of the gods. As early as 1875 he takes pleasure in emphasizing that the holy men of India had no time for the gods and demigods venerated by popular religion (*KSA* 8, 5[26]), and a fragment from the spring of 1888, inspired by the *Laws of Manu*, echoes the idea: "Where is the god who would be capable of withstanding the solemnity and prayers of the Yati who has withdrawn into the forest?" (*KSA* 13, 14[198]). It is interesting to note in this context that other elements of

traditional Brahmanic ideology—in particular, the belief in the power
of rituals correctly executed and conjoined with impeccable Vedic knowledge—are included, for Nietzsche, in the same perspective, as if they
themselves represented particular types of asceticism (see also D 96).

These are in fact the most typical intellectual procedures of Indian
philosophy, and especially of Vedanta, which end up being interpreted as
borderline cases or extreme forms of asceticism. This is especially the
case with the critique of the phenomenon of the ego which Vedanta
undertakes for the purpose of revealing the reality of the Self (*ātman*)
concealed by the false appearances of the "I." In a remarkable passage
from *On the Genealogy of Morals*, after saying that "the ascetics of
Vedanta philosophy" dared to deny multiplicity, corporeality, subject and
object, and pain itself, Nietzsche continues:

> To renounce belief in one's ego, to deny one's own "reality,"—what a triumph!
> not merely over the senses, over appearance, but a much higher kind of triumph,
> a violation and cruelty against *reason*—a voluptuous pleasure that reaches its
> height when the ascetic self-contempt and self-mockery of reason declares:
> "*there is* a realm of truth and being, but reason is *excluded* from it!" (*GM* III, 12)

It would, however, be a major misunderstanding to see Nietzsche here
as distancing himself on account of its delirium and extravagance from
a certain kind of Indian metaphysical thought. For one thing, he claims
constantly that there cannot exist purely intellectual values at any time
or place, that every scientific or philosophical inquiry, however "disin-
terested" it may appear to be on the surface, is sustained by a host of
affective interests that are ultimately reducible to particular forms of the
will to power. Knowledge never represents an end in itself but only a
means, among many others, of feeling oneself exist with a heightened
vivacity and intensity, thanks precisely to a more assured grip on external reality. And this is why the kind of self-negation or self-humiliation
of reason evoked in this text does not, properly speaking, represent for
him an aberration, but rather the beginning of the accomplishment of
extreme possibilities that are included from the start in the very essence
of human consciousness. On the other hand, there is no lack of texts in
which Nietzsche explicitly undertakes this project of a radical dissolution of the agency of the "I." His critique of the Cartesian *cogito*—and
especially of the grammatical prejudices (thinking is an action, which
requires a subject, and so on) upon which the *cogito* is, without knowing
it, based—is too well known to be rehearsed in detail here.[8] It is worth
mentioning, however, that at the points where he sketches something

like a genealogy of this new "ego-less" philosophy the advent of which he longs for, Nietzsche hardly ever fails to acknowledge (along with Kant) the Vedanta thinkers, whom he considers his real precursors on this issue.[9]

There is a final way in which Nietzsche values Brahmanic asceticism, and that is by elevating it to a principle of government, or seeing in it an ensemble of methods to which the Brahmins had recourse in order to discipline themselves and thereby render themselves capable, or worthy, of ruling over the other castes. This theme is especially prominent in the writings of 1888, a time when Nietzsche was impressed by his recent discovery of the *Laws of Manu*, although the idea had been nascent in him for some time. As early as *Human, All Too Human* (1876) he showed himself to be concerned with the phenomenon of asceticism, the truth about which he seeks to unmask behind a conventional appearance of heroic sanctity. More specifically, he tries to show that the ascetic, whatever he may himself think and say, does not simply sacrifice himself for a cause or for the service of others, but that like everyone else he gains from his behavior an affective or "libidinal" satisfaction, as we would say nowadays. It is true that during this period it is primarily Christian asceticism that Nietzsche is concerned to demystify. But it is also clear that the religious figure of the Brahmin is by no means unknown to him, as the following passage shows:

In many respects the ascetic too seeks to make life easier for himself: and he does so as a rule by complete subordination to the will of another or to a comprehensive law and ritual: somewhat in the way in which the Brahmin decides nothing whatever for himself but is guided every moment by holy writ" (*HA* I, 139).

And so just as he had assimilated into asceticism the speculative boldness of Vedanta philosophy, Nietzsche interprets this whole network of rules of hygiene and ritual prescriptions which regulate the day—and the entire life—of the Brahmins in terms of asceticism.

The texts of 1888 only confirm and make more precise this intuition in the light of a similarly passionate and highly selective reading of the *Laws of Manu*. Nietzsche is fascinated by the historical success of the Brahmanic caste, which he imagines to have ruled over Indian society for millennia—still the same presumption of extremely high antiquity!—and without being challenged from outside. Now the secret of such success could only lie in a certain ascetic regime patiently adhered to, through all kinds of trials and tribulations, in prehistoric times, and then transmitted unchanged from generation to generation, inculcated by an education from a very early age to the point where it becomes second nature. The Brahmins are supposed to have understood that certain partial renunciations—pertaining to diet, sexual activity, and so on—a certain frugality, a disdain for riches and honors insofar as they conduce to ostentation, represent the price that has to be paid for a monopoly on higher and rarer forms of satisfaction: leisure, the respect of all, study, the power to determine values and direct morality. A note from the spring of 1888 takes up this train of thought:

The highest caste, as the most accomplished one, has also to represent happiness: thus there is nothing less appropriate than pessimism and anger . . . no rage, no nasty retorts—asceticism only as a means to higher happiness, to the redemption from multiplicity. The highest class has to uphold a *happiness*, at the price of portraying unconditional obedience, every kind of hardness, self-control, and strictness with oneself—they want to be seen as the most venerable type of human being—also as the one most worthy of admiration: as a result they may need just any kind of happiness.[10]

Collectively the Brahmins at best incarnate one of the favorite figures of the Nietzschean imagination: members of small groups of elitists, aristocratic, united by an iron discipline freely consented to, close to the centers of power, but in retreat from the stage upon which the great figures of the world play their parts, and entirely devoted to a historical task that transcends individuals and generations. The austere and imperious Brahmin caste would thus be situated somewhere between the Order of the Jesuits and the Prussian Officer Corps. But, viewed as an individual, the Brahmin bears a strange resemblance to the philosopher of the future, or even to the *Übermensch*, as Nietzsche imagines him. Gentle, frugal, self-effacing, he voluntarily lets the Shudra wallow in vulgar pleasures, the Vaishya parade his opulence, and the Kshatriya strut upon the political stage. His sole preoccupation is with justifying the world as it is, with its monstrous incoherence and its apparent injustices, and with inciting others to affirm, according to their power and lucidity, this eternal cosmic order (see *AC* 57).

If we turn now to the image of Buddhism that Nietzsche constructs for himself, we find ourselves in a complex and paradoxical situation. While by no means ignorant of the Indian origins of Buddhism and of its founder, he takes hardly any account whatsoever of these basic data and, for example, hardly ever draws the parallels between Buddhism and Brahmanism.[11] At the same time, although he was aware of the vast diffusion of this religion throughout South Asia and the Far East, Nietzsche makes no attempt to ground it in the social structure and mode of life of these peoples. Moreover, the fact that Buddhism had a historically attested founder, conjoined with its "missionary" character, leads Nietzsche, like many of his contemporaries, to see it constantly as comparable with Christianity, whereas Brahmanism lends itself less comfortably to such an approach. All in all, it seems that Nietzsche at least tacitly sees Buddhism above all in its Indian setting, but makes of it something like an elitist sect that at some point detached itself from Brahmanism. The choice of this kind of interpretation has the consequence of downplaying the expansionist vocation of Buddhism as well as the "popular" aspects with which it was invested both in India and in other countries as well.

In short, Buddhism is seen as an individualist reaction taking place in the midst of Brahmanism after the latter had exhausted its secular domination of Indian society. As the inverse of Christianity, it would come not from a revolt from below, from the oppressed classes, but rather from physiological exhaustion, skepticism, and disenchantment on the part of the elites in power, or at least of their more lucid elements. All the traits of the "Indian character" mentioned above, as Nietzsche represents them, are found again in Buddhism, beginning with that of *Reizbarkeit*, which sums them all up. Buddhism would above all be an expression of the immense lassitude engendered in the higher castes by centuries or even millennia of austerities, of renunciation, of physical and intellectual discipline, by the immensity of sacrifices undertaken for the enjoyment of spiritual power. This pathos of exhaustion and disgust, when dignified as a principle of explanation, accounts in turn for the apolitical, nonviolent, hedonist, and fiercely intellectualist character of the Buddhist reaction: "In the teaching of Buddha egoism becomes a duty: the 'one thing needful,' the 'how can you get rid of suffering?' regulates and circumscribes the entire spiritual diet" (AC 20).

Under these conditions how could it still be a question of asceticism? In one sense the answer to this question has to be negative: "Prayer is excluded, as is asceticism." On the other hand, Buddhism cannot be reduced to a flight from the world, passive and undeceived. Insofar as it is a religion, it has to propose to its adepts a supreme goal—the definitive eradication of suffering—and rules for living that are appropriate to the attainment of such a goal. Nietzsche characterizes these rules not as asceticism but as physical and mental *hygiene*. Its principle is simple: to avoid—in the realm of diet, for example—everything that excites and heats up the system, to renounce thoughts that awaken and nourish the passions, to abstain from all undertakings that may engender internal tensions and conflicts with the external world. In this logic of refreshment and relaxation one will also avoid alcohol as much as violent yogic exercises—we are here at the antipodes of the *tapas*!—or as much as the intense emotions that come from ambition, *ressentiment*, and so on. Virtue then no longer represents a value in itself, but simply constitutes one element in a regimen adapted to the search for the cessation of suffering.[12]

It is appropriate to emphasize here the astonishing softening to which Nietzsche submits the Buddhist rules of living. In particular, he maintains an almost complete silence with respect to an essential given: namely, that Buddhist doctrine is addressed primarily to renunciates, to monks (Pali: *bhikkhu*) who alone are supposed to be equal to satisfying all its exigencies, thereby standing a chance of attaining nirvana in this life. A much less demanding discipline is enjoined upon the laity who compose the rest—in fact the majority—of the Buddhist community, or *saṅgha*. In sustaining materially the monastic establishments and satisfying certain minimal exigencies of decency and honesty, the laity can hope to accumulate sufficient merit to let them be reborn in a future existence animated by the monastic vocation. But Nietzsche is ignorant of, or else ignores, this great split, which is nevertheless clearly presented in works such as Oldenberg's *Buddha*.[13]

The result is that Nietzsche cleaves to a kind of middle term that is neither truly monastic nor truly secular, some poetic phantasm that floats between the two types of rules. For example, the obligation for the monks to live, at least at first, "in the woods, at the foot of a tree, in an exposed place or a cremation ground" becomes "life in the open air." Where the texts dealing with monastic discipline (*vinaya*) emphasize the obligation to be "without a home" and to wander ceaselessly from village to village (except during the monsoon), Nietzsche speaks simply of "the wandering life." And the obligation to be content with food obtaining by begging—that is the meaning of the term *bhikkhu*—and to take only one meal a day, is reduced to "moderation and fastidiousness as regards food" (*AC* 20).

Nietzsche could no doubt invoke the numerous passages in which the Buddha presents himself as a "physician of souls" rather than as a judge or a legislator. It is also true that Buddhism has always claimed, in matters of asceticism, to follow a middle way (*madhyamā pratipad*) between laxity and self-torture, but it is no less true that the Buddha is unrecognizable in the role of the Asiatic Epicurus which Nietzsche would like to have him play. The origin of this contradiction, or at least this tendentious refraction, is plain enough to see. If Nietzsche "domesticates" Buddhism, if he erases everything severe and intransigent about its monastic asceticism, if he points up its simple wisdom and downplays its properly religious aspects, it is because he needs it as a foil in his interminable polemic against Christianity.

More precisely, Nietzsche wants to show that all early Christianity "basically was aiming at the same thing as Buddhism" (*KSA* 13, 11[367])—at a retreat from the tumult of the city, an abandoning of worldly ambition, and a return to the delights of interiority—but that it lost its way because, being too much bound to the misery and lack of culture of the lower classes, it did not have sufficient awareness of its own goals (see *KSA* 13, 11[364]). The Buddha would then be a Christ who, benefiting from more favorable circumstances, "succeeds"—having obtained for himself and made accessible to his disciples the kind of ataraxy that Jesus knew for a moment, but which he had to abandon on the Cross and of which the Church subsequently lost even the memory:

One sees *what* came to an end with the death on the Cross: a new, an absolutely primary beginning to a Buddhistic peace movement, to an actual and not merely promised *happiness on earth*. For this remains—I have already emphasized it— the basic distinction between the two *décadence* religions: Buddhism makes no promises but keeps them, Christianity makes a thousand promises but *keeps none*.[14]

Laicized in this way, Buddhism takes on the allure of an atheistic wisdom, purely earthly, in many respects close to what Nietzsche himself is looking for: "In the idea of Buddhism the getting away from good and evil appears to be essential: it elaborates a refined transcendence of morality which coincides with the nature of perfection. . ." (*KSA* 12, 10[190]). At several points in the course of his last years of lucidity, in evoking the spiritual situation of Europe, the failure of Christianity as well as the moral values and political regimes inspired by it, Nietzsche announces that the time is ripe for a new Buddhism. A well-known fragment even proclaims: "I could become the Buddha of Europe" (*KSA* 10, 4[2]).

Nevertheless this fragment concludes with the remark, "which would certainly be a match for the Indian one." There is really a cleft between Buddhism, and Indian thought in general, and Nietzsche's philosophy. The underlying misunderstanding expresses itself, it seems to me, in two ways. On the one hand, Nietzsche is sometimes inclined to think that Buddhism simply represents a sketch of a genuine nihilism, that it "does not have behind it a fundamentally moral evolution," and thus certain moral values that have not been surpassed are to be found in the very innards of its pessimism—such as the idea that all reincarnation is punishment for mistakes made in one's previous existences (*KSA* 12, 2[127]). On the other hand, if he praises Buddhism for having been able, in its theory of knowledge, to reject the idea of an independent external reality and substitute for it constructions of the human mind oriented toward practical goals, he nonetheless denounces the Buddhist renunciation of all kinds of perspectivism and all temptation to appropriate the real through mental constructs as "a symptom of weakening of the will" (*KSA* 12, 9[62] and 5[14]). Sharing the incomprehension of his contemporaries on this issue, Nietzsche does not manage to confer a positive signification on this refusal of the Buddhists to act and prior to that project an interpretation upon bare reality. This is why he too understands nirvana as annihilation pure and simple (*GM* I, 6). The Buddha's nihilism is supposed to have stopped halfway, and his pessimism to have been a "pessimism of weakness" that everywhere flees in the face of suffering—a view that fails to see that this too is a necessary ingredient in the supreme joy, the joy of ecstatic acquiescence in the real.

Notes

1. In *On the Genealogy of Morals* Nietzsche returns to the exemplary case of Vishvamitra in order to extract from it this general piece of wisdom: "whoever has at some time built a 'new heaven' has found the power to do so only in his *own hell*" (*GM* III, 10).

2. In *The Gay Science* Nietzsche sets the pair rice/opium in India alongside the pair potatoes/brandy in modern Europe! (*GS* 145).

3. Nietzsche opposes to the Greek notion of joyful and gratuitous competitive exertion (*agon*) the Brahmanic maxim according to which all activity is painful in itself (and is thus justified only by the benefits one hopes to gain from it).

4. This second implicit generalization is prevalent throughout *On the Genealogy of Morals* (especially I, 6 and III, 17); see also *The Antichrist* 30.

5. In fact Nietzsche presents at this point, following Deussen, a veritable "montage"of Upanishadic citations, in which one can recognize at least three passages from the *Br̥hadāraṇyaka*: IV, 3, 9–10; IV, 3, 21; and IV, 4, 22, as well as two passages from the *Chāndogya Upaniṣad*: VIII, 3, 4 and VII, 4, 1.

6. See, for example, *KSA* 12, 6[7] and 11, 26[198].

7. See M. Hulin, *Hegel et l'Orient* (Paris, 1979), pp. 159–62 and 187–90.

8. See, especially, *BGE* 12–20.

9. See, especially, *BGE* 54 and *KSA* 11, 40[16]. Nietzsche also speaks of his affinity with Vedanta with regard to another metaphysical theme, that of the world's being divine play that is beyond good and evil (*KSA* 11, 26[193]).

10. *KSA* 13, 14[215]; see also 13, 14[212–221].

11. A few notes from the *Nachlass* constitute exceptions to this general rule: one from the spring of 1888, for example, opposes Buddhism to Brahmanism as an Aryan religion of negation to an Aryan religion of affirmation, both, however, issuing from the ruling classes (*KSA* 13, 14[195]).

12. *AC* 20; see also *Ecce Homo* I, 6 and *KSA* 12, 10[190].

13. Hermann Oldenberg, *Buddha: Sein Leben, seine Lehre, seine Gemeinde* (Buddha: his life, his teaching, his community) (Berlin, 1881). Nietzsche does make one mention of the monastic community as such, but only to remark straight away that it is possible, in contrast with the "perpetual vows" of Christianity, to leave it at any time.

14. *AC* 42. A note from 1885 or 1886 reads: "What seems to distinguish Christ and Buddha: it seems to be inner happiness that makes them religious" (*KSA* 12, 1[5]).

6

Nietzsche's Trans-European Eye

Mervyn Sprung

According to a tenacious tradition, still apparently alive in our day—though Eastern allusions are not quite the popular fashion they were a few years ago—Nietzsche had a lifelong interest in Sanskrit philosophy and Indian thought. His early adoration of Schopenhauer, who *was* a serious student of Buddhism and the Upanishads, and his persistent, if broken, acquaintance with Paul Deussen, who *was* an academic sanskritist and comparative philosopher, from their schooldays until after Nietzsche's breakdown, have fed this tradition with plausibility. Most convincing, however, is Nietzsche's own use of passages and sayings from Sanskrit texts and his recurrent adductions, some repudiative, some grudgingly favourable, of Buddhism.

In a vivacious letter to Paul Deussen of 3 January 1888 Nietzsche speaks of his "trans-European eye" which enables him to see that "Indian philosophy is the only major parallel to our European philosophy." Some thirteen years earlier (January 1875) he had assured Deussen of his "eagerness, myself to drink from the spring of Indian philosophy which you will one day open up for all of us." A normal reading of such passages would suggest a persistent concern for Indian philosophy on Nietzsche's part throughout this span of years, and most of those who have been aware of the question have indeed so inferred. Alsdorf [1] relied heavily on the widely held belief that Deussen and Nietzsche were "lifelong close friends" and yet offered Nietzsche's praise of the *Laws of Manu* (with which Deussen had nothing to do and which he must have found repugnant) as evidence of his interest in India. Even Glasenapp, despite his straight-laced criticism of Nietzsche, found it encumbent to praise his serious and penetrating study of Indian thought: "He penetrated deeply into its essence"; "He reflected a great deal on Buddhism."[2]

Quite recently the common presumption has been both tacitly and explicitly reinforced. Ryōgi Ōkōchi in *Nietzsche-Studien*,[3] though remarking on Nietzsche's limitations as a scholar of Buddhism, believes he was, through Deussen, in direct contact with the findings of German Sanskrit philosophy of his time and had a rather large number of books on Indian philosophy and Buddhism in his personal library (which is, regrettably, not the case: Hermann Oldenberg's *Buddha: Sein Leben, sein Lehre, seine Gemeinde*, the *only* book on Buddhism still there, appears never to have been opened). A current note[4] on Nietzsche and Deussen accepts the statements and protestations in letters and the use of Indian concepts in Nietzsche's published work at face value, and quite naturally concludes to a major impact of Indian thought on Nietzsche due to his "life-long friendship" with Deussen.

When we recall that the rhetoric, if not the argument in *The Birth of Tragedy* virtually turns on the Sanskrit term *māyā* (world illusion), that the title page of *Daybreak* carries a line from the *Ṛg Veda*, and that, in a note to Rohde a few days after his final collapse, the underlayers of Nietzsche's mind could produce the sentence "Taine composed the Vedas," the impression is virtually irresistible that Indian thought was formative in Nietzsche's intellectual destiny, although to a much lesser extent than Greek and German philosophy, Judaism, and Christianity. Sharing this impression, I thought it worthwhile to search out whatever might tell us more about this area of Nietzsche's thought. During a few weeks in Weimar, assisted invaluably by my wife, I worked through the dossiers of letters between Nietzsche and Deussen and searched Nietzsche's personal library for any trace of his interest in or knowledge of Indian thought. This included leafing through every relevant book to note marginal comments, underlinings, and any other indicator of interest or lack of it, such as uncut pages.

The reflections stimulated by this brief search easily broadened to form a set of related questions. It seems to me now that these questions have some interest for Nietzsche research in general.

1. What was the nature and extent of Nietzsche's interest in Indian thought?
2. What Indian texts did Nietzsche *know*?
3. How adequate was Nietzsche's understanding of Indian thought?
4. What importance did Indian thought have in the formation of Nietzsche's own thought?

5. What, if anything, has Nietzsche done for Western access to Indian thought (this not necessarily scaled to his knowledge of it)?

Such a wide-ranging questionnaire presupposes mastery both of the Nietzsche corpus and of the secondary literature, a mastery I would certainly not claim for myself. It is only the first two queries—those concerning Nietzsche's interest in and knowledge of Indian thought— which this brief report and discussion can deal with, and even so, in some points only partially. It is convenient to consider what might be called "evidence" in these two matters according to the following grouping and sequence.

1. Nietzsche's own statements in the published works, including the notebooks.
2. Nietzsche's library.
3. Nietzsche's correspondence with Deussen.
4. Nietzsche's correspondence with others.
5. The correspondence of Nietzsche's friends among themselves.
6. The memories and observations of Nietzsche's friends expressed elsewhere than in letters to or about him.

As I proceed it will become clear which of these kinds of evidence I believe I have considered thoroughly and which only partially. In either case I shall proceed through these various types of evidence in the order given and begin with the published works, considering quotations first and afterwards references and allusions.

Though he speaks of or alludes to Indian thought frequently enough to arouse the presumption that it was alive in his mind, Nietzsche seldom quotes from an Indian text: I have found some nine or ten such quotations, though this is perhaps not exhaustive. Precise references are, of course, never given, and what Nietzsche puts between quotation marks is more often than not drawn from several points in the original text and composed by him into one quotation to intensify the power of his argument.

In his *Untimely Meditation* on Schopenhauer, Nietzsche introduced the Upanishadic sentence "Men are born, in accordance with their deeds, stupid, dumb, deaf, misshapen"[5] (*UM* III, 8) to beat German academics with, but without a flicker of interest in the principle of *karma*, a *leitmotiv* of Indian philosophy. The title page of *Daybreak* carries the line "There are so many days that have not broken" from the Ṛg Veda. This verse fragment is, I judge, drawn from Ṛg Veda VII 76, although Nietzsche's version of this obscure passage does not correspond to the interpretation of the German and English translators. Geldner and Griffith agree that the thought is rather "There are so many dawns that have *already* dawned," a version not quite so appropriate to Nietzsche's mood of 1881. In the *The Gay Science* Nietzsche uses the mantras *"oṃ mane padme hum"* and *"Ram, Ram, Ram,"* though they are hardly quotations, derisively, to belittle prayer (*GS* 128). With the approval often vouchsafed Buddha, the admonition "Do not flatter your benefactor" (*GS* 142) is quoted in disparagement of Christian practice.

The only passage in which Nietzsche quotes substantially from Indian philosophy is in *On the Genealogy of Morals* during his discussion of asceticism. He first introduces a Buddhist statement "Good and evil, both are fetters: the Perfect One became master over both"; then the *Vedanta* believer is said to hold "What is done and what is not done give him no pain; as a sage he shakes good and evil from himself; no deed can harm his kingdom; he has gone beyond both good and evil" (*GM* III, 17). This latter quotation is drawn from the *Kauṣītakī Upaniṣad* but is Nietzsche's own composition.

Immediately following this Nietzsche adduces three considerable "quotations" from Deussen's *Das System des Vedanta*. They are all taken from Shankara's Commentary on the *Brahma Sūtras* and consist, in fact, of passages from the *Chāndogya Upaniṣad* (VIII 3, 4, 11, 12) with one sentence unidentified: "For the man of knowledge there is no duty." Nietzsche finds praise for the Indians' recognition that virtue does not suffice for redemption, but believes that their doctrine of release is at bottom Epicurean, a valuation of the hypnotic experience of nothingness as supreme. In this passage Nietzsche, uncharacteristically, names Deussen and praises his work.

In *Twilight of the Idols* Nietzsche reports on the *Laws of Manu* (which he had read in French translation) and composes a "quotation" from it (*TI* VI, 3). He focuses exclusively on the genetic engineering (*Züchtung*) implicit in Manu's decrees casting out the *Chaṇḍālas* from normal communal life. Finally, in *Ecce Homo*, discussing *ressentiment* Nietzsche praises Buddha as the physiologist whose teachings are more a hygiene than a religion and quotes from the *Dhammapada*: "Not by enmity is enmity ended; by friendliness enmity is ended" (*EH* I, 6).

Thus the meagre list of Nietzsche's quotations from Indian texts so far as I can find them. What do these quotations tell us about his reading? Excepting the three brief Buddhist quotes and the line from the Ṛg *Veda* in *Daybreak*, none presupposes more than Deussen's book *Das System des Vedanta* backed up by DuPerron's Latin version of the Upaniṣads, and a French translation of the *Laws of Manu*. Compared with the assiduous and persistent efforts of Schopenhauer to keep himself abreast of the lively Indian scholarship of the day, the evidence from quotations does not support the view that Nietzsche's "trans-European eye" was scanning the Indian horizon with much interest.

But then Nietzsche *quotes* little from any source. It is the frequency, spontaneity, and unpredictability of his naming of ideas, philosophical schools, and religions of India, invariably with a strong argumentative twist, that persuades the casual reader that Nietzsche drew substantially on a strong, if nontechnical, sympathy with Indian thought. *The Birth of Tragedy*, studded as it is with "the veil of Māyā" and "Buddhistic denial of the will" and structured on the key concept of "Buddhistic culture," reads as if the author were *approaching* the Greeks from a point of departure in classical India. This impression is, of course, not sustained in the pieces that followed. "On Truth and Lie in the Extra-Moral Sense," the early piece which Nietzsche never published, though its theme longs for nurture and support from the skeptical epistemologies of India, is written as if classical Sanskrit did not exist. In his *Untimely Meditation* on Schopenhauer Nietzsche does of course have India in the background much of the time. He thinks Indian history is virtually the history of Indian philosophy; he beats at the German philologists for ignoring Indian philosophy "as an animal [ignores] music"; he sees Schopenhauer as a hero of the spirit whose will should find its end in nirvana. The comment which, unwittingly, reveals most about Nietzsche himself is his opinion that Schopenhauer, in expounding his own philosophy, resorted to Buddhist and Christian mythology simply as "an extraordinary rhetorical instrument" (*UM* III, 7).

Daybreak not only carries the *Ṛg Veda* quote mentioned earlier but has a fine passage (aph. 96) on the religious history of India, which praises a height of culture capable of abolishing gods and priests and of producing a religion of *self*-liberation (Buddhism), an achievement Nietzsche urges Europe to emulate. In *The Gay Science* it is clear that neither Buddhism nor Vedanta, however "scientific," qualifies as "gay." Nirvana is "The oriental nothing," "rigid resignation . . . self extinction" (*GS* Prologue, 3), which nevertheless can induce a new self-mastery and stronger will to live, and which is the condition of a higher humanity. Nietzsche seems to imply he has made this passage himself. A tendency to positivistic sociology and history is unmistakable in Nietzsche's use of the vegetarian diet to explain oriental lethargy and indulgence in opium, and in relating these to the spread of Buddhism (*GS* 145).

From *Beyond Good and Evil* on, the influence of Deussen's first major book, *Das System des Vedanta* (the copy in Nietzsche's library bears, in some sections, the marginal marks of his attentive reading) is quite unmistakable. Nietzsche recognizes that the liberated man of Vedanta is beyond good and evil, but regrets that he is still within the framework of morality; he finds Vedanta an example of the way dogmatic philosophy becomes "a mask," as Platonism did in Europe (*BGE*, Preface); he believes that Europe is threatened by a softening of the mind, "a new Buddhism" (*BGE* 202); he approves of the Brahmins using religion to win power over kings (*BGE* 61). In *On the Genealogy of Morals* Nietzsche continues his attack on nirvana as a "nihilistic turning away from existence" which is creeping into Europe (*GM* II, 21); he writes vehemently against Vedanta asceticism, holding it to be Epicurean, "a hypnotic feeling of nothingness," but again praises the Indian schools for going beyond good and evil (*GM* III, 17).

The last of Nietzsche's published works, including the notebooks, are dominated, so far as India is concerned, by his reading, in the spring of 1888, a French translation of the *Laws of Manu*. In *Twilight of the Idols* he says the Bible should not be mentioned in the same breath with it; it is *"vornehm"* (noble) and has a philosophy behind it; the caste system reflects the order of nature and excretes useless products; it is a "holy lie"; "the sun shines upon the entire book." Only this once in all his writing does Nietzsche speak unreserved praise of anything Indian. He acquired the concept of *chaṇḍāla*—an outcast misbegotten—and uses it liberally during the last year of his work, even seeing himself as chaṇḍāla (*TI* VII, 2). In *The Antichrist* Nietzsche uses Buddhism to make disparaging comment on Christianity the easier. Buddhism is the only positivistic religion we know of; it ripens after a long tradition of philosophic thought; it has transcended the self-deception of morality: it is beyond good and evil; and all this in spite of its being a religion of decadence (*AC* 20). In *Ecce Homo* Buddha is praised as a great physiologist and Buddhism is said to be more a hygiene than a morality (*EH* I, 6). The notebooks of the last years contain a number of observations that emphasize much the same conclusions as we have already noted. Buddhism is more frequently taken up than Vedanta, and Nietzsche more than once draws a historical parallel between Buddha's position in Indian cultural history and his own position in Europe, implying that the doctrine of the eternal recurrence, in its negative aspect, is analogous to Buddhist nihilism (or perhaps vice versa) (*WP* 55).

This hasty scanning of Nietzsche's writings supports, in the main, the impressions gained from reviewing the quotations themselves. Noteworthy is the absence of India from the two works which are most spontaneous and least historically argumentative: *Human, All Too Human* and *Zarathustra*.[6] Nowhere are there references to Vedanta which imply wider reading than the quotations did: i.e., Deussen and at least two or three Upanishads. The case of Buddhism is slightly more complex. Though Nietzsche's grasp of Buddhism does not go beyond Schopenhauer, so that he betrays no awareness of a Buddhist philosophy beyond the doctrine of release from suffering, nonetheless the perspicacity he shows in sensing the freedom from moral self-deception in the words of Buddha suggest some reading of the original discourses, although there is no hint left us which ones, if any, he may have read. He quotes from the *Dhammapada* and quite conceivably knew nothing else.

The books still held in Weimar as Nietzsche's own library are a fascinating, if limited, further source of information about his knowledge of and, especially, interest in India. No volumes are presently held which offer evidence of any reading not apparent from Nietzsche's writings. Indeed, some precisely relevant books bear no sign of having been opened, e.g., Böhtlink's *Indische Sprüche*, Oldenberg's *Buddha*, Deussen's *Sutras des Vedanta*, and Max Müller's *Essays*, all published before his collapse. Even though one bears in mind the possibility that these copies are not the ones Nietzsche possessed, the consistency of the absence of evidence of reading together with the absence of reference to these works in Nietzsche's own writings cannot be dismissed. The volume which rivets one's attention is, of course, Schopenhauer's *The World as Will and Representation*. The extant copy is the fourth edition (1873), so that Nietzsche's student copy, in which he will have revealed his early reaction to the master, is not available. This makes the prolific marginal markings and underlinings in the 1873 edition all the more clearly the voice of Nietzsche's second and mature response to the Schopenhauerian *Weltbild*. This is, of course, a study in itself. For present purposes it is enough to note that Nietzsche's markings occur consistently in the passages dealing with the travail and death of the genius and with biological observations. Goethe is the person most frequently singled out. In spite of the rich sprinkling of allusions to Indian thought and mythology throughout Schopenhauer's pages, none catches Nietzsche's eye excepting only three: (1) "The creators of the Vedas and Upanishads were scarcely human" (underlined); (2) "Nirvana alone makes it possible to willingly surrender the will to live" (marginal comment: "false"); (3) "Death is *Schein*, as in the *Bhagavad Gītā*" (marginal strokes).

It is only too clear that even in these three instances Nietzsche was not interested in the ideas of the Indians but in the problems of the genius and of death. Taking the weight of evidence of the entire work, nothing could be more clear than that Nietzsche is quite insensitive to, indeed virtually deliberately ignores, the philosophical possibilities of the Indian material which Schopenhauer introduces. It is like a man striding through an exhibition of modern painting bent on finding the Greek sculpture. The conclusion from Nietzsche's copy of Schopenhauer, as from an examination of his library in general, for what these devices are worth, is quite unavoidable: Nietzsche's trans-European eye was more European than "trans." Or, one might say, his trans-European eye saw India through a powerful Nietzchean lens.

The outward signs of a "life-long friendship" between Nietzsche and Deussen have been universally accepted as evidence of Nietzsche's life-long interest in Indian thought. However trustworthy these outward signs may prove to be, it is true that the acid test of Nietzsche's interest in Indian thought must be his relationship to Deussen. The long acquaintance of the two men, from schooldays to the years after Nietzsche's collapse, is a theme worthy of a monograph, and until that has been written perhaps the last word about the significance of India for Nietzsche cannot be spoken. Restricting my survey to the exchange of letters between the two, and drawing on Deussen's two autobiographical books[7] marginally, I find that the evidence here is not different from that so far noted, and indeed is surprisingly confirmatory.

The Weimar Archives hold twenty-seven letters and two postcards from Nietzsche to Deussen and thirty-two letters from Deussen to Nietzsche. The bulk of this correspondence dates from their *Studentenzeit* up to Deussen's disastrous visit to Nietzsche in Basel in July of 1871. During the next sixteen years—the creative period in the lives of both men—Nietzsche wrote Deussen four letters, two of which were gracious acknowledgements of the receipt of Deussens's first two books. In the last year of his activity, 1888, Nietzsche wrote Deussen four letters and one postcard, the fresh stimulus being Deussen's visit to Sils Maria the previous summer, the first meeting of the two since 1872, and his offer of an anonymous gift of two thousand Deutschmarks.

Apart from gracious and perspicacious words of recognition and praise on receipt of Deussen's books—followed of course immediately by a blunt rejection of their content for himself—Nietzsche never in the course of twenty-four years broaches the subject of India and never asks one question, nor ever solicits Deussen's opinion, about Indian philosophy. The two revert again and again to Schopenhauer, and Deussen reports from time to time on his progress in Sanskrit studies, referring on one occasion to the "clear, luminous Indo-German world" without touching a sympathetic nerve in his classical friend.[8] Nietzsche was quite aware of Deussen's eminence and unique ability to interpret Indian ideas in European terms, but never once bothered to seek information from or discuss issues with him. In short, the correspondence gives no evidence not available from his own writing of any reading Nietzsche may have done, and no indication of a more active or wider interest. The correspondence, indeed, does rather the reverse: it suggests a much lesser interest than the published writings do. Without the latter as corrective, one could study the letters of Nietzsche to Deussen and conclude that his interest was not so much in the subject matter of Deussen's work as it was in remaining loyal to an old school friend.

And indeed this is the final, if surprising, impression which Nietzsche's relation to Deussen makes on one. Nietzsche never takes Deussen seriously as a thinker; he often scolds him, lectures him on the elements of philosophy, sometimes barely, sometimes not at all, concealing his slight regard for, not to say scorn of Deussen's ideas. Nietzsche plays the part of the impatient teacher and imperious father. During a breathless midnight visit of Deussen to Basel in the summer of 1871, Nietzsche told him "You are not gifted philosophically."[9] Deussen, although himself a man of great ambition and self-esteem, never fights back; he humbles himself in front of his great friend and, when deeply hurt, suffers in prolonged, tortured silence.

It may, of course, have been precisely this unhappy lack of respect which made it impossible for Nietzsche to learn from Deussen; one cannot say. But the fact is that Nietzsche made no attempt to exploit his acquaintance with the most competent comparative philosopher of the time in order to study critically the ideas of the Sanskrit philosophers. Oddly, Deussen, who has generally been seen as concrete evidence of Nietzsche's "trans-European vision," and whom I certainly so regarded before working through his correspondence with Nietzsche, turns out to be, as I now believe, the most crucial evidence we have of Nietzsche's lack of interest in trans-European ideas.

Nietzsche's letters to his other acquaintances—primarily Overbeck, Meysenbug, Rohde, Gast, von Gersdorff—present a mass of material with which I would make no claim to be critically familiar. Hasty scanning emboldens me to risk merely a few cautious generalizations. No aspect of Indian philosophy, excepting, of course, his loyal mention of Deussen's books, arises in Nietzsche's lively correspondence with precisely those fellow scholars with whom he would have discussed such matters had they been questions of genuine interest. He enthuses about the *Laws of Manu* to Peter Gast.[10] It appears that Nietzsche made no attempt to interest his friends in things Indian, with one further notable exception. In a letter to Gersdorff of 13 May 1875 he mentions borrowing an English translation of the *Sutta Nipāta,* a collection of early Buddhist poetry and anecdotes. At that time only fragments were available, I believe. Nietzsche mentions one poem, with the refrain, "Let one wander alone like a Rhinoceros," and intimates he has taken it to heart. He quotes it "I wander lonely as a Rhinoceros," a typical Nietzschean rereading of a text. The idea of nirvana as "clarity of mind" is drawn to Gersdorff's attention.[11] The passing mention of Deussen's *Elemente der Metaphysik* to Meysenbug, and of *Das System des Vedanta* to Overbeck and *Die Sutras des Vedanta* to Gast, Overbeck, Gersdorff, and sister Elizabeth, has more the character of a report to a small circle of friends of the noteworthy achievements of one of its members. Nietzsche does not appear to have gone even this far in his letters to Rohde: in the twenty years of their correspondence not one mention of Indian philosophy has come to my attention.

From correspondence with his closest friends I move to the last source of evidence available to us: reports on Nietzsche's conversations and activities by these same friends in letters to one another or in their own publications. Of Deussen we have said enough already; Franz Overbeck must be the most fruitful remaining source and Malwida von Meysenbug close after him. These two should suffice to contradict or confirm what has already been said.

Bernoulli's wonderful book[12] allows us to picture Nietzsche in the circle of the Overbecks, light-heartedly improvising on the piano, relating lively episodes from his reading, discussing Byron, Shelley, Hobbes, and Hume as well as Goethe and Schiller, arguing repeatedly about music and language though never about sculpture, architecture, or painting, and from time to time declaiming principles of his own philosophy (e.g., "to be able to amalgamate one's Yes and one's No").

In all the close and loving documentation from the years of this lively friendship, even in Overbeck's expansive and moving letters to Nietzsche's family and friends, there appears not one mention of books or ideas concerning India. Overbeck's historical and religious interests would have been receptive to a trans-European turn in the discussions and his personal tolerance would have invited it, yet there is no indication, that I am aware of, that Nietzsche and the Overbecks ever betrayed the slightest suspicion that outside of the Greek-Christian tradition there might be other worlds of ideas and culture from which Europeans could learn anything seriously relevant to their own problems and from which might come fresh critical perspectives.

Malwida von Meysenbug's reminiscences[13] permit essentially the same conclusion, but add more incisive evidence. Meysenbug recounts, fascinatingly, some weeks she passed together with Nietzsche in Sorrento in the autumn of 1877 after the Bayreuth season had concluded. The Wagners had left, as had Paul Rée, leaving Nietzsche alone with the woman he had once said should be his mother. Large portions of *Human, All Too Human* were in draft and Meysenbug was shocked at their tone and content; she thought Nietzsche was much too much under the influence of Rée and of the exclusive claims of the natural sciences; she urged the wisdom of the Upanishadic *tat tvam asi* against Nietzsche's one-dimensional historicism. At one point, after much talk about Goethe, Schiller, and Cervantes, she gave Nietzsche a copy of Kālidāsa's play *Śakuntalā* and requested his response to it. Nietzsche read it and his subsequent comments, as recounted by Meysenbug, are, for myself, the single most revealing episode in the entire documentary evidence available to us concerning his stance in matters of European and trans-European philosophy and culture. For one thing, Meysenbug says Nietzsche had never read the play, *the* play which German poets and scholars had enthused over from the times of Schlegel and Goethe onward. He refused to concede much worth to it because it violated European dramatic rules of plot, motivation, and temporal unity. He was incapable, in spite of Meysenbug's urging, of sensing the irrelevance of the European canons in the face of the quite different Indian mythological background, lyrical freedom, ethical presuppositions, and, above all, in the face of the Indian treatment of time as dream time. Even allowing for a certain reluctance on Nietzsche's part to concede a point in argument, it seems bluntly true that in this episode he disclosed no sensitivity to aesthetic and philosophic values lying outside his classical European upbringing. This is, as far as I know, the one passage in Meysenbug's writings where Nietzsche and India are brought together in more than a casual way.

And with this Sorrento episode, Nietzsche being thirty-three years old, I will close this brief report on Nietzsche's interest in and knowledge of Indian thought.

There may well be much more to say than this sketchy survey of the complex material has turned up; and I may have too easily inferred an absence of interest from an absence of documentary evidence; again my initial assumption of a substantial, if minor, concern with Indian thought on Nietzsche's part may have led me to undervalue or overlook anything less than this. However this may be, a summing up of my impressions from the sources used turns out something like this.

We can conveniently name four areas of Nietzsche's interest—Buddhism, Vedanta, *Laws of Manu*, historical parallels—in descending order of frequency of reference.

Buddhism means to Nietzsche essentially what it meant to Schopenhauer, though his appreciation is more superficial: a religion of release from the inevitable suffering of human existence; a religion of pity based on the refined hedonism of the experience of nothingness. Nietzsche praises Buddhism for showing no trace of Semitic *ressentiment*, for being more a hygiene than a morality, and for rejecting the ultimacy of good and evil (though he quite fails to grasp the radical nature of this rejection). Often the word Buddhism can be read as a synonym for pessimism and this in turn as shorthand for Schopenhauer. One can apply Nietzsche's comment on Schopenhauer, that he used Buddhist mythology as a "rhetorical instrument," to himself. The term "Buddhism" functions most frequently as a focus of Nietzsche's abuse, as a counterpole to his own Dionysian ideas, as a device for saying succinctly what it is he disapproves of and thinks must be overcome ("European Buddhism"). That Buddhism is so often a scapegoat derives perhaps from Nietzsche's tendency to attack most relentlessly what he most feared as his own weakness.

Vedanta served Nietzsche as the perfect model of a world-denying way of thought. It was conveniently remote, and the swift perusal of two of Deussen's books confirmed his suspicion that Schopenhauer's pessimism was rooted in such philosophy. He made little attempt to grapple with the mysteries of negation as a strong form of affirmation, the "pivotal point" of Indian philosophy. He found the asceticism of Vedanta too extreme; in denying the body as well as subject and object, it was guilty of an "assault on reason." Its rejection of good and evil as ultimates was however a saving mark of its realism, Nietzsche thought. Here, too, as in the case of Buddhism, one must conclude from Nietzsche's disinclination to penetrate the issues raised by Vedanta, that the term served him more as a shibboleth, useful for denouncing what he believed to be his arch-enemy.

Little can be added to what has already been said about the *Laws of Manu*: Nietzsche seized on it as a happy and unexpected confirmation of an aspect of his own thinking. It was the radical hierarchy of human worth that aroused his enthusiasm; one has to admire Nietzsche's sensitive "nose," when he says "Plato reads like one who had been well instructed by a Brahmin."

The explicit references to Indian history attempt either to apply a blunt materialist theory or to draw parallels with the Europe of Nietzsche's own time. Both Buddhism and Vedanta as historical phenomena are accounted for by the rice and vegetarian diet of the Indians, which so enfeebles that it exposes those who follow it to the temptations of opium, and thus to a withdrawal from life. Such comments are, however, merely thrown off in passing. More than once Nietzsche sees in the rise of atheistic, amoral Buddhism, at a time of crumbling Vedic religions, a parallel to his efforts to create a new basis for humans in the face of the collapse of Christian culture in Europe, a parallel which does not quite extend to the philosophic content of the two doctrines. That Nietzsche accorded Indian history and ideas so much importance that he found it worthwhile to draw them into his own thinking, even if only in an impressionistic way, is perhaps the appropriate concluding observation on the nature and extent of his interest in these matters.

This perhaps somewhat pedantic exposure of Nietzsche's acquaintance with Indian philosophical literature leaves the remaining questions, stated at the beginning of this paper, for further and more probing consideration: (1) The adequacy of Nietzsche's grasp of Indian thinking; (2) the nature and importance of any influence Indian thinking may have had on Nietzsche's own work; (3) the extent to which, or at least the possibility that Nietzsche, in spite of his fragmentary and second-hand knowledge of the Sanskrit texts, has made Western access to them easier. These questions demand a fully-rounded grasp of Nietzsche's own life-long thought struggles, no less than a careful study of the reluctant rapprochement of Western thought since Nietzsche, and the available texts from India's classical age. Indeed they demand a sure grasp of the volcanic changes in Western thought itself since Nietzsche. There can be no question of these matters being discussed here. If I can give a useful edge to the questions themselves, based on the limited research of this paper, that will be all.

1. Nietzsche's conceptions were probably not greatly different from those prevailing in his time, or at least not greatly less adequate. After all, Max Müller argued that nirvana did not exclude the possibility of personal immortality in heaven! Nietzsche's hard and courageous comments have the merit of silhouetting the contrast between the European Faustian man and the Indian liberated man. At the same time they reveal the inadequacy of setting up an absolute polarity between yes and no in philosophical thought. The Indians are wary of this and would remind us that Nietzsche's enthused yes-saying Dionysian is suppressing human capacities no less, perhaps more, than the composed Bodhi-

sattva who is master of his enthusiasms. No injunction is more common in Buddhist literature than to summon the courage and the virility to make passions one's servants, not one's master. Nietzsche's repudiation of Buddhism and Hinduism as "life-denying" is hardly adequate to the Indian conception.

2. How important was Nietzsche's knowledge of Indian thought for the development of his own thought? This must remain a problem for a full-length study of the growth of Nietzsche's thought from Röcken to Sils Maria. However, the first impression one has is that ideas from India penetrated Nietzsche as little as drops of water penetrate a goose's feathers. Certainly the conclusions of this study appear to support that impression. When one re-reads the *The Birth of Tragedy*, however, one can be struck by the force of Nietzsche's conviction that the person conventionally understood as *das Ich* (the "I")—the free agent of thinking and of action—was purely phenomenal, a part of *māyā*, and was not a metaphysical absolute. This conviction never weakened, I believe, in spite of the primary place he accords the individual. Nietzsche tried to be sceptical toward all Greek-European categories, but the one he attacks most vehemently and which he appears to regard as the key is the Cartesian and Kantian *Ich*, the grammatical subject of the *cogito*. The hallowed concepts "being," "knowledge," and many others are equally repudiated. Could it be that Nietzsche was sustained in these heresies by knowing that Indian thinkers shared them with him? Perhaps, but I would not hazard an opinion.

3. Finally, has Nietzsche, in spite of his inadequacies or even misconceptions, made Western access to Indian thought any easier? It is difficult to believe that he understood himself in this way, but often enough a thinker's influence is quite other than his intentions. Nietzsche was the first European to sweep through the inherited systems of Greek categories with a disconcerting, disintegrating scepsis. Being, truth, causality, person, whatever he found in use, he rejects as "fictions, unusable." This is a striking parallel to the Vedantist and Buddhist treatment of concepts, a treatment which Westerners, almost without exception, take to be irresponsible or eccentric, and at the very least irrelevant. That a great Western thinker has been driven to this conclusion must shake our complacency somewhat and alert us to the odd fact that in some matters Nietzsche is in substantial agreement with thinkers from another, remote, tradition. Ironically, he denied this throughout, with vehemence. Is it possible that Nietzsche's historical sense was acute when he surmised that Europe might now be in a cultural phase comparable to India at the time of the Upanishads and Buddha, a phase in

which a radically altered self-understanding is needed if humans are to continue to believe in themselves?

Notes

1. Ludwig Alsdorf, *Deutsch-Indisch Geistesbeziehungen* (Heidelberg, 1944).

2. H. Von Glasenapp, *Das Indienbild Deutscher Denker* (Stuttgart, 1960), pp. 102, 106.

3. Ryōgi Ōkōchi, "Nietzsches Amor Fati im Lichte von Karma des Buddhismus," *Nietzsche-Studien* 1 (1972):36–94.

4. Hans Rollmann, "Deussen, Nietzsche and Vedanta," *Journal of the History of Ideas* 39/1 (1978):125–32.

5. I cannot locate this precise sentence, but it reminds one of the *Kauṣītakī Upaniṣad* I, 2.

6. Freny Mistry, *Nietzsche and Buddhism* (Berlin, 1981), p. 142, note 9, draws attention to an entry in the note books from the time of *Zarathustra*— KSA 11, 26[220]. Nietzsche mentions pages in Oldenberg's *Buddha* which deal with the Upanishadic problem of suffering, infinite rebirth, and freedom, in connection with his own thinking about the eternal return.

7. Paul Deussen, *Erinnerungen an Friedrich Nietzsche* (Leipzig, 1901); *Mein Leben* (Leipzig, 1922).

8. Deussen to Nietzsche, 6 January 1867.

9. Deussen to Nietzsche, 5 January 1872.

10. Nietzsche to Peter Gast, 5 May 1888.

11. I owe the details of this letter to Mistry, *Nietzsche and Buddhism*, p. 17.

12. Carl Albrecht Bernoulli, *Franz Overbeck und Friedrich Nietzsche: Eine Freundschaft* (Jena, 1908).

13. Malwida von Meysenbug, *Individualitäten* (Berlin, 1902).

7

Deconstruction and Breakthrough in Nietzsche and Nāgārjuna

Glen T. Martin

Skepticism has a long tradition in Western thought from the ancient Greek thinkers like Cratylus and Gorgias, through the Greek and Roman disciples of Pyrrho, to the Renaissance rediscovery of Sextus Empiricus and Cicero's *De Academica*, down to the modern skepticism of Gassendi, Hume, and their followers.[1] Yet Nietzsche's work goes beyond traditional skepticism's doubt about human knowledge to the identification of a crisis at the heart of Western civilization in which the highest values which sustained culture invert themselves and become, ultimately, negative valuations of existence. With the removal of the categories "aim," "unity," and "being," he says, the world begins to look "valueless" (*WP* 12). A yawning "abyss" has opened up at the center of human existence that calls into question the entire ontological tradition on which Western culture has been founded. In the final years of his philosophical activity Nietzsche invested a great deal of effort in finding a way beyond this nihilistic devaluation of existence and in searching for a breakthrough to a new mode of affirmation.

Similarly, Nāgārjuna's dialectical analysis of the common categories by which people understand existence carries radical implications, somewhat comparable to those of Nietzsche's philosophy, in which a deconstructive process ultimately leads to the realization that both everyday existence and the categories by which we comprehend it are self-contradictory and incoherent. Nāgārjuna, however, claiming constancy with the original inspiration of the Buddha, advances his analysis with the object of liberating the reader to nirvana, a mode of being fully within the world while simultaneously free of the burdensome character of ordinary existence. This essay examines each of these subjects in turn and hopes to shed light on the relation between the respective methods of these thinkers and their ideas of spiritual break-through. Finally, it hopes to indicate something of the relevance of Nāgārjuna's work for Nietzsche's "problem of nihilism" in particular and for the historical situation of the modern world in general.

I

Nietzsche's critique of traditional ideas does not simply involve a positivistic or atheistic attack on the religious and metaphysical traditions. Rather, his writing creates a new kind of hermeneutic that goes beyond taking epistemological issue with traditional ideas to a *reading* of those ideas that sees them as having a disguised meaning hiding a more primal meaning which this special hermeneutic is meant to decipher. Most frequently traditional ideals and concepts are understood as a response to hidden fears, resentments, and, in general, a suffering from existence (*WP* 579). The entire edifice of culture is not based on a representation of the way the world is; nor is it grounded in any metaphysical substratum in which human beings can rest. Rather, the primal meaning behind the surface text of our concepts involves only the mobile and ever changing responses of suffering human beings to the historical and existential conditions of life (*WP* 461). This primal meaning behind our metaphysical ideas, therefore, represents no more fundamental truth but only the dynamics of the constructive process by which human beings generate a conceptual world within which they can live (*GS* 110). In this conceptual world, a world ever changing and effervescent, any subtext can in turn be treated as surface text and read by the same hermeneutic, creating an unending series of texts within texts, interpretations within interpretations, "caves within caves," ultimately serving to expose the "perspectival" and nonsubstantial character of existence itself. "Behind every one of a philosopher's caves," Nietzsche writes, is "again a deeper cave, . . . another ground behind every ground, and beneath every attempt to provide grounds" (*BGE* 289). In this skepticism, all language, and ultimately meaning itself, begins to disintegrate. "Each word," he continues, "is also a mask." There are no extra-linguistic realities, no "being," to which our ideas ultimately correspond, a notion which Nietzsche symbolizes in the 1886 Preface to *The Gay Science* with the Greek figure of "Baubo," the hole, the abyss beneath the veneer of existence. Unlike traditional skepticism, which often had the goal of *atar-*

axia, or living comfortably and unattached within the conventional character of existence, Nietzsche's deconstructive hermeneutic opens up an abyss at the core of existence. All human values are called into question. Human life has come upon an ever more penetrating sense of its own nothingness (*GM* III, 25). God is dead.

Although this hermeneutic expresses itself in a variety of genealogical, psychological, and epistemological forms in Nietzsche's writings, it is nearly always couched in a dialectical manner in which opposing ideas are presented in agonistic competition with one another, creating a dynamic form of philosophizing that serves to deconstruct both sides of every equation and to illuminate the arbitrary and mutable character of the concepts themselves. Thus Socrates as the great lover of life and advocate of skepticism is dialectically opposed to Socrates as the initiator of the emasculating rule of reason and devaluation of the instincts (*TI* II). And Christianity, through promoting sickness and weakness, is seen as the great destroyer of all that is noble and rare in human existence, while dialectically it is responsible for spiritualizing human beings and making them deep, its weakness becoming the possiblity of a new mode of strength on a higher level (*GM* I, 10). In Nietzsche's philosophizing an often passionately defended position is likely to be developed in a direction which leads to its negation and disintegration. This clash of perspectives in turn generates new perspectives which are themselves developed into a counter-position and dialectically disintegrated. One perspective does not annihilate the opposing perspectives but supersedes it only to be opposed by its contradictory, or to be read in turn as surface text concealing a subtext—creating a movement which mirrors the very texture of existence: perpetual becoming, without metaphysical essence; a becoming, like the interpretative process, eternally without aim, meaning, or goal.[2] Nietzsche sometimes metaphorically characterizes this impermanent existence without substantial nature as "will to power" (*WP* 1067). The formula "God is dead" does not merely reflect the subjective responses of the atheist Nietzsche. It is the dialectical and dynamic character of existence itself which destroys, and in the end will destroy, all metaphysical beliefs and ideals.

This vision of existence revealed by Nietzsche's deconstructive hermeneutic reflects one of the main uses of the word "truth" in his writings. "Truth" is ugly, but demands, nevertheless, to be told. A person's strength and courage are revealed by the degree with which they can endure this truth, the truth that all meanings and all values have disintegrated along with the disintegration of the notion of "being" and its religious correlate "God" (*BGE* 39). The greatest and most fundamental tension within his writings involves the struggle with this "truth," and his attempt to overcome its nihilism in favor of a new unheard of spiritual vision not grounded in metaphysical illusions and not a denial of "becoming" by its logical antithesis, "being."

In the earliest writings the unrestrained drive for "truth at any price," which progressively reveals the emptiness of all human valuings, is opposed by Nietzsche to the need for "genuine culture." Such a "genuine culture" would include the possibility of the continued "improving of mankind" and the production of a "nobler humanity" (through the creation of "unifying goals" provided by such "geniuses" as the artist, the saint, or the philosopher).[3] As early as the second *Untimely Meditation*, however, the paradigm of "genuine culture" begins to be replaced by a conception of fullness of "life" in the present and its implications for the future. History must be used in the service of life, he says, and not regarded as "pure knowledge." It is vital to the present in terms of our struggles and actions, our reverence, and "our suffering and longing for deliverance" (*UM* II, 2). These needs of present life always demand that history (and the drive to "objective" truth in general) be placed in their service. This theme evolves, in the later philosophy, into the notion that the demands of "life" are necessarily perspectival and interpretive (*WP* 481). Yet truthfulness requires that we confront these demands of life with the continual realization that our perspectives give us nothing but "lies" and "illusions." The conflict between truth and culture in the earliest writings becomes the nihilistic conflict between "truth and life" in the later: there is no "truth"; yet we cannot give up the demand for a representational truth in order to affirm "life." The 1886 Preface to *The Gay Science* recounts the myth of those Egyptian youths who "at nighttime endanger temples, embrace the statues within, and by whatever means wish to unveil, uncover, and illuminate whatever for good reasons is kept concealed." But this is a mistake, Nietzsche says, for "this poor taste and will to . . . truth at any cost . . . no longer have charm to us: we are now too much experienced, too serious, gay, burned, and *profound*."

It is this "profundity" which gives rise to the vision of Zarathustra and the concept of the "Dionysian" as symbolic paradigms reflecting complete and unreserved life-affirmation, affirmation not only of suffering, death, and becoming, but of the necessarily perspectival character of existence itself which constitutes the "most dreadful insight" (*EH* III, "Z"). Nietzsche as a nihilist trapped in a metaphysical skepticism concluding that "there is no truth" is therefore to be distinguished from Nietzsche as visionary whose third period is animated by a vision and an exegesis of a state of being beyond nihilism. If nihilism is pushed to its limits, becoming fully conscious through a deconstruction of any notion of "reality-in-itself," then we are faced with the possibility of a transformation of our being-in-the-world beyond nihilism and the death of God. The phenomena of everyday existence, devalued by traditional metaphysics, can and must take on a new "sanctity" (*WP* 1044), not in connection with any new materialistic or positivistic doctrine, but through a "transfiguration" of our relation to life itself.

II

The possibility of this new relation to the world of becoming is articulated through a number of metaphors in the late philosophy including the well-known notions of "overman," "will to power," and "eternal recurrence." For the present discussion, we shall focus on three related metaphors which are also central to the symbology of transformation that characterizes Nietzsche's late philosophy: the metaphor of alchemy and the alchemist, that of art and the artist, and that of play and the playing child. Each of these metaphors attempts to illuminate a new relation to a world which no longer has any character of "self-existence" or "reality-in-itself." "The alchemist," Nietzsche writes in a late note, "is the only true *benefactor* of mankind" (*KSA* 13, 16[43]). While the others merely "exchange" one perspective for another, the alchemist "transfigures" values and hence our relation to the phenomenal world. Similarly, *Thus Spoke Zarathustra* can be read as a work articulating a spiritual alchemy from our human-all-too-human condition of "resentment" towards phenomenal existence into the "superhuman" condition of a transformed relation to existence.[4] Zarathustra's dream in Part Two of the book portends just such a transformation in the image of the shepherd who had bitten off the head of the black snake of resentment: "No more a shepherd, no more merely human—one changed, illuminated, *laughing*! At no time on earth has any human being laughed as he laughed!" (*Z* III, 2). This spiritual alchemy engenders a new relation to that world which nihilism has revealed to us. For there is no returning to any traditional conception of "being" or of representational "truth." "Parmenides," Nietzsche writes, "said 'a person cannot think what is not';—we are at the opposite pole, and say 'whatever can be thought is necessarily a fiction'" (*WP* 539). In an 1888 letter to George Brandes, he writes, "the alchemist [*der Goldmacher*] is the worthiest kind of person that exists: I mean him who out of what is trifling, even despicable, creates something valuable, like gold. He alone enriches, the others only exchange" (*KSA* 7, 318–19). Whatever "gold" that mankind once possessed in its great metaphysical values of the true, the good, and the beautiful has become devalued and converted into its opposite, into the "base metal" of "lies, illusions, and falsehoods." This nihilistic understanding of existence obviates the possibility of merely exchanging the old values for new ones on the same order of being. The alchemist does not exchange but transfigures, creating new values out of next to nothing. The holiness of Being that once permeated and grounded phenomenal existence is lost in nihilistic devaluation, never to be restored. Our only hope lies in finding a new sanctity through a transvaluation of our relation to this groundless existence.

Similarly, the artist (living in a "Dionysian" relation to the world) does not find "truth" in representing the supposed structures of existence but in the creative process itself: in "creating truth," and in transfiguration (*EH* III, "Z" 6). "The essential characteristic of art," Nietzsche writes, "is its perfecting of existence, its production of perfection and fullness; essentially art is affirmation, blessing, and deification of existence" (*WP* 821). The truth within creative power is the truth that we are not condemned to a flawed and all-too-human existence, but contain within us the revolutionary potential to create new values and transform our mode of being-in-the-world. Dionysian and artistic truth replaces a discredited and devalued metaphysical truth as a metaphor indicating the possibility of a transfigured human relation to life. Art does not determine the phenomena once and for all, but rather enhances through the intensified presencing of the phenomena in the art work (or in the creative act) what already characterizes the phenomena: their "presence," what Heidegger calls "the shining."[5] In calling art "the real task of life" (*WP* 853), Nietzsche intimates the possibility of a new relation to the phenomena in which we have learned to leave them be, on the one hand, in their pristine and unsayable integrity, and to transform them, on the other, through continually renewed mythic and artistic renderings. The result may be an ability to live fully in the world for the first time, alive with the dance of life and ever new creation of meaning.

Alternatively, the ultimate result of the deconstructive process for Nietzsche may be a possible transformation of our relation to existence into a "play" relation. Zarathustra's keynote speech "On The Three Metamorphoses of The Spirit" defines the movement of life from "the camel," who bears the weight of traditional metaphysical values, to the "lion" of deconstructive nihilism, to the playful "child" of renewed affirmation (Z I, 1). Nietzsche's writings from early to late are permeated with the theme of creative play and the symbol of an innocent, game-playing child. The creative play of the "genius" in the early writings becomes the playful wandering of the "free spirit" in Nietzsche's middle period and, in the third period, finds its culmination in Zarathustra's vision of the playing child as the highest stage of the spirit. This symbol articulates some of the essential qualities of the overman and his new relation to existence. Instead of our human resentment of life, the child is "innocence and forgetting." Instead, of the seriousness, clumsiness, and heaviness with which we "work" at life, the child is "a game and a self-moving wheel." Instead of our reliance on traditional values and ideals, the child is "a new beginning, a first movement." And instead of our burdened and suffering relation to the world, the child is "a sacred Yes" to all existence.

Intertwined with the theme of play and the artist-child in the later writings is that of the will to power both as animating the creative activities of the artist-child and as a mythic symbol, beyond good and evil, for the world process itself. The world as play, or as the play of a "child-god," is looked at as a "monster of energy" with "the most complex forms arising out of the simplest structures . . . and then returning again to the simple, from the play of contradictions back to the delight of harmony" (WP 1067). In *Ecce Homo* Nietzsche suggests that Heraclitus may have been the only one to have previously taught these doctrines (EH III, "BT" 3) And in Nietzsche's early writings on Heraclitus, we find the seeds of his will to power in its role as symbol for the cosmic play of the world. Like Nietzsche, whose mature philosophy "denied being" and developed a cosmic metaphor which saw the world as a "monster of energy" beating rhythmically up and down, Nietzsche's Heraclitus sees the world as the divine game of the child-god Zeus, overfull of strength, with cosmically creative and destructive energies (BT 24). In at least two of his late notes, Nietzsche continues to point to his connection with Heraclitus, in the first using a Greek phrase which is a direct reference to the Presocratic thinker: "'Play,' the useless—as the ideal of the person who is overfull with power, as 'childlike'. The 'childlikeness of God, *pais paizōn'*" (WP 797). "That the world is a divine game and beyond good and evil: in this the Vedanta and Heraclitus are my predecessors."[6] Nietzsche here recognizes not only Heraclitus, but the Vedanta, as his predecessors. Why the Vedanta? Why the great mystical religion of India? Because one of the cosmic metaphors through which its sacred scriptures characterize the world is *līlā*, play. S. Radhakrishnan, speaking of Brahman as "The Supreme," writes that:

The Supreme is described as *kavi*, a poet, an artist, a maker or creator, not a mere imitator. Even as art reveals man's wealth of life, so does the world reveal the immensity of God's life. The *Brahma Sutra* refers to the creation of the world as an act of *līlā*, play, the joy of the poet, eternally young.[7]

The "play" relation to existence for Nietzsche involves no new interpretation of the phenomena but a transfigured relationship to them: a playful engagement with ideas and perceptions free of attachment to them as representations of some final "truth."

Nietzsche's hermeneutical deconstruction of the idea of a "being" beyond the "becoming" of the phenomena, together with his recognition of the metaphoric character of all language, finds its reverse side in a realization of the transforming potential inherent within ourselves and the human existential situation. Indeed, Nietzsche seems to intimate that it is only if the phenomena are *not* locked into a hard and fast reflection of some underlying reality that there can really be the possibility of genuine transformation. Just as in the Vedanta the world is *līlā*, the play of Brahman, eternally creating and destroying with equal vigor and delight, so the play of the artist-child, freed from slavery to a single apprehension of "reality," is able to transfigure and be transfigured. Perhaps for the first time, after our relation to existence has lost its conditioned and determinate character, are we available for an ever renewed opening into the possibilities of our being-in-the-world.

III

The spiritual quest of human beings has often taken one or more of three general forms: (1) a religious intuition of a "sacred dimension" transcending the everyday world; (2) a critical and intellectual deepening of the understanding to the point where a "transforming wisdom" is awakened; or (3) participation in a set of symbols, myths, and metaphors which point to the possibility of "redemption."[8] (One should add, however, that such a division will always be somewhat arbitrary and made with certain purposes in mind. There may be dozens of forms that "religious apprehension" can take.) The spiritual implications of Nietzsche's philosophy can be said to most clearly involve the last two. His deconstructive hermeneutic progressively destroys the metaphysical foundations of the traditional Western ontology, giving deeper and deeper insight into the "problem of truth" with its nihilistic implications and simultaneously into the possibilities of a new, this-worldly wisdom. Secondly, the unheard of possibilities of a transformation in our relation to the world intimated by this hermeneutic give rise in his philosophy to a series of interconnected symbolic paradigms pointing, on the one hand, to these possibilities, and designed, on the other, to initiate this transformation.

The overwhelming force of Nāgārjuna's philosophical activity clearly lies with the second form of critical and intellectual deepening of the understanding. The logical and conceptual austerity of his writings precludes the third of these forms (so fundamental to Nietzsche's experimental philosophy), and is carried to such an extreme (sometimes compared with Wittgenstein)[9] that Nāgārjuna can be seen as refusing to participate in any form of discourse that might misleadingly carry ontological implications. Just as the metaphoric and symbolic richness of Nietzsche's writings makes them difficult to interpret, the very paucity of Nāgārjuna's positive assertions makes for a comparable difficulty. This difficulty is reflected in the wide disagreement among his interpreters as to whether the direction of his critical dialectic is intended to realize in the reader the first of these religious forms: an intuition into something like an "ultimate nonsensuous reality."

That the import of Nāgārjuna's writings is "spiritual" or "soteriological," however, is not at issue. Nāgārjuna stands firmly within the Buddhist tradition and takes as his starting point, he tells us, the statements of the Buddha himself. As an early Mahāyāna Buddhist (and philosophical founder of the Mādhyamika tradition) he is creating a literary corpus with the intention of leading the reader out of bondage and suffering toward the liberation and peace of nirvana. The "place" from which people must be brought, samsara or the wheel of suffering, birth and death, involves a psychological clinging to their own thought constructions (and concomitantly what they take to be a real multiplicity of substantial things in the world) which generates in turn the suffering connected with greed, desire, and all forms of attachment. Nāgārjuna's work, therefore, falls squarely within the impulse articulated in the Four Noble Truths of Buddhism: that there is suffering, that suffering has a cause, that this cause can be eliminated, and that there is a path or a way to do this. In this spirit he opens the *Mūlamadhyamikakārikās* with a devotional salute to the Buddha which takes the very essence of the Buddha's teaching to be directed toward "the blissful cessation of all phenomenal thought constructions."[10] There are no philosophical views to be put forward by the Buddha (or by any fully awakened one). As Nāgārjuna states in chapter 25: "No *dharma* anywhere has been taught by the Buddha of anything" (*MMK* 25.24). His work would seem to result only in this series of negations which are not to be taken in any way as a negative philosophical view. The method by which he achieves these negations involves the dialectical deconstruction of the central categories by which language seduces us into accepting its "thought constructions" (*prapañca*) as realities and concomitantly leads us into forming attachments to these seeming realities. Nāgārjuna examines a "thought category" and attempts to show that the category makes no sense when looked at on the assumption of having "self-existence" or "own-being" (*svabhāva*). Nor, he argues, is the category coherent without this assumption. In this manner not only is every possible positive assertion negated, but the negation of that assertion is also negated.

The source of that clinging and attachment which generates suffering is precisely this tendency to attribute "self-existence" to the entities named in thought or in language. Nāgārjuna writes in chapter 15 that "those who perceive self-existence and other-existence, and an existent thing and a non-existent thing, do not perceive the true nature of the Buddha's teaching" (*MMK* 15.6). It is the metaphysical assumption of "existence" itself, attachment to the idea that something substantial "is," which is the root cause of human delusion and ignorance (*avidyā*). With each set of categories examined, he attempts to show that conceiving of any of these as having a reality of its own is unintelligible and impossible, and since the notion of "non-existence" is logically dependent on the notion of existence, one cannot conceive of any of these things as non-existent either (*MMK* 15.5). Ultimately things neither exist, nor do not exist: "'It is,' he says, 'is a notion of eternity.' 'It is not' is a nihilistic view. Therefore, one who is wise does not have recourse to 'being' or 'non-being'" (*MMK* 15.10).[11]

Using this method Nāgārjuna examines twenty-seven different thought categories (comprising the chapters of *MMK*), which may be included under three general headings which form traditional topics of discussion in Buddhism: (1) the basic factors categorizing the world of *becoming* (such as causality, universal and irreducible elements, composite products, producer and product, pre-existent reality, past and future, conditioned elements, self-existent things, time, and aggregates); (2) the basic categories with which we characterize the human *self* (such as goer and going to, sense faculties, desire and one who desires, sorrow, and the "self"); and (3) the basic concepts of Buddhist *enlightenment* (such as *tathāgata*, errors, the holy truths, and nirvana). Hence, the most fundamental categories through which humans construct the "phenomenal world," "the self," and "enlightenment" are shown to be "empty" (*śūnya*). He wishes to convince us, as Frederick Streng puts it, that every assertion can be negated, "without admitting its opposite."[12] Nāgārjuna in every case, therefore, examines the dichotomies by which we characterize our world (origination and extinction, permanence and impermanence, identity and difference, enlightened and unenlightened people) and shows that we cannot logically accept either category but must face the paradox, as Richard Robinson phrases it, "that two entities in a relation are neither identical nor different." [13] Since he claims to hold no philosophical views whatsoever, everything he writes would seem to serve as *upāya* or "skillful means" for bringing the reader beyond thought constructions to nirvana. He explicitly denies that he is hypostasizing "emptiness" (*śūnyatā*) and says that his language in this regard is operating only on the level of conventional meaning and truth (*VV* 20–29). Not only does he have no "propositions" or theses to advance, but if he did advance any, *that* in itself would constitute a "logical error" (*VV* 29).

Neither does the concept of "conditioning causes" or "dependent co-origination" (*pratītyasamutpāda*), through which impermanence had been analysed in the Abhidharma tradition, represent an actual state of affairs beyond conventional designations. We characterize the phenomenal world as being thoroughly dependent on the interaction of innumerable causal conditions, obviating the possibility of any entity having "own-being" or "self-existence." But this is a conventional way of understanding the emptiness of all things and should not lead us into attributing any mode of self-existence to the causal process itself. If existing things are empty, then, Nāgārjuna asserts, so is the process by which they are said to arise and pass away (*MMK* 1.10–11). The idea of "conditioning causes" or "originating dependently" becomes a way of expressing the emptiness of impermanent existence (*MMK* 24.18). The person who understands the emptiness of all conditioned things (*saṃskāra*) is the person, liberated from sorrow, for whom "constructed phenomena" no longer come into existence (*MMK* 26.11–12).

The full realization of emptiness, therefore, means awakening to "ultimate truth" in contradistinction to conventional or "mundane truth." But "ultimate truth" does not indicate a self-existent dimension of reality beyond the everyday. Nāgārjuna's dialectical analysis of the key Buddhist terms, such as "nirvana," the "*tathāgata*," and "emptiness" itself indicates that none of these points to anything that might be said to have self-existence. None refers to, or suggests intuition of, an alternative reality beyond the conventionally constituted everyday reality: just as "nirvana" refers neither to an existing nor to a non- existing thing (*MMK* 25.5–8), so "emptiness," he says, neither exists nor does not exist (*MMK* 22.11). The difference between samsara and nirvana is not an ontological one. The only difference between an awakened and an ignorant person is this realization of "emptiness," the term itself being merely another linguistic device "for the purpose of conveying knowledge" (*MMK*, 22.11) and without metaphysical significance.

IV

Clearly, then, what is most at issue in Nāgārjuna's philosophy is the question of "emptiness." It is well known that his emphasis on this notion (which had its roots in the Prajñāpāramitā literature before him) became central to Mādhyamika philosophy and a great influence on the development of the Mahāyāna tradition. But the question of what he "meant" by this term is far from clear if, indeed, any cognitive meaning can be assigned at all. Some modern commentators have interpreted the idea in Nāgārjuna's work as indicating a direct intuition of a metaphysical reality comparable to Kant's "noumenal" realm. T. R. V. Murti, for example, argues that the notion of *śūnyatā* in the Mādhyamika tradition is the result of an "intellectual intuition" of the *Ens realissimum* which Kant took to be the unknowable thing-in- itself.[14] This metaphysical interpretation of "emptiness" is certainly a possible rendering of Nāgārjuna's philosophy, especially if certain plausible inferences are made beyond what he actually says. But we have seen that Nāgārjuna does not speak in terms of "intuitional knowledge of unconditioned reality." His writings are a continual denial of the "being" not only of the categories of the so-called "conditioned" world but of those Buddhist categories that might be interpreted as pointing toward an unconditioned reality. Murti understands Nāgārjuna as developing a "critical philosophy" in response to the *anātman* doctrine of the Abhidharma schools which had themselves been responding to the *ātman* doctrine of the Brahmanical systems, in the same way that Kant had responded with a critical philosophy to British Empiricism which had in turn been responding to uncritical Continental Rationalism.[15] But whereas Kant speaks of "noumenon" in *many* places, and often seems to treat the notion as indicating a metaphysical reality "behind," so to speak, the phenomena, Nāgārjuna says extremely little that might indicate this sort of orientation.

When Nāgārjuna says that "there is nothing whatever which differentiates samsara from nirvana" (*MMK* 25.19), therefore, he would seem to be equating "emptiness" entirely with the everyday world, leaving no metaphysical residue whatsoever. As Streng puts the matter: "Mundane truth is not rejected in the sense that it is replaced by another 'truth', but it is rejected in the sense that it is transformed into 'no self-existent truth'. The things of the apparent world are not destroyed, but they are reevaluated in such a way that they no longer have the power emotionally and intellectually to control human life." [16] A new attitude toward "all mundane and customary activities" is required if our perception of the everyday world is to be transformed from that of a "samsaric" world of bondage and suffering to a "nirvanic" world of freedom and peace. Everything "works," and everything is in order as it is, when we live from the standpoint of "emptiness" (*MMK* 24.14). "You deny all mundane and customary activities when you deny emptiness" (*MMK* 24.36).

On the other hand, the aforementioned austerity of Nāgārjuna's approach, which refuses to make any remarks that might be construed as indicating a view about the ultimate nature of things, has led some modern interpreters of his thought to construe his philosophy as a thoroughly empirical and pragmatic philosophy. Such interpreters argue that there are no grounds for interpreting Nāgārjuna as describing an intuition of a nonsensuous dimension "behind" the phenomena as Murti and others tended to do. David Kalupahana, for example, sees Nāgārjuna (and the Buddha before him) as holding "a pragmatic theory of truth or reality." [17] Kalupahana sees Nāgārjuna's rejection of the *svabhāva* orientation as a rejection of the traditional idea that "freedom was . . . reached on the basis of a non-sensuous insight, and the 'freed one' (*nibbuta*) is one who has developed a form of knowing that transcends all forms of sensory perception, including the duality of subject and object." [18] Thus Nāgārjuna's embracing of the "middle way" between the *sat* (being) and *asat* (non-being) orientations means an affirmation of empirical becoming alone and a rejection of the idea that nirvana "transcends all descriptions and characterization." [19]

This view wishes to take at face value what Nāgārjuna actually says rather than to infer beyond the text in terms of those traditional religious categories which Nāgarjuna seems to be rejecting. However, it seems to be as little faithful to the actual text as the traditional view. Whereas the traditional view interpreted *śūnyatā* in the categories of transcendental metaphysics, this view interprets the notion as a critique of any form of metaphysical thinking which might obscure a clear view of the process of empirical becoming and our ability to live our lives in a pragmatically detached way within this becoming. But if the *Mūlamadhyamikakārikās* were a defense of empiricism and a critique of metaphysics in the modern (empiricist and pragmatic) sense of these words, it would be a strangely incoherent work. The basic force of its analyses is not a defense of what is observable but an analysis concluding that what is observable is paradoxical and self-contradictory. With each category by which we describe our world the conclusion is the same. Neither the category nor its opposite is logically possible. Thus, for example, in his examination of "origination" (*saṃbhava*) and "disappearance" (*vibhava*) Nāgārjuna concludes that things neither originate nor disappear, and neither do things not originate nor not disappear (*MMK* 21.6–10). Human beings mistakenly cling to the entities which confront them in phenomenal reality because they do not see that phenomenal reality is epistemologically and metaphysically groundless. As Edward Conze suggests, Nāgārjuna's work is "a perpetual concentration on the self-contradictory nature of all our experience." [20] This focus is not empirical and pragmatic but revolutionary in the sense of pointing to the "inexpressible" which confronts us directly in the living present, not as an alternative reality, and not "in front of us" as an object, but so to speak, "everywhere and nowhere" as our groundless-ground. "Self" and "object," Nāgārjuna is saying, are "thought constructs" obscuring non-dual awareness.

For Nāgārjuna liberation is the ability to live fully and directly in the world without the mediation of representative thinking and conceptualization, in "the blissful cessation of all phenomenal thought constructions" (*prapañcopaśamaḥ*). The range of implications carried by this phrase indicate precisely the non-dual emphasis of his thought. What Inada renders for this term as "the blissful cessation of thought constructions" is rendered by Streng variously as "not elaborated by discursive thought" (*MMK* 18.9) and as "the salutary cessation of phenomenal development" (*MMK* 25.24). "Discursive thought" and "phenomenal development" are fundamentally identical. The variety of translations of this key term into English indicates something of its usage by Nāgārjuna to include both aspects of the conventional "self-world" dichotomy. It has been rendered, for example, as: "cessation of the world" (of "verbal elaboration" or "the phenomenal world") (Murti), "cessation of conceptual proliferation" (Jones), "a complete recovery from the malady of manifoldness" (Matilal), and as "the coming to rest" of "the manifold of all named things" (Sprung). [21] Coming upon the emptiness of "thought constructions" is simultaneously coming upon the emptiness of the "world." It is a "breakthrough" to non-duality: the cessation of *both* "verbal elaboration" and "the phenomenal world" (Murti). On the other hand, Kalupahana's consistent rendering of *prapañcopaśamaḥ* as "appeasement of obsessions" (dedication to *MMK*) or as "unobsessed by obsessions" (*MMK* 18.9) does not capture the paradox of non-duality which this phrase carries. Just as Murti's metaphysical view has difficulty in not formulating its interpretation in dualistic terms, so an empiricist interpretation would seem to ignore the implication of non-duality entirely.

Both traditional metaphysics and empiricism can remain within the domain of "metaphysical" thinking insofar as they have not realized the absolutely unsayable "suchness" (*tathatā*) of things. This is the reason why Nāgārjuna does not devote a chapter, as Kalupahana suggests he might have, to the epistemological foundations for the perception of *śūnyatā*. *śūnyatā*, like phenomenal existence, is epistemologically and metaphysically groundless. (More exactly, it is neither grounded, nor groundless, nor both, nor neither both nor neither.) It is the human tendency to cling to "thought constructions" which generates the demand for a grounding where none is to be had. There is no danger, therefore, of the notion of "emptiness" becoming "as abstract and unidentifiable as a substance (*svabhāva*)." For Nāgārjuna, "emptiness" is not a notion or a concept at all. "It" is not conceptualizable, any more than phenomenal existence (with which it is identical) is conceptualizable. This is what constitutes the basic force of the *Mūlamadhyamikakārikās* taken at face value: not metaphysics, nor empiricism, but the inexpressibility and non-duality of things seen in their immediacy at the point of the groundless-ground prior to thought.

V

Perhaps one of the goals of all the great religions has been the spiritual transformation of human beings. That the human condition is in need of transformation has been indicated by such ideas as "fallenness" in Christianity and "karmic suffering in endless rebirths" in Buddhism. There is something drastically wrong with each of us in our ordinary human condition which can be remedied through spiritual transformation, through the transfiguring "grace" of Christ, for example, or through "awakening" and the elimination of defiling ignorance (*avidyā*). Nietzsche's philosophy, focusing on Western history, suggests that the drive for transformation all along took on a perverted form which was itself a kind of latent nihilism. For after the Biblical drive for salvation from our fallen condition was synthesized with the Platonic drive to think "eternal being," Christianity tended to generate an otherworldly orientation which focused on the Biblical God as a metaphysical being, a being whose predicates of perfection, unchangeability, simplicity, and infinitude devalued and denigrated the imperfection, changeability, complexity, and finitude of the phenomenal world. Since the rise of science, however, there has been a progressive realization that there is no epistemological ground for the idea of eternal being. Indeed, since all our concepts are "constructs" which form and shape the phenomena into a world that is livable for us, not only is there no eternal being but there is no "truth" at all in the sense of our ideas corresponding with some objective reality independent of those ideas. Nietzsche's statement "God is dead" indicates the former as well as the latter realization.

If Nietzsche's philosophy has insight at all into the situation of modern man, then his insight applies to Oriental as well as Occidental history. For the emerging world culture of the twentieth century has seen the gradual realization of the relativity of all ideas and the arbitrariness of all concepts, including traditional religious concepts. In the Kyoto school of philosophy in contemporary Japan, most notably in its foremost member Nishitani Keiji, Nietzsche's significance is interpreted in just this way. In reference to contemporary atheism with its nihilistic doubting of all claims to truth or to being, Nishitani agrees with Nietzsche that our situation can be likened to a cataclysm of natural history which requires of creatures "a fundamental reorientation in their way of being and valuing." "The shift to atheism," he says, "represents a change so fundamental that not only the human mode of existence but even the very visible form of the world itself must undergo a radical transformation."[22] This shift will require, Nishitani says, a "fundamental conversion" in our way of being in the world which involves a new kind of "religiosity," the impulse toward which is seen in Nietzsche's symbol of the Dionysian affirmation of existence (RN 56).

In his own thought Nishitani addresses this contemporary crisis in meaning and intelligibility from the "standpoint" of śūnyatā, an approach to emptiness that harkens back to the "Copernican Revolution" in Indian thought effected by Nāgārjuna.[23] His style and method, however, differ significantly from those of Nāgārjuna. Whereas Nāgārjuna refuses to use any empirical or ontological terminology without the immediate negation of that terminology as self-contradictory and "empty," Nishitani uses Occidental as well as Oriental ontological categories freely and at length in a style that continually emphasizes the paradoxical status of these categories when seen from the "standpoint" of śūnyatā. The result can add to our understanding of Nāgārjuna's work through coming at the notion of "emptiness" in an entirely fresh manner.

Nietzsche's insistence on facing nihilism and living through its implications to the end, Nishitani says, is a correct one: "It is here that Existenz seeks to draw forth the strength . . . to stand its ground unswervingly amidst the absurdity of life. In place of the image of God, the image of the 'Overman'. . . " (RN 93). What is required for the nothingness of nihilism to reach the absolute affirmation in which the emptiness of all things is simultaneously their ecstatic "fullness"[24] is the *radicalization* of the negativity of nihilism in the direction of "absolute negativity," a negativity which Nishitani compares with the generation of the "great doubt block" in Zen Buddhism (*RN* 111–12). The ontological tradition of Western thought, called into question by Nietzsche and the advent of nihilism, will only receive the entire world back in a transformed way if it accepts the fact of its own death and the possibility of rebirth on an entirely new field (*RN* 97). But this possibility (beyond the duality of being and nothingness) which speaks to the modern world from the heart of nihilism does not merely require an intellectual paradigm shift but more fundamentally "a change of heart" within man himself: "The shift of man as person from person- centered self-prehension to self-revelation as the manifestation of absolute nothingness . . . requires an existential conversion . . ." (*RN* 70). It is here that all "interpretations" of *śūnyata* break down, and the Kantian intepretation of Nāgārjuna is seen to be just as much an intellectualization of his thought as the empiricist interpretation. The deconstructive process, whether of Nāgārjuna's dialectic or Nietzsche's hermeneutics, can only bring us to the edge of a breakthough to the field of *śūnyatā*. The process can destroy our *svabhāva* or "being" orientation and lead us into nihilism and doubt about all our former conceptualizations. But in the last resort *prajñā* is not a form of intellectual comprehension or intellectual intuition; it is the result of a existential conversion from a being-centered (and person-centered) field, to "self-revelation as the manifestation of absolute nothingness." This religious conversion, according to Nishitani, is the task that faces modern man. It is what Nietzsche was looking for: "the field of *śūnyatā* is nothing other than the field of the great affirmation" (*RN* 131).

This is where the appropriateness of Nietzsche's transformative metaphors of alchemist, artist, and play becomes clear. The alchemist, or the artist, does not merely exchange one thing for another on the same level, but transforms them onto an entirely different plane. In the same manner "play" involves a transfiguration of our relation to the present moment in a way entirely dissimilar from our "work" orientation which is always escaping the present reality in its drive to achieve a goal or to attain the "purpose" of its work. A new possibility of being-in-the-world shows up which Nietzsche characterizes as ecstatic living in "innocence, freedom, and power." [25] Similarly, Nishitani uses the metaphor of "play" to indicate life on the other side of the conversion to *śūnyatā* (*RN* 252–55). "Play" as a symbol indicates a being-in-the-world transformed in such a way that its existence is no longer a burden to itself. Action no longer accumulates the "debt of karma" and the feeling of suffering in existence as an "endless payment" (*RN* 252), but takes on the qualities of innocence and freedom for which Nietzsche had also used the symbol of play. This "personal" conversion to the field of emptiness (in which the "burden of existence" is transmuted into a playful earnestness) is simultaneously a conversion in the way we see the world. The personal spontaneity of "sheer elemental doing" is mirrored in the cosmic metaphor of the world itself as spontaneous play. Nishitani again recognizes Nietzsche, as well as Heraclitus, in their symbolic vision of the world as cyclical and as a kind of play, as pointing in the direction of this conversion. But ultimately any such conversion awaits its confrontation by modern man. Even Heraclitus and Nietzsche, he says, did not attain true playfulness because they had not yet realized "absolute emptiness" (*RN* 265).

Drawing on the philosophical inspiration of Nāgārjuna and the Mahāyāna Buddhist tradition in general, therefore, Nishitani sees *śūnyatā* as the result of an existential realization in which nihility is pushed to its limits until it reverses itself in the form of a great awakening in which, for the first time, we face an "absolute uniqueness of things, their reality" where "there is no distinction . . . between phenomena and thing-in-itself" (*RN* 146, 138). Emptiness is absolutely inconceivable and inexpressible. It is not a philosophical, an ontological, or an empirical concept; nor, indeed, is it a "concept." It does not escape the everyday world but involves, as Nietzsche insisted, a breakthrough and a transformation of our relation to this world. It can only be come upon through existential conversion and direct realization. As Nāgārjuna says, the "true perceivers" find all those who hold "emptiness" as a viewpoint to be "incurable" (*MMK*, 13.8).

For Nāgārjuna there is no sense to speaking of an intellectual or conceptual separation between an objective metaphysical situation (the way the world "really" is) and the orientation of the human spirit. Human comprehension is not separable from what we take the world to be. There is a non-duality between language and world, subject and object, samsara and nirvana, which has very few associations with the intellectual presuppositions of Western thought. Nietzsche comes close to Nāgārjuna here, in that for him there is an unprecedented non-duality between human action, language, and grammar, on the one hand, and the world on the other. Thus, there is for Nietzsche no metaphysical residue of the way the world is apart from the ways we do and can talk about it except for its sheer "becoming" which is "formless" and "unformulable" (*formlos-unformulirbar*).[26]

If we transform our relation to the world through attaining the state

of *Übermenschen* (as intimated in the symbolic meanings of the alchemist, the artist, or the playing child), then our sense of the rootless or
abyssal quality of existence will take on simultaneously the quality of
absolute affirmation, and we will no longer be torn between the alter-
natives of "being" and "nothingness." We will attain the capacity to live
fully within the everyday world without being enslaved by an ontolog-
ized conception of that world. Similarly, for Nāgārjuna, "liberation"
means living in the ordinary world in a transformed way which makes
one free of bondage to that world, a bondage perpetuated precisely because we do not realize the "emptiness" of all our thought constructions.

Nietzsche's articulation of the phenomenon of nihilism makes us realize that the world has moved historically to a point where the realization of "emptiness" is no longer simply the privilege of the exceptional
human being whose insight into our condition of perpetual suffering
and bondage leads him or her onto the Buddhist path. And *śūnyatā* is
no longer a term belonging solely to a particular religious tradition but
has become a fundamental part of twentieth century spiritual reflection.
Nihilism not only blocks the way of any return to traditionally conceived religions or to a secularized anthropocentric existence, it also
opens up unheard of creative possibilities latent within the human situation, possibilities which may be beyond anything the human intellect
can conceive. Perhaps history itself dictates, at its current juncture and
with its current crisis of meaning, that we move beyond the relativity
of concepts and ideas to the non-dual standpoint of *śūnyatā*.

Notes

1. For Nietzsche's view of skepticism see *The Antichrist*, sections 12–13.
Translations from the German are my own, from the *Kritische Gesamtausgabe*.

2. A detailed description of Nietzsche's method, including a critique, can be
found in Peter Heller, *Studies on Nietzsche* (Bonn, 1980), pp. 1–49. See also
Paul de Man, "Nietzsche's Theory of Rhetoric," *Symposium* (1974):37–47.

3. See "Schopenhauer as Educator" (*UM* III, 5) and "The Greek State" (*KSA*
1, 764–77).

4. A detailed treatment of this metaphor in relation to Nietzsche's final philosophy is developed in two papers by Richard Perkins, "Nietzsche's *opus al-
chymicum*," *Seminar* 23/3 (1987):216–26, and "Analogistic Strategies in *Zarathustra*," in David Goicoechea, ed., *The Great Year of Zarathustra* (Lanham,
N.Y., and London, 1983), pp. 316–38.

5. Heidegger, *Nietzsche: The Will to Power as Art*, trans. David Farrell Krell
(New York, 1979), p. 216.

6. Quoted in Johannes Klein, *Die Dichtung Nietzsches* (Munich, 1936), p. 225.

7. *The Principal Upanishads* (New York, 1978), p. 86.

8. See Frederick J. Streng, *Emptiness: A Study in Religious Meaning* (Nashville, 1967), chapters 7, 8, and 9 for a similar division which he calls "the mythical," "the intuitive," and "the dialectical" "structures of religious apprehension." Unless otherwise noted, translations from Nāgārjuna will be from Streng's text, the *Mūlamadhyamikakārikās* abbreviated as "*MMK*" and the *Vigrahavyāvartanī* as "*VV*."

9. See, for example, Ives Waldo, "Nāgārjuna and Analytic Philosophy II," *Philosophy East and West* 28/3 (1978):296–97. See also Hsueh-Li Cheng, "Nāgārjuna, Kant, and Wittgenstein," *Religious Studies* (1981):67–85.

10. Kenneth K. Inada, *Nāgārjuna—A Translation of his Mūlamadhyamikakārikā with an Introductory Essay* (Tokyo, 1970), p. 39. (Streng's *Emptiness* omits these verses.)

11. For informed discussions of this negation of both "being" and "nonbeing" see chapter 2 of *Nāgārjuna's 'Twelve Gate Treatise,'* trans. Hsueh-Li Cheng (Dordrecht, 1982), and the Translator's Introduction in *Lucid Exposition of the Middle Way*, trans. Mervyn Sprung (Boulder, 1979).

12. Streng, p. 96.

13. Richard Robinson, *Early Madhyamika in India and China* (New York, 1978), p. 42.

14. T. R. V. Murti, *The Central Philosophy of Buddhism* (London, 1980), pp. 300–301.

15. Murti, pp. 8–9.

16. Streng, p. 96.

17. David Kalupahana, *Nāgārjuna: The Philosophy of the Middle Way* (Albany, 1986), pp. 85 and 88–89.

18. Ibid., p. 76.

19. Ibid., p. 73.

20. Edward Conze, *Buddhist Thought in India* (Ann Arbor, 1967), p. 22.

21. See the works listed in the notes to this paper for each of these translations.

22. Nishitani Keiji, *Religion and Nothingness*, trans. Jan Van Bragt (Berkeley and Los Angeles, 1982), p. 55 (hereafter abbreviated as "*RN*").

23. See Hans Waldenfels, *Absolute Nothingness*, trans, J. W. Heisig (New York, 1980), pp. 15–16. See also Jan Van Bragt's Introduction to *Religion and Nothingness*, p. xxvi.

24. The idea of *śūnyatā* as simultaneous "fullness-emptiness" is present throughout Nishitani's work and is reflected in the quotations given below in his notion of the identity of being and emptiness. For an informative discussion of the correlation of emptiness with "fullness" see Ueda Shizuteru, "Emptiness and Fullness: Śūnyatā in Mahayana Buddhism," *The Eastern Buddhist* 15/1 (1982):9–37.

25. An exposition of these "ludic" aspects of Nietzsche's philosophy can be found in Richard Perkins, "The Genius and the Better Player: Superman and The Elements of Play," *International Studies in Philosophy* 15/2 (1983):13–23.

26. *WP* 569. However, in the view of the present writer there is a *logical* "residue" (certain conceptual presuppositions) which makes Nietzsche's thinking retain its metaphysical character in spite of his explicit denials of metaphysics. See Glen T. Martin, "A Critique of Nietzsche's Metaphysical Scepticism," *International Studies in Philosophy* 19/2 (1987):51–59.

CHINA

8

Zhuang Zi and Nietzsche:
Plays of Perspectives

Chen Guying, *translated by James D. Sellmann*

I

The main thrust of Zhuang Zi's philosophy is the pursuit of spiritual freedom. It was Zhuang Zi's conviction that while human beings are naturally inclined toward freedom, they constantly get entangled in every kind of artifice and self-contrived constraint. On the one hand, people suffer from being ensnared in layer after layer of artificially and externally imposed regulations, and on the other they consciously or unconsciously fall into the trap of pursuing fame and fortune, thereby limiting and impoverishing themselves. In this way they create obstacles between themselves and the world and impede communication between the subjective and the objective. They thereby create an egocentric system, limiting the free movement of the human spirit. Zhuang Zi employs the power of literary imagination to shape a human ideal—the *zhi ren* (consummate person), or the *shen ren* (spiritual person)—in order to break out of the various kinds of snares that bind humanity, and to close the gap between the person and the external world, thereby gaining a sympathetic harmony with the environment. When Zhuang Zi says, "The consummate person is without self. The spiritual person is without accomplishments. The sage is without a reputation" (2/1/20–21),[1] he is urging people to extricate themselves from the values of the social market place. And when he says, "mounted on the regularity of heaven and earth, and charioting the changes of the six cosmic forces (*liu qi*)," he means that such a person is free without limitation in his

115

spiritual movement, coming together to form one body with the cosmos and the myriad things.

From a philosophical perspective, Zhuang Zi is looking at the relationship between external things and the human being as a continuum. In the *da zong shi* (The Great and Venerable Teacher) chapter, he says: ". . . wandering in the single vapor of heaven and earth . . . a person's life and death is a gathering and a dissipating of this vapor" (18/6/68). A later passage reads: "Human life is a gathering of vapor (*qi*); upon gathering, there is life; with dispersing, there is death" (58/22/11). This is to say that the basic stuff of human beings, heaven, earth, and the myriad things is the same, so that the relationship between subjective and objective is not one of opposition and separation, but rather of continuity and unity.

Nietzsche's ideal of the *Übermensch* has a completely different cultural context. The condition of the *Übermensch* involves an expression of one's own pent-up strength and a relentless self-overcoming. Nietzsche was concerned to pitch his philosophy of the *Übermensch* against the Christian world view, whose contempt for the physical he regarded as a degeneration of life. In the "Prologue" to *Thus Spoke Zarathustra*, he characterizes the *Übermensch* as "the sense of the earth," which implies an affirmation of this human world and a criticism of the Christian belief in an afterlife. His criticisms of the Platonic-Christian tradition are developed in a number of Zarathustra's speeches: in "On the Afterworldly," "On the Despisers of the Body," "On the Higher Man," "On Enjoying and Suffering the Passions," and "On the Gift Giving Virtue" in particular.

II

Zhuang Zi and Nietzsche both make a model of the ideal person as a way of expressing their philosophical ideas. Nietzsche creates the character Zarathustra, and Zhuang Zi in his *Inner Chapters* constructs persons such as Ai-Tai To, Zi Yu, and Zi Lai. The kinds of personalities and characters the two thinkers present can be compared under several different headings: the stance toward the emotions, dreaming, solitude and eccentricity, autonomy and fate, and the healthy body.

The character of Nietzsche's Zarathustra is unique. At times he strides along expressing the intense joy of his heart, and at other times he distances himself from the crowd and seeks seclusion, sinking into painful thoughts. In chapters such as "The Stillest Hour" and "On the Vision and the Riddle" the depth of Zarathustra's sadness is powerfully portrayed. It has been said that the true measure of a person who can fathom himself and his age is how much pain he has endured. The character of Zarathustra is a vivid expression of the relentless pain endured by his creator.

Zhuang Zi's attitude toward the emotions is more or less antithetical to Nietzsche's. Zhuang Zi considered the emotional constraints attendant upon human life—especially the feelings of trepidation which we associate with life and death—to be an enormous restraint on human beings. He therefore advocated "forgetting feelings" (*wang qing*) as a way of extricating oneself from these kinds of constraints. In his *yang sheng* (The Secret of Caring for Life) chapter, he relates how "when Lao Dan died, Qin Shi went to mourn for him; but after giving three cries, he left the room" (8/3/14–15); and in the *da zong shi* chapter he borrows the words of Zi You when he was deathly ill: "one acts according to the times without grief or joy" (17/6/52). The idea is that one ought to adopt an attitude of compliance to nature in the question of life and death, and not be constrained by the emotions of grief and joy. Chapter six also contains the story of Master Sang-hu's death, in which his friends gather around the corpse and sing. The *zhi le* (The Perfect Happiness) chapter records that when Zhuang Zi's wife died, he drummed on a pot and sang. These anecdotes all express, at least indirectly, an attitude of not fearing death and according with what is natural.

At the end of chapter five, *de chong fu* (The Sign of Virtue Complete), there is an encounter between Zhuang Zi and Hui Shi in which they discuss the question of harming one's feeling (*qing*) or one's character (*xing*). Zhuang Zi says: "What I mean by having no feelings is to say that one does not allow feelings of likes and dislikes to get in and thereby injure one's person" (15/5/57–58). This is a clear expression of Zhuang Zi's idea that human beings should comply with nature, not be distressed by the feelings of grief and joy, and should maintain a peaceful and balanced state of mind.

Since Zhuang Zi wants people to cast off the fetters of the emotions, his ideal of the *zhen ren* (genuine person) is one who "sleeps without dreaming and wakes without worry" (15/6/6). A person in his waking hours has too many desires and anxieties, and these are necessarily reflected in his dream world. (One might think here of Freud's theories concerning the production of dreams.) "The *zhen jen* is without dreams" means that a person's release from the world of mundane affairs is such that no amount of stimulation can arouse the emotions.

At the end of the *qi wu lun* (Discussion on Making All Things Equal) chapter, Zhuang Zi tells the anecdote of Zhuang Zhou's dreaming he is a butterfly. When Zhuang Zhou awoke from having dreamed that he was a butterfly fluttering happily from one place to the next, he was not sure whether he was Zhuang Zhou who had dreamed he was a butterfly or else a butterfly who had dreamed that it was Zhuang Zhou. The story conveys the idea of *zi you shi zhi* ("being happy with himself and doing as he pleases"). The transformation of Zhuang Zhou into a butterfly is a metaphor for the natural simplicity of human nature, and also symbolizes the carefree freedom of a person unconstrained and unregulated. From Zhuang Zi's perspective the cosmos is like a grand garden, in which the butterfly can enjoy the flower beds without any constraints.

In the writings of Nietzsche there are no dreams evoking the carefree freedom of the butterfly. In direct contrast is the report of Zarathustra's nightmare in the chapter entitled "The Soothsayer":

And amid the roaring and whistling and shrilling the coffin burst and spewed out a thousandfold laughter.
And a thousand grimaces of children, angels, owls, fools, and butterflies as big as children, it laughed and mocked and roared at me.
Then I was terribly frightened; it threw me to the ground. And I cried in horror as I have never cried.
And my own cry awakened me—and I came to my senses. (Z II, 19)

This kind of dream world expresses the struggle to make headway against obstacles and the "life-draining weariness" that Zarathustra encounters in the process of human life.

As for the function of the dream, Nietzsche thought that it is a compensation for the pleasures and beauty that one has missed during the day: "the meaning and value of our *dreams* is precisely to *compensate* to some extent for the chance absence of 'nourishment' during the day" (D 119). Nietzsche goes on to suggest that the inventions of dreams are "interpretations of nervous stimuli we receive while we are asleep, *very free*, very arbitrary interpretations of the motions of the blood and intestines . . . and so on." He observes further that the same nervous stimuli might, under different circumstances, produces a different dream realm. The same thing happens in the light of day where different people confront the same event, and their different reactions and different demands give rise to differing interpretations. Nietzsche claims that to this extent "there is no *essential* difference between waking and dreaming." Insofar as they both suggest that waking and dreaming are not substantially different, Nietzsche and Zhuang Zi would seem to be in agreement, although Zhuang Zi puts forward the idea that life and death are one, and that dreaming and waking are indistinguishable, from the perspective of the great organic unity of things.

Before Freud, Nietzsche had already suggested the importance of the mental activity of the unconscious: "For the longest time, conscious thought was considered thought itself. Only now does the truth dawn on us that by far the greatest part of our spirit's activity remains unconscious and unfelt" (*GS* 333). In this same passage Nietzsche criticizes Spinoza, rejecting his idea of something "divine that eternally rests in itself." He goes on: "*Conscious* thinking, especially that of the philosopher, is the least vigorous and therefore also the relatively mildest and calmest form of thinking; and thus precisely philosophers are most apt to be led astray about the nature of knowledge."

With respect to this concept Nietzsche and Zhuang Zi are fundamentally at odds. Zhuang Zi's position on wisdom is relatively close to that of Spinoza's, while Nietzsche's emphasis is on instinctual activity and the unconscious, devaluing the "mildest and calmest form of thinking" of the philosopher.

Nietzsche and Zhuang Zi are both profoundly eccentric. The eccentricity of Nietzsche is entirely overt and is expressed in the distance between him and the mob, and in his distance from traditional culture. The penultimate aphorism of *Daybreak* reads: "The higher we soar the smaller we appear to those who cannot fly" (*D* 574). This expresses his distance from the multitude at a spiritual level. The many passages in *Zarathustra* which depict the protagonist's frequent flights away from "the market place" and into solitude are powerful expressions of Nietzsche's dissatisfaction with and resistance to the period in which he lived. Zarathustra goes further by recommending solitude to anyone engaged in the task of self-creation:

> Go into your loneliness with your love and with your creation, my brother; and only much later will justice limp after you.
>
> With my tears go into your loneliness, my brother. I love him who wants to create over and beyond himself and thus perishes. (ZI, 17)

Zhuang Zi, like Nietzsche, felt isolated from the multitude and was vehemently dissatisfied with and critical of the period in which he lived. Although his "doing whatever pleased him" shows he was eccentric, one does not get from him the sense of loneliness that we find in Nietzsche. Zhuang Zi recommends a dissolution of the solitary condition, and a transcendence of disputes over right and wrong in the world of human relations in the direction of a communing with nature. A passage in the *tian xia* (The World) chapter describes Zhuang Zhou as "coming and going along with the pure spirit of heaven and earth, yet he did not scold over 'right' and 'wrong', but lived with the age and its vulgarity" (93/33/65–66). This shows that Zhuang Zi was not an escapist but a person of this world.

Zhuang Zi's conception of an accommodation with nature goes hand in hand with a tolerance of what is fated, an understanding of life and death, existing and perishing, and even poverty and prosperity as the working out of fate. In the *da zong shi* chapter, he says: "Life and death are fated (*ming*)." This means that both life and death are naturally so and cannot be avoided. In the *ren jian shi* (In the World of Men) chapter, he describes a person living in an environment of political turmoil in which he is powerless to do anything, and who yet finds peace in that which is fated. "Fate" in the *Zhuang zi* invariably refers to those encounters which are natural and cannot be avoided. His overall attitude is one of accommodating what is natural and of being receptive to it.

Nietzsche, in contrast, would reject this notion of tolerating fate. He has Zarathustra proclaim: "I am Zarathustra the godless. . . . All those are my equals who give themselves their own will and reject all resignation" (Z III, 5 3). In this passage, Nietzsche advocates a development of one's subjective powers in order to overcome difficulties and create one's own ideal environment.

A major ground of Nietzsche's opposition to Christianity is its denigration of the body as "the flesh" in favor of the spirit. Against "the despisers of the body" he has Zarathustra say:

> The body is a great reason a plurality with one sense, a war and a peace, a herd and a shepherd.
> An instrument of your body is also your little reason, my brother, which you call "spirit"—a little instrument and toy of your great reason. (Z I, 4)

And later in the book Zarathustra repeatedly sings the praises of the healthy body:

> There your body is elevated and resurrected; with its rapture it delights the spirit so that it turns creator and esteemer and lover and benefactor of all things. . . .
> With knowledge the body purifies itself; making experiments with knowledge, it elevates itself. . . . (Z I, 22, §§1, 2)

Although the *da zong shi* chapter of the *Zhuang zi* expresses a pessimistic view of life as a tumor and of death as the bursting of a boil

(18/6/68), in the *da sheng* (Mastering Life) chapter one finds the opposite idea of "the body as whole and the spirit as renewed." This is to say
that when the body is in good condition, the spirit is complete. Zhuang
Zi considers Shan Bao's "nurturing the inside while a tiger ate up his
outside," and Zhang Yi's "looking after the outside while sickness attacked him from the inside," to be biased, and suggests that humanity
must nurture life and give equal weight to both the physical and the
spiritual (49/19/31–32).

Numerous anecdotes in the *Zhuang Zi* describe people perfect in
physical form but deficient in spirit and wisdom, as well as people who
are complete and beautiful spiritually in spite of their being physically
deformed. The many crippled and handicapped persons portrayed there
are meant to subvert the notion that one can evaluate a person from
external characteristics. The *de chong fu* chapter in particular advocates
that "one should roam within the realm of forms and bodies," and rejects the prejudice that "one should seek life beyond the physical person"
(13/5/23). But Zhuang Zi further recommends that one not stop with
the physical body but rather go on to extend one's own spiritual space
and develop one's intellectual life.

III

While Nietzsche's attitude toward life involves an active engagement
with the world, Zhuang Zi tends to be more escapist and quietistic. The
method of Nietzsche's "engagement" with the world is by no means
straightforward as is evidenced by Zarathustra's constant alternations
between coming down from the mountain to engage the world and then
retiring into his solitude. Zarathustra's retreats are not to be understood
negatively, since their purpose is reflection and introspection, self-
realization and self-articulation. Nietzsche's own sense of alienation
from the group increased his sense of being alone. When he did go into
society, it was for no other reason than to seek out creatures of his own
kind.

Zhuang Zi's notion of withdrawal involves a radical separation from
ordinary values. Zhuang Zi was not a person without a patriotic heart
or a person who did not find meaning in society. It was because he lived
in such a turbulent age in which people (especially intellectuals) were
not able to live out their natural life spans, that Zhuang Zi himself came
to adore freedom. His notion of withdrawal has several aspects. First, in
a troubled world it provided a way to preserve life. He speaks of people
who "if they encountered a period of order, they did not run away from

public office; but if they encountered an age of disorder, they did not try to hold on to an office at any cost" (80/28/84).

Second, Zhuang Zi was concerned to extricate himself from the snares of government and society, a move he describes as *wu yung zhi yung* (the utility of the useless), which means not to take what other people regard as useful to be useful in actuality. Zhuang Zi's attitude toward those who hold power was simply uncooperative, and the biography in the *Shi ji* describes him as "enjoying alone his own purposes" and "doing whatever suits himself." He was concerned not to be trapped by the common values and power structures of his times, because he wished to maintain a place for his own spiritual activity. In sum, he felt that in pursuing social values dominated by rank and reputation one invariably loses sight of oneself.

IV

The pre-Chin philosophers faced tumultuous historical circumstances, and the *Zhuang zi* painfully describes the difficult circumstances of warfare in the Warring States Period (481–221 B.C.E.), the violent excesses of government, and the misery suffered by the common people. Of particular interest in the context of a comparison with Nietzsche is the passage about carpenter Shi's visit to Qi, in which an extended simile characterizes the person of talent:

The cherry apple, the pear, the orange, the citron, the rest of those fructiferous trees and shrubs—as soon as their fruit is ripe, they are torn apart and subjected to abuse. Their big limbs are broken off, their little limbs are yanked around. Their utility makes life miserable for them, and so they don't get to finish out the years Heaven gave to them, but are cut off in mid- journey. They bring it on themselves—the pulling and tearing of the common mob. (11/4/69–71)

This gives a vivid sense of the abuse that talented people suffered at the hands of the society in which Zhuang Zi lived. Born into a disorderly age, Zhuang Zi's mental state was one of suffering and contradiction. If he had not cared about the fortunes of society and its people, he would not have "written a work of more than 100,000 characters" to express his feelings for the age and to outline his philosophical tenets (*Shi ji*, "Zhuang Zi biography").

The social environment of the age in which Nietzsche lived was nothing like that rugged world into which Zhuang Zi was born. Nietzsche lived in a period in which the capitalism of his own country was developing, and economically and politically the nation was in ascendance. And so even though he was dissatisfied with the government and was a

polemical figure with respect to political affairs, his situation was nowhere near as tenuous as Zhuang Zi's. Although Nietzsche's dissatisfaction with social and political conditions is forcefully expressed in his
writings, they do not offer any deep response to the situation.
Nietzsche's attitude toward life was not primarily political, but rather
grew out of his concern with culture and philosophy.

V

Nietzsche called himself a free spirit, and he said: "Wherever we may
come there will always be freedom and sunlight around us" (*GS* 343,
294). Zhuang Zi's *xiao yao you* (Free and Easy Wandering) chapter also
expresses the freedom of the human spirit. The *ren jian shi* (In the
World of Men) chapter recommends that one "just go alone with things
and let one's heart-mind move freely" (10/4/52), where "letting the
heart-mind move freely" (*you xin*) means preserving the freedom of
one's spirit. Even though both Zhuang Zi and Nietzsche exalt spiritual
freedom, the idea has radically different features and philosophic content
in each case. Nietzsche was exasperated by what he called "fixed habits":
"Every habit lends our hand more wit but makes our wit less handy"
(*GS* 247, also 295). His antipathy toward the moral categories of Christianity also had to do with habits and customs: "Morality makes people
stupid and is a hindrance to the creation of new and better customs" (*D*
19). In general, he saw morality as the product of a "diseased will":

Conversely, one could conceive of such pleasure and power of self-determination, such a freedom of will that the spirit would take leave of all faith and every
wish for certainty, being practiced in maintaining himself on insubstantial ropes
and possibilities and dancing even near abysses. Such a spirit would be the *free
spirit* par excellence. (*GS* 347)

When Nietzsche talks about spiritual freedom, he is in fact confronting
the unfree person produced by Christian thought and morality.
    When Zhuang Zi talks of spiritual freedom it is from several perspec-
tives. First, he held that what fetters people and prevents them from
realizing their spiritual freedom are human factors, the constraints and
proscriptions that the categories of traditional culture and social relations impose on them. He criticizes the ideas of *ren, yi, li,* and *zhi* representative of the Confucian school as violating and constricting human
nature and preventing the liberation of the human spirit. Many of the
anecdotes concerning animals in the *yang sheng* (Cultivating Life) and
the *qiu shui* (Autumn Floods) chapters are allegories of the pedant confined by his one-sided teachings.

Zhuang Zi believes further that there are other, self-imposed factors which constrict human beings and preclude their freedom, factors stemming from the sealed heart and mind of the egoist. What is meant by the "sealed heart and mind of the egoist" is the *cheng xin* (completed mind) (4/2/22) of the *qi wu lun* chapter, or the *feng zhi xin* (heart and mind full of undergrowth) (3/1/42) of the *xiao yao you* chapter. The *cheng xin* refers to the subjective prejudices of all humans, which constitute the framework of the limited ego. The *feng xin* refers to the myopic field of view and tunnel vision which constitute the encasement of the egoist's heart and mind.

In the *tian-di* (Heaven and Earth) chapter, Zhuang Zi describes the situation of those who get into difficulties:

> If what you have gotten has gotten you into trouble, then can you really be said to have gotten something? If so, then the pigeons and doves in their cages have also gotten hold of something. With likes and dislikes, sounds and colors you cripple what is on the inside; with leather caps and snipe- feathered bonnets, batons struck in belts and sashes trailing, you cramp what is on the outside. The inside hemmed in by pickets and pegs, the outside heaped with wraps and swathes, and still you stand in this tangle of wraps and swathes and declare that you have gotten hold of something? If so, then the condemned and the leopard in their pens and prisons have also gotten hold of something! (3/12/99ff.)

A person who suffers from constraints of his own making cannot be said to have liberated himself and achieved spiritual freedom.

The *qi wu lun* chapter challenges the limitations of ego-centeredness by invoking the method of understanding called *ming* (clarity). In discussing whether or not the myriad things have some shared standard, Zhuang Zi encourages people to abandon the anthropocentric attitude toward things and to adopt many different perspectives in order to broaden the basis of their value judgments. He employs the image of ten suns coming out at once, thereby illuminating the myriad things, in order to portray the potential breadth and texture of the human heart. It is only when one opens the horizons of one's perspective and liberates one's heart and mind that one is able to achieve the condition of "pure spirit flowing in all four directions" (40–41/15/18–19) and attain true spiritual freedom.

VI

Zhuang Zi and Nietzsche both assume the posture of relativism (*sheng-zhi zhuyi*), rejecting the absolutist values previously accepted by their respective traditions. Zhuang Zi employs an "ethical relativism" to reject the right and wrong of ritually ordered culture, while Nietzsche uses something comparable to reject the right and wrong of Christian culture and the acceptance of God as the standard of absolute value.

Nietzsche's radical skepticism causes him to doubt the fundamental tenets of the Christian teachings. In *Human, All Too Human*, he expresses the important insight that there are no absolute values in the world, no transcendent truths or standards, and that good and evil exist only as a function of human activity and, moreover, develop only in their relationship to one another. The figure of Zarathustra affirms that human beings are the sole creators of values:

Only man placed values in things to preserve himself—he alone created a meaning for things, a human meaning. Therefore he calls himself "man" which means: the esteemer.
To esteem is to create. . . .
Transformation of values—that is a transformation of creators. (Z I, 15)

In this passage Nietzsche advocates "the transformation of values" and the "renewal of values." Throughout his works he accuses the Christian doctrine of self-restraint of suppressing all natural talent and desire and of constraining human beings from soaring to spiritual heights. And in general he criticizes the Christian tradition for causing a "total loss of life and vitality" (AC 7) and for leading to absolute nihilism.

The *Zhuang zi* exemplifies a similar turn away from and sustained critique of conventional values. In the *xiao yao you* chapter, the anecdote about the great Peng Bird and the little sparrows sharply outlines the difference between conventional and ideal values and gives a sense of the distance between the ordinary person and the one of enlightened purpose. In the *zhi le* chapter, Zhuang Zi suggests that all the world covets and chases after wealth and status, long life, and reputation and calculates how to acquire fame, stability, fine clothes, and hedonistic pleasures "as though they cannot help it." For this reason people break their bodies, agitate themselves, and worry their minds while their spirits are constantly disturbed by concern over gain and loss: "Those who don't get these things fret a great deal and are afraid."

The *shan xing* (Mending the Inborn Nature) chapter contains a succinct expression of Zhuang Zi's critique of conventional values:

Nowadays, however, when men speak of the fulfillment of ambition, they mean fine carriages and caps. But carriages and caps affect the body alone, not the inborn nature and fate. Such things from time to time may happen to come your way. When they come, you cannot keep them from arriving, but when they depart you cannot stop them from going. (41/16/18ff.)

Zhuang Zi considers that this kind of "sacrificing oneself to other things and losing one's nature to the common world" is characteristic of the "upside-down people"—of people whose values have been inverted.

In the first aphorism of *The Gay Science* Nietzsche writes that "all ethical systems hitherto have been so foolish and anti-natural that humanity would have perished of every one of them if it had gained power over humanity. . . ." This corresponds to Zhuang Zi's critique of the constraints on human nature imposed by ethical systems, and especially those imposed by the Confucian morality. The *da zong shi* chapter says, "Yao has already tattooed you with benevolence and righteousness and cut off your nose with right and wrong" (19/6/83–84). The *ma di* (Horses Hooves) chapter says: "Then along comes the sage huffing and puffing after benevolence, reaching on tiptoe for righteousness, and the world for the first time has doubts; mooning and mouthing over his music, snipping and stitching away at his rites, and the world for the first time is divided" (23/9/11).

Throughout the entire *Zhuang zi*, the author's critique of the virtues *ren* and *yi* of Confucian morality invariably proceeds from the perspective of what is natural to human nature, suggesting that such a morality goes against the grain of the human condition. In general Zhuang Zi's thought breaks through the web of values of traditional, ritually ordered society, and from a much broader cosmic model grasps the meaning of human existence to elevate human spirituality and expand the purviews of human thought.

In sum, both Zhuang Zi and Nietzsche take issue with the various philosophies that constitute their respective cultural traditions. Nietzsche initiates his own transvaluation of values in the face of Christian and traditional Western values, while Zhuang Zi initiates his transvaluation of values against the values of the vulgar world and traditional Confucian morality.

VII

I should like to conclude this comparison by recapitulating the points of similarity between Zhuang Zi and Nietzsche, then contrasting their major differences, and finally criticizing their shortcomings.

1. Both Zhuang Zi and Nietzsche are literary philosophers; they belong to a Romantic style of philosophizing, employing as they do highly

figurative language to express their understanding of the world and human experience, thereby moving the reader to reflect seriously and sincerely upon her or his own life.

2. They are both severe critics of their respective historical traditions and the values that undergird them. The function of each in his own tradition is to breathe new life into the ossified intellectual orthodoxy.

3. Both Nietzsche and Zhuang Zi are of a solitary intellectual character, rejecting as they do both authoritarianism and personality cult. Zhuang Zi rejects the traditional sages and ridicules Confucius, and Nietzsche sings his requiem mass for God.

4. Zhuang Zi and Nietzsche both reject conservativism and the classics. Nietzsche says: "The snake that cannot slough its skin, perishes. Likewise spirits which are prevented from changing their opinions; they cease to be spirits" (D 573). Zhuang Zi in the *tian yun* (The Turning of Heaven) chapter suggests that conservatives who promote institutions that are not in keeping with the times are like people pushing boats in the mountains.

5. They both criticize—though from different standpoints—the conventional nature and lack of originality of the academic world. While Zhuang Zi takes Confucius as his target, Nietzsche criticizes "aristocrats, priests, and teachers" as being "poor in spirit" (D 198).

6. Nietzsche and Zhuang Zi both aim at promoting the liberation of the individual. Just as Nietzsche emphasizes the importance of the individual and individual differences, so Zhuang Zi elevates the individual to the status of "being a companion with heaven and earth," and also stresses that "each has different talents, each has different occupations" (47/18/39).

7. Both thinkers emphasize the importance of spiritual freedom. Their notions of freedom should not be confused with the concept of legal freedoms, but are rather literary and aesthetic notions.

8. With respect to political positions, one could characterize Nietzsche as an "aristocratic anarchist," as Russell did, while Zhuang Zi (unlike Lao Zi in this respect) is very definitely a political anarchist.

9. Cosmologically, there is some degree of correspondence between Nietzsche's eternal recurrence and the notion of cyclical return in the philosophies of Lao Zi and Zhuang Zi. Similarly they both reject a dualistic world view, seeing the world as an organic whole devoid of any transcendent reality. Insofar as Zhuang Zi holds that "the *dao* pervades all things" and Nietzsche vigorously opposes the transcendent world of Plato and the other world of Christianity, both are affirming the reality of this world of change.

1. Although the philosophies of these two thinkers have much in common, they are articulated from utterly different cultural and social backgrounds. Nietzsche's philosophy is shaped against the background of the convergence of the tragic spirit of the Greeks and the Judeo-Christian culture; Zhuang Zi's philosophy, on the other hand, critiques the constraints imposed on human nature by artificially contrived clan culture, seeking as it does freedom for the human spirit.

2. Nietzsche's "down-going" takes the descent from the mountain as its key metaphor, and eventuates in an engagement with the human world, however changing and sporadic that might be. Zhuang Zi, on the other hand, confronted with the turmoil of the Warring States Period, in which the lives of the commoners were as so much fodder, tended to be reclusive at heart—sometimes to the point of escapism.

3. Nietzsche's thought is pervaded with a feeling of contest (agon), while Zhuang Zi in dealing with his world adopts the posture of complying with what is natural.

4. Nietzsche's thought constantly evokes the "creative will of the human spirit," while Zhuang Zi advocates "a fasting of the heart" and "sitting and forgetting" with respect to life experience. The former advocates an external assault, while the latter advocates an internal purification.

5. Zhuang Zi's egalitarianism contrasts with Nietzsche's promotion of an "order of rank." Central to Zhuang Zi is the ideal of the "parity of all things" (in the qi wu lun chapter). Nietzsche, on the other hand, rejects the notion of equality advocated in the Christian context, proposing instead that people exert themselves and transform themselves through effort into something higher and more noble.

1. Both Zhuang Zi and Nietzsche promote philosophies of individualism. When Zhuang Zi discusses the human being's relation to the natural world he is open and conciliatory, taking the natural condition of one's world to be the conditions of one's self. The objective is really subjective and vice versa: "Heaven and earth and I were born together, and the myriad things and I are one." But when he discusses the person's relation to society, his antisocial and anticonventional attitude lead him to withdraw. He assumes the position that the wise person who knows what is best for himself can best safeguard his own personal security. Although Nietzsche has the courage to want to improve his world, by demanding that the self constantly transcend itself, he grossly exaggerates the role of the self. As a consequence one senses in his dealings with the human world and society an extreme isolation and loneliness, which tend to lead to demoralization and defeatism.

2. Both Nietzsche and Zhuang Zi suggest that there are no limits to the elevation of the individual human spirit by creating an enormous gap between the individual and society. Nietzsche's position leads to isolation and misanthropy, and Zhuang Zi's to a retreat into emptiness. The kind of thought that leads one away from community and abandons social development ultimately arrives at what Lu Xun critically calls "deserting the community and submerging oneself in malaise."

3. Both Zhuang Zi and Nietzsche are critical of social institutions. There is no doubt that Zhuang Zi is keenly penetrating in his evaluation of human experience and discerning in his articulation of social ills. But whether in response to problems inherited from the past or social problems current in his time, having launched his critical attack he refuses to enter the fray but rather retreats to the high ground of the imagination. Zhuang Zi is good at identifying social ills but offers no remedy. Nietzsche is rich with the spirit of the fight, whether it be against God above or the devil below; his sword has been sharpened for them. But it is one man's battle—he stands alone. Neither Zhuang Zi nor Nietzsche is able to harness the strength and intelligence of the masses to lift society out of its morass.

4. The greatest problem with the *Zhuang Zi* its lack of fighting spirit. Zhuang Zi was born into troubled times in which intellectuals lived in the shadow of danger, and so his escapist attitude is understandable. However, if a thinker encounters human society in crisis, he surely has an obligation to take up arms to change the situation. Nietzsche was certainly cognizant of the spiritual demoralization of the contemporary Western world. But what he did not see was that the capitalistic and imperialistic direction of the Western powers encouraged them to become strong at the expense of other nations. And so when Nietzsche emphasizes the human need to exercise without limit the creative will, even though his intention lies in healing the sick human being produced by Christian culture, he is failing to recognize the expansionism of the Western nations which characterizes the history of the modern period.

Note

1. TN—All references to *Zhuang Zi* will follow the Harvard-Yen Ching Institute, *A Concordance to Chung Tzu*, no. 20, 1956. The citation gives the page/chapter/line of the original; by following the middle number it will be easy to find the passage in question in any translation.

9

Nietzsche's "Will to Power" and Chinese "Virtuality" (*De*): A Comparative Study

Roger T. Ames

I

This paper is an exercise in comparative philosophy. I want to juxtapose and contrast two obscure yet seemingly resonant notions: the early Chinese conception of *de*, commonly rendered "virtue," and Nietzsche's notion of will to power (*der Wille zur Macht*). This comparative approach recommends itself for the following reason.

Both terms are painfully recondite. "Will to power," like many of the central themes in Nietzsche, undergoes a process of gradual development. Although it is adumbrated in the middle works beginning with *Zarathustra*, and some definition is offered in several of the later works—*Beyond Good and Evil* in particular—these occurrences are far from definitive. In fact, corroboration for a viable interpretation has often required reference to the sometimes conflicting fragments collected in the later *Nachlass*, Nietzsche's unpublished works.[1]

Another source of ambiguity shrouding "will to power" arises from Nietzsche's explanatory medium—in its earliest appearances, it is suggested imagistically through fable.[2] Nietzsche, in rebelling against many fundamental presuppositions that have undergirded and framed the evolution of Western thought, and in challenging the very categories out of which his interpreters can construct their commentaries, has almost guaranteed his own misinterpretation. For Nietzsche, language is quite simply an insurmountable problem. He claims explicitly that the terms used to define his central ideas cannot be understood in any conventional sense, and in fact must be disengaged from the prevailing meanings that attend them. The locution "will to power" is a case in point. In attempting to illuminate his usage of "will," he states:

Willing seems to me above all something *complicated*, something that is a unit only as a word— . . . Inasmuch in the given circumstances we are at the same time the commanding *and* the obeying parties, and as the obeying party we know the sensations of constraint, impulsion, pressure, resistance, and motion. . . . (*BGE* 19)

He attempts to release will from its common psychological moorings: "My proposition is: that the will of psychology hitherto is an unjustified generalization, that this will *does not exist at all*" (*WP* 692). Rejecting a conativist interpretation, he suggests that will is some primitive drive that impels phenomena—a life internal to all things:

The struggle for existence is only an *exception*, a temporary restriction of the will of life; the struggle, great and small, everywhere turns on ascendancy, on growth and extension, in accordance with the will to power, which is precisely the will of life. (*GS* 349)

But the problem of language is even more fundamental for Nietzsche than the inappropriateness of available terminologies. According to Nietzsche, the very syntax of the Indo-European languages which have articulated our civilization are themselves infected with an incurable "metaphysics" that subverts the very expression of the ideas that he is attempting to communicate:

The strange family resemblance of all Indian, Greek, and German philosophizing is explained easily enough. Where there is affinity of languages, it cannot fail, owing to the common philosophy of grammar—I mean, owing to the unconscious domination and guidance by similar grammatical functions—that everything is prepared at the outset for a similar development and sequence of philosophical systems; just as the way seems barred against certain other possibilities of world-interpretation. (*BGE* 20)

While our subject-predicate grammar insists that "will" must have a subject that wills it, Nietzsche requires that there is no subject or superordinate faculty that "wills" power—rather, "will" is categorial, the impetus underlying the process of existence and the phenomena that constitute it. The reader intent on understanding Nietzsche must struggle relentlessly against the language in which this philosopher's insights are couched, in full knowledge that in exponential degree, the more profound the insight, the less appropriate will be the language.

The notion of *de* is hardly less obscure. Confucius states specifically,

"Few indeed are those who understand and realize *de* "(*A* 15/3). In fact, this concept *de* is an uncomfortable puzzle in the early texts. Many scholars have not really determined what to make of it, and as a consequence, have tended to give it short shrift.[3]

The prominence and the ambiguity of this term, *de*, in the corpus of pre-Chin literature is adequately illustrated in F. W. Mote's translation of Hsiao Kung-chuan's *A History of Chinese Political Thought*, in which he renders *de* in the following ways: "ethical nature," "spiritual powers," "Power," "moral excellence," "power imparted from the *Tao* [*Dao*]," "*virtus*" (in the sense of a thing's intrinsic and distinctive character), "moral force" (citing Waley), "the powers native to beings and things," and frequently, perhaps in despair, simply as "*te* [*de*]."[4]

To generalize from Mote's translations, for the Confucians and Mohists, *de* is most often translated "virtue," while for the Daoists it is usually some order of "power." Beyond these two general categories which imply something cultivated within, *de* also refers to "favor" or "bounty" extended outward, and further, the "gratitude" it evokes as a response. In other words, *de* encompasses both efficient force and its effects. On this basis, I want to suggest "virtuality" in the archaic sense of "having inherent virtue or power to produce effects" as our working translation of *de*.

II

I want to begin our comparison of *de* and will to power from a reconstruction of the less familiar "virtuality" (*de*) because it provides the occasion to articulate several fundamental assumptions grounding classical Chinese cosmology. We tend to regard Nietzsche as an increasingly important player in setting the agenda for our own philosophical reflections, and expect him as such to share with us certain unannounced yet determinative assumptions. In this familiarity, there is a real danger of undervaluing his originality. In exploring the Chinese world view, on the other hand, we are quite willing (if not entirely able) to suspend our presuppositions in the anticipation of a more formidable cultural and linguistic divide. The exoticness of the classical Chinese "virtuality" might serve to prime us for the more difficult task of getting behind what we might initially take to be familiar in Nietzsche only to discover that he too is very exotic indeed. It might enable us to give Nietzsche his difference.

J. L. Austin once remarked that "a word never—well, hardly ever—shakes off from its etymology and formation. In spite of all changes in and extensions of and additions to its meaning, and indeed rather pervading and governing these, there will persist the old idea."[5] To understand Austin as making the hard claim that a word, independent of context and usage, is inhabited by and retains some univocal and unchanging meaning is, for me, rather suspect, and probably not fair to Austin. A softer version of this same claim, however, seems plausible. Extending Austin's insight somewhat, I would suggest that linguistic continuities are often traceable etymologically to some concealed metaphor or image, or to some cluster of correlations, that constrains the range of possible applications. It is the project of this section, then, to attempt to pursue a more fundamental level of meaning for *de*, and, while eschewing the possibility of identifying some univocal meaning, to excavate a core meaning against which its several specific historical interpretations can be understood.

Many sinologists have tacitly disagreed with Austin's claim. They have made much of the disparate meanings of *de* for the Confucians and for the Daoists even to the point of disengaging them entirely, claiming that for these schools *de* "had a totally different meaning."[6] While the Confucian and Daoist philosophers clearly use *de* in a variety of different ways, I want to suggest that this term still has an underlying continuity that can be discerned and articulated.

The weight of the Daoist discussion tends to be cosmological, not in the abstract sense of "a science of first principles," but in the aesthetic sense of *ars contextualis*, "the art of contextualization" or "composition." *De* denotes the correlation of particular vectors—of "this's and that's"—in the ceaseless process of change.

In the Confucian *Analects*, on the other hand, *de* is more specifically ethical and social in its applications. When we lay bare the cosmological and aesthetic presuppositions underlying Confucian ethical sensibilities, however, and when we draw out the social and political implications of *de* in the Daoist texts, we find that the distance between their interpretations of *de* closes significantly.

III

As a basis for reconstructing *de*, we need to lay out several "uncommon" assumptions that are pervasive in the classical Chinese world view. First, existence is a ceaseless and continuous process or field of change (*dao*) made determinate in the interdependent particulars (*de*) that constitute it. This is not a "one-many" cosmology. In fact, in this tradition there is no "cosmos" in the sense of a single-ordered world—no "uni"-verse.

Dao is always interpreted from some particular perspective, a perspective which makes *dao* determinate for itself. *Dao* is always "this" world or "that" world, and never "the" world. As such, each interconnected particular constitutes and construes its own field.

Secondly, there is no assumed distinction between what is and how it is—between the *stuff* and the *order* of existence. There is no Being that underlies and explains Becoming; no Reality that both recommends and falsifies Appearance; no unchanging first principles that provide existence with unity and system. There is no formal *archē* which, by virtue of some ontological priority, marshals a cosmos out of chaos, and which, when grasped, renders the world intelligible and articulatable. Rather, in Daoism, particulars are *kosmoi*—both *what* they are and *how* they are. They constitute their own creative source and their own emergent ordering structures.

And thirdly, *dao* is hylozoistic—a psychophysical world in which mental and physical describe differences of degree rather than kind.

IV

Before attempting to reconstruct "virtuality" (*de*) at a conceptual level, I want to follow Austin's insight and explore *de* philologically in order to uncover what he calls the "old idea." In the *Shuo-wen*, one of the earliest extant lexicons, *de* is defined as "to ascend," "to climb," "to arise" or "to presence" (*sheng*). Knitting the various strands of the philological data together, it would seem that *de*, at a cosmological level, denotes the arising of the hylozoistic particular in a process vision of existence. The particular is the unfolding of a *sui generis* focus of potency that encompasses and makes determinate those conditions within the field and parameters of its particularity. The range of its particularity is variable, contingent upon the way in which it is interpreted both by itself and by other environing particulars. That is to say, its context in whatever direction and degree can be construed as either "self" or as "other."

The particular is a compositor, always composing its world. Its direction is "appropriate" to the extent that it is efficacious for the constituent elements and is able to maximize their possibilities. There is an openness of the particular such that it can suffuse to become coextensive with other willing particulars, and absorb an increasingly broader field of "arising" within the sphere of its own particularity. This then is the "getting" or "appropriating" aspect of *de*. As a particular extends itself through patterns of deference to encompass a wider range of "presencing" or "arising," the possibilities of its conditions and its potency for self-construal are proportionately increased.

In a "one-many" cosmology, the basic question tends to be: how is the particular related to and derived from the superordinate one? But in the *dao-de* cosmology, we ultimately must ask: what is the difference between the focus and the field?

The *Zhuang Zi* can help us to sort out this terminology:

Dao is the arrangement and display of *de*; the process of birth, life and growth (*sheng**) is the radiating of *de*. Natural tendency (*xing*) is the raw ingredients of the process of birth, life and growth. The activity of natural tendency is called "to do" or "to make" (*wei*); "doing" or "making" which departs from natural tendency is called "to lose" (*shi*). (ZZ 64/23/70; W 259)

In this passage, the *Zhuang Zi* plays with the homophonous relationship between *de* and its cognate, *de**—"to gain," and with the homophonous relationship between "life and growth" (*sheng**) and its cognate, "natural tendency" (*xing*).[7] The process of birth, life, and growth—the expression of *de*—is constrained by a thing's natural conditions and tendencies. When the "doing" or "making" of one's self and one's world expresses the integrity of these conditions, the "poietic" activity of self-disclosure is "gaining"; when the "making" of oneself is inauthentic and contrived, it is "losing." The highest *de* is efficacious, maximizing the participating elements. The *Zhuang Zi* passage continues:

Activity that issues from what is inevitable is called *de*; activity that is wholly expressive of oneself is called proper order.

This passage characterizes the "doing" or "making" of the particular in a seemingly contradictory way. On the one hand, this activity of "making" is deterministically "inevitable"; on the other, it is creative—"wholly expressive of oneself." As a product issuing out of its natural tendencies and conditions, the course of the particular's activity can be characterized as "inevitable." The context out of which the particular "makes" itself constrains its range of possibilities. But, if we alter the focus which defines the particular, these same conditions are constitutive of its own autogenerative particularity and, hence, are not something "other." There is nothing which is not a condition of one's own process of existence (*wu-fei-wo*). When the particular is understood in this way, there is no conflict between inevitability and self-expression. Hence, the *Zhuang Zi* passage concludes by collapsing this very distinction:

By definition, inevitability and self-expressiveness seem to be contraries, but in fact, they are coincident.

V

Any suggestions gleaned from the philological analysis must necessarily be tested in the philosophical literature. Across the corpus of pre-Chin literature, *de* seems to have a fundamental and consistent cosmological significance from which its other connotations are derived. In the Daoist literature, it is explicitly described as a variable field or focus of potency in the process of existence. As viewed from the perspective of any particular, this dynamic process *in toto* is called *dao*, but when discussed as individuated existents, these particulars are *de*. Although the Confucians were reluctant to engage in metaphysical speculation, the functional equivalent of *dao* implicit in their human world view is *tian*— conventionally translated as "Heaven." In our reading of both the *Dao de jing* and the *Analects* and of the world view that these texts express, we must guard against the comfortable and all too familiar slide into the Creator/creature cosmogonic model in which an independent transcendent deity engenders and endows a dependent world. Creation and destruction, life and death, part and whole, far from being understood in dualistic categories of Creator and creature, *creatio ex nihilo* and *destructio in nihilum*, are interdependent categories. Existence is the unbounded totality of particular fields on which each particular with its own impetus and matrix of conditions is describable in focal language: growing and declining, waxing and waning, condensing and dissipating, densifying and rarifying.

The particular analogy is like any note or phrase in the performance of a piece of music which can be extended or contracted depending upon how it is interpreted and construed. Not only does a symphony have notes, but each note has a symphony. Implicate within each note is the entire performance as its defining conditions. The symphony conditions each of the particular notes, and each note construes the symphony from its own particular perspective. When disclosing its own uniqueness and difference, the note can be entertained as a particular focus within the symphony; when considered in terms of the full complement and consequence of its determining conditions, the note is its own interpretation of the entire symphony.

VI

As we have seen, *de* is a means of interpreting *dao* and making it determinate and unique. Hence, it is discriminatory. But it is also a principle of synthesis and integration. While *de* is most often used to define *dao* as a particular focus, this focus is elastic, and can be extended from its center even to the extent of embracing its whole. In the *Dao de jing*, for example, locutions such as "constant *de*" (*chang de*), "perpetual *de*" (*heng de*), "dark *de*" (*xuan de*), and "superlative *de*" (*shang de*) all denote the coincidence of *dao* and *de*—the extension of *de* such that the distinction between *de* and its *dao* is indiscernible. The *Dao de jing* states:

> If you are a river gorge to the world,
> Your constant *de* will not desert you.
> When your constant *de* does not desert you,
> You will again return to being a babe. . . .
> If you are a valley to the world,
> Your constant *de* will be sufficient.
> When your constant *de* is sufficient,
> You will again return to being the uncarved block.
>
> (*DDJ* 28)

When *de* is cultivated and accumulated such that the particular is integrated efficaciously into its environments, the distinction between *dao* and *de*—between field and focus—collapses, and the individuating capacity of *de*, in a gestalt-like "duck-rabbit" way, transforms into its integrating capacity. That is to say, the focus of *de* extends without discontinuity to embrace fully the indeterminate field of its context. *De* is both particular and its particular whole.

Perhaps a concrete example would make this point clear. The Chinese tradition—political, religious, intellectual—has regularly been defined in terms of "supreme personalities." Given the centripetal order characteristic of the Confucian world view, the ruler or the magistrate or the father or the canonical text derives its authority from being at the center, and having implicate within it the order of the whole. The attraction of the center is such that, with varying degrees of success, it draws into its field and suspends the disparate and diverse centers that constitute its world. Although the family, the society, the state, and even the tradition itself, as the extended "group" or "field," is indeed ambiguous *as a group or field*, the vagueness of the abstract nexus is focused and made immediate in the embodiment of the group or field by the particular father, the communal exemplar, the ruler, and the historical model. It is by virtue of this "supreme personality's" embodiment of his world that he lays claim to impartiality—his actions are appropriate (*yi*), accommodating the interests of all rather than being self-interested (*li**). Just as the conceptions of *dao* or Heaven (*tian*), encompassing within themselves the world order, are described in terms of impartiality, so the "Sage-ruler" or "Son of Heaven" (*tian-zi*) with similar compass is devoid of egoism. As long as the center is strong enough to draw the deference or tribute of its environing spheres of influence, it retains its position of authoritativeness—that is, not only the willing acknowledgement of its order but active participation in reinforcing it. Standing at the center, the ruler acts imperceptibly, constituting a bearing for the human order, yet appearing to be unmoved and unmoving himself (*A* 2/1, 15/5).

In the *Dao de jing*, the indeterminacy of *dao* is frequently alluded to by appeal to images such as the uncarved block (*pu*), water (*sui*), darkness (*xuan*), the abyss (*yuan*) and the newly born baby (*chi zi*). For example, "one who possess *de* in abundance is comparable to a new born babe" (*DDJ* 55). The point here is that an infant with its "oceanic feeling" does not distinguish itself from its environment. There is no circumscription or separation from its whole. Such being the case, because the infant is a matrix through which the full consequence of undiscriminated existence can be experienced, it can be used as a metaphor for the *de* which is *dao*. Throughout the early literature, this collapse of *de* into *dao*—of focus into field—is often expressed in paradoxical language:

> The person of superior *de* does not get *de*,
> And that is why he has *de*.
> The person of inferior *de* does not lose *de*
> And that is why he has no *de*. . . .

> (*DDJ* 38)

The *Zhuang Zi* also describes *de* as a unifying principle:

> This man and this kind of *de* will enfold all things
> within itself as one.

> (ZZ 2/1/32; W 33)

The "oneness" referred to in this passage is the coherence discernable in the concrete particular rather than some systemic unity. It is a harmonious order, a regularity, a discernable pattern that is emergent in the process of existence which brings coherence to diversity, oneness to plurality, similarity to difference.

The early Confucian tradition expresses a similar idea within the human sphere. In this tradition, personal activity directed at integration with one's community is called humanity (*ren*). This kind of activity overcomes discreteness and discontinuity in the direction of integration and harmony. In the *Analects* we read:

To discipline oneself and practice ritual action is to realize one's humanity. . . . One's humanity emerges out of oneself; how could it emerge out of others? (*A* 12/1)

In a manner analogous to the continuous relationship between *de* and *dao* in Daoism, persons express their humanity to the extent that they overcome the limitations of the ego-self to extend themselves through integrative ritual action into human community. In this explicitly social and political model, the particular person is the focus, and the community is the field. As the patterns of one's relationships are extended and deepened, one becomes increasingly definitive of humanity.

It is significant that for Confucius the possibilities for humanity are open-ended: "It is the person who extends *dao*, not *dao* that extends the person" (*A* 15/29). This means that the human being is a world-maker, and the greater one's proportions, the greater the influence of one's interpretation.

This sense of "enlarging" oneself defines the political attitudes of classical Confucianism. The capacity of a ruler to attract the loyalty of his people and the goodwill of the barbarians on the frontier is often described in terms of *de*. To the extent that the people defer to the values and purposes embodied in the ruler, the people have, in the language of Wayne Booth, built themselves into the ruler's "field of selves," and the ruler is said to have "gotten them" (*te**) in the sense of having won them over.[8] On the other hand, where the concerns of the parental ruler derive from and are coextensive with those of his subjects, he responds with generosity and impartiality. As the people's *de* is embraced within his own, his potency is thus enhanced and he becomes a wind that overwhelms the weaker *de* (*A* 12/17), the north star around which the other stars revolve (*A* 2/1), the maker and transmitter of culture to which other persons subscribe (*A* 7/1).

The Daoist tradition is critical of the Confucian willingness to limit its concerns to the human world alone. It does not reject the "extension" of oneself in the development of one's humanity (*ren*), but seeks to go further in extending oneself to all things by "acting authentically and without coercion" (*wu-wei*). Perhaps the most helpful metaphor available in the Daoist texts to elucidate this notion of "extension" is that of the tally. The fifth chapter of the *Zhuang Zi* ie entitled *"De* Satisfies the Tally." This chapter is a series of anecdotes about mutilated cripples who, under normal circumstances and under the sway of conventional values, would be ostracized from their communities. Their mutilated physical forms, often the result of amputatory punishments, would be certain grounds for societal rejection. Having overcome discreteness and extended their *de* to contribute to and integrate themselves with the community, however, they "satisfy the tally" with their *de* and not only blend harmoniously with their societies, but further come to exercise considerable influence in establishing the importances of their respective worlds. The extent and quality of their *de* is such that they are important factors in the ongoing process of defining values and establishing an aesthetic and moral order.

In the Daoist tradition, the extension of one's *de* is described in more pervasive terms than in the Confucian literature. As in the Confucian tradition, a person becomes the embodiment and protector of the human order, a styler of new culture and a source of new meaning. But the Daoists take it beyond this into the natural world. The *zhen ren*—the Daoist version of the consummate person—embraces the *de* of the natural as well as of the human environment. By becoming coextensive with the *de* of the ox, for example, Cook Ding in butchering it is able to penetrate and interpret its natural lineaments and interstices without distraction, and to become an efficacious butcher (ZZ 7/3/4, W 50–51); by becoming coextensive with the *de* of the wood, Carpenter Ching is sensitive to the quality and potential of his materials without distraction, and is able to become an efficacious craftsman (ZZ 50/19/54, W 205–206). The absence of a "dis-integrating" ego-self makes these exemplars open to the *de* of their natural environments, so that the environment contributes to them, making them potent and productive, and they contribute to their environments, interpreting and maximizing the possibilities of those things which constitute their world.

With this reconstruction of the classical Chinese notion of *de* in hand, we can now turn to the Nietzschean conception of "will to power." Hopefully, the similarities that lead us to associate these ideas will, on exploration, assist us in highlighting their important differences.

VII

Nietzsche tends to disdain "power" in the early writings because it frequently entails a conformity of the weak and suffering to an established table of values as a means of rescuing oneself from one's own wretchedness. For Nietzsche, the unattractive and unacceptable element in this notion of power is the abandonment of one's own capacity for creating value—one's *true* will to power—in exchange for worldly applause: Wagner's unforgivable crime. Far from being "power," this sense of power is surrender; far from being victory, it is defeat; far from it being self-assertive, it is self-abnegating. Such power is "external" in that self becomes a instrument through which an external, competing will to power is reified in the world.

A starting point for a discussion of Nietzsche's later conception of will to power is its radical transformation from a purely psychological explanation for perverse human conduct to a "cosmological" description of the process of existence. I use the term "cosmological" not in the classical sense of positing some underlying ahistorical *archē* that stands as the determinative origin and ordering principle of a universe. Cosmology need not be dogmatic in the sense that it pronounces on some unalterable feature of the world that wants unconditional affirmation. I want to rehabilitate the notion of "cosmological explanation" and to argue that cosmology is not necessarily inconsistent with an aesthetically sensitive, coherent, and yet nonsystematic interpretation of Nietzsche.

Will to power is clearly characterized in categorial terms—categorial in the claim that nothing more fundamental can be said than to allow the full expression of the uniqueness of the particular in its world. Because will to power cannot be further analyzed without distortion, it is categorical as explanation. All we can do is point to the "this's and that's." In Nietzsche's own language: "Will to power is the ultimate *factum* to which we come." [9]

Nietzsche's cosmology is biographical and genealogical. It refers to the determinate character and coherence that emerges in the course of a particular existence. This cosmology is profoundly aesthetic: it traces the composition and coherence of the unique particular, not as the expression of some universal theory, but as one perspectivally specific interpretation. Whenever the cosmologist abandons the particular perspective and moves to a level of unity or univocity, an ambiguity is introduced by the suspension of the irreducible continuity between the particular world and its implicate order. Nietzsche's alternative, then, to a cosmological dogmatism that pretends to explain unconditionally the underlying nature of the world, is to write creatively as an artist and, out of one's own conditions, to interpret and assert a particular world. The affirmation of the artist, inseparable from the world that he fashions, is only to cry out: "choose me!" Nietzsche does precisely this.

Having outlined his will to power as an alternative to mechanistic physics, Nietzsche concludes: "Supposing that this is also only interpretation—and you will be eager enough to make this objection?—Well, so
much the better" (*BGE* 22).

I would contend further that this "aesthetic" understanding of "cosmology" is tolerable within the etymology of "cosmology" itself. After
all, "*kosmos*" is both an ordered world and an elegant world. It can
mean both "single-ordered universe" (which is not appropriate to
Nietzsche), and a bottom-up, emergent "cosmetic" or "ornamental order" that entails both what is ordered and how it is ordered (which does
seem consistent with Nietzsche). Further, it is seldom advertised that
the "*logos*" in "cosmology" too has a "rational" and an "aesthetic" side.
It can mean both *ratio* and *oratio*. There is the familiar technical sense
of *logos* as a reasoned or theoretical explanation which, in exposing ana-
lytically the organizational principle of the universe, claims univocality.
There is also the less familiar sense of *logos* as rhetoric—the unique
"word" itself. The rational-aesthetic equivocation derives from the fact
that *logos* can refer to both the word by means of which the inward
thought is expressed, and also to the inward thought itself. That the
"aesthetic" side of cosmology is generally overlooked reflects a prejudice
in the way in which we tend to read our tradition.

VIII

As I have suggested above, cosmology, like *all* of the traditional philosophical areas, has to be radically recast in order to accommodate the
recalcitrant Nietzsche. It is significant that this cosmological notion of
will to power is most fully developed in Nietzsche's later writings—
some of them being the unpublished *Nachlass*. In recent times, the appropriateness of using the *Nachlass* as a source for Nietzsche's thought
has become a point of debate among Nietzsche scholars. Some, on the
basis of its relative lateness in his career, regard it as containing some of
the fullest and most coherent of Nietzsche's reflections, and others regard it not only as Nietzsche's rejected remainder but also as being positively subversive of the insights that he had wanted to communicate.[10]
Without joining this debate, I take a fundamental continuity between
the later published works and some of the ideas expressed in the *Nachlass* as a warrant for using the *Nachlass* as a corroborative resource for
Nietzsche's thought.

One can certainly make the case that a robust understanding of a text such as *Beyond Good and Evil* is dependent upon a cosmological understanding of will to power, and that it contains several rather specific references:

Suppose nothing else were "given" as real except our own world of desires and passions, and we could not get down, or up, to any other "reality" besides the reality of our drives. . . . [S]uppose all organic functions could be traced back to this will to power and one could find in it the solution to the problem of procreation and nourishment—it is *one* problem—then one would have gained the right to determine *all* efficient force univocally as—*will to power.* (BGE 36)

The idea of will to power is itself a pervasive although not necessarily explicit element in the text as a whole.

IX

For Nietzsche, existence is a seamless and unbounded dynamic continuum that is entertained and interpreted from always unique perspectives. It is this continuum between the perspective of "self" and the conditions of self which we identify as "other" that makes any notion of either "free will" or "unfree will" suspect. Nietzsche articulates his insight in language that is immediately reminiscent of the *Zhuang Zi* passage cited above:

The desire for "freedom of the will" in the superlative metaphysical sense, which still holds sway, unfortunately, in the minds of the half-educated; the desire to bear the entire and ultimate responsibility for one's actions oneself, and to absolve God, the world, ancestors, chance, and society involves nothing less than to be precisely this *causa sui* and, with more than Münchhausen's audacity, to pull oneself up into existence by the hair, out of the swamps of nothingness. Suppose someone were thus to see through the boorish simplicity of this celebrated concept of "free will" and put it out of his head altogether, I beg of him to carry his "enlightenment" a step further, and also put out of his head the contrary of this monstrous conception of "free will:" I mean "unfree will," which amounts to a misuse of cause and effect. (BGE 21)

Perhaps the most felicitous way of describing the "part-whole" relationship in will to power is to invoke the language of "field and focus" that we used for *dao-de* above. "Field and focus" is felicitous because it dispenses with the language of "whole" and the assumptions of univocity and necessity that the notion of bounded "whole" introduces into cosmological speculation. Instead, Nietzsche perceives existence as a forcefield: a dynamic quanta of interconnected relationships that are themselves the product of difference. J. Hillis Miller describes this "field" of force or power by appeal to a Saussurean linguistic metaphor:

Will there is, for Nietzsche, but not will in the sense of an intention directed by a conscious, unified, substantial self. Will is rather a name for force, for the forces, inner and outer (but the distinction no longer makes sense), which make things happen as they happen. Will as force (the will to power) is the product of difference, of the differentiation of energies, as an electric current flows only if there is a difference of potential between two poles, though the "poles" exist not as things in themselves but as their difference from one another, as in the case of two letters, phonemes, or other signs in structural linguistics.[11]

Miller is making several important observations. There is no subject that "wills" the "will": only the will itself. Hence, there is no intention that separates subject from object or agent from action in a psychological sense. Secondly, given that there is no severe and final "inner"-"outer" or "subject"-"object" dichotomies, each "focus" entails within itself the full field of its conditions. And thirdly, since determinacy in the force-field is the function of difference, all such configurations are unique.

It is Nietzsche's own articulation of will to power that inspires this "focus-field" characterization:

No things remain but only dynamic quanta, in a relation of tension to all other dynamic quanta: their essence lies in their relation to all other quanta, in their "effect" upon the same. (WP 635)

Alexander Nehamas comments on this passage:

The will to power is then an activity that affects and in fact constitutes the character of everything in the world and that is itself the result of such effects. Since these effects embody, establish, and carry forth the character of whatever effects them, Nietzsche characterizes them generally as "power."[12]

Any particular focus can only be understood in terms of what distinguishes it from everything else. At the same time, implicate in each particular is the entire field of conditions as construed from its particular perspective. There is no alternative to interpretation, and yet it is by misconstruing the act of interpreting as reifying either subject or object that we separate cause and effect, and distinguish self from other, agent from action, will from act. The penalty paid for unifying a self—privileging some conditions while excluding others—is to make a break with the *sui generis*, continuous process of existence and insinuate univocity and necessity into our worlds. Any particular focus is only one contingent interpretation among many:

'This is *my* way; where is yours?' thus I answered those who asked me 'the way'. For *the* way—that does not exist. (Z III, 11)

To assert that there is one world would be to deny the inseparability of style and content, of how and what, "as if a world would still remain over after one deducted the perspective" (*WP* 567). Ultimately, each focus is holographic, including within itself the full field of conditions, and yet each hologram is itself unique in that it is construed from some particular perspective. Both the hologram and the uniqueness of perspective are alluded to in eternal recurrence:

In every Now, being begins; round every Here rolls the sphere There. The center is everywhere. (Z III, 13)

Nietzsche's perspectivism underscores the inevitability of interpreting a world from *some* perspective, but a perspective that is fluid and constantly being recast (*GM* II, 12). At the same time, we are unable to entertain this world from *every* perspective, or, equally, from no perspective. He challenges the familiar assumption in "reality/appearance" cosmology that because the project of interpretation necessarily introduces a subjective element, it can only make claims to appearance rather than reality itself. In Nietzschean perspectivism, there is interpretation, and nothing else.

It does not follow, however, that all interpretations are of equal merit. Within the welter of changing conditions, each self-revising interpretation is a compositing. And compositions have both character and coherence that can be valued in qualitative terms—in terms of nobility and baseness. That is, in this process of constantly reconfiguring our worlds, Nietzsche posits the notion of "power" to provide a standard that distinguishes his aesthetic perspectivism from an anything-goes relativism.[13] Will to power is the drive to interpret and hence "create" a world on one's own terms. It is to impel and produce an ever higher product. This production is measurable in the influence and determinacy of a particular focus as a center of force. And at the highest end is the philosopher as artist, sculpting a novel future:

Genuine philosophers . . . are commanders and legislators: they say, "*thus it shall be!*" They first determine the Whither and For What for man, and in so doing have at their disposal the preliminary labor of all philosophical laborers, all who have overcome the past. With a creative hand they reach for the future, and all that is and has been become a means for them, an instrument, a hammer. Their "knowing" is *creating,* their creating is a legislation, their will to truth is—*will to power.* (BGE 211)

X

There is no difficulty in identifying a resonance between Nietzsche's will to power so described and the classical Chinese notion of "virtuality" (*de*), although the echo is somewhat muted by a difference in emphasis and by the language that articulates this difference. The creative project central to the aesthetic cosmology entails both disjunction and continuity which are read then as a gestalt. The disjunction, more prominent in Nietzsche, is captured in the vocabulary of overcoming and mastery, where the quality of the creative product is proportionate to its tensions. Since composition is necessarily a function of manipulating differences, not only disjunction, but both the tension and the force or power required to establish and sustain this tension among the competing details, are significant to the quality of the product.

By contrast, through a gestalt shift, we can read the same composition in terms of its coherence and coordination—the efficacious harmony that obtains among the constituent elements. This then is the emphasis that we find in the classical Chinese context.

Take communal harmony as an illustration of the conjunctive/disjunctive distinction. The composition of the community can be articulated by emphasizing the degree of productive tension that characterizes the relationships that obtain among its members. A community constituted through the interactions of persons of widely divergent yet mutually enhancing accomplishments is presumably richer than a community of clones. This tension, if we focus on the particular persons, can be expressed in terms of a calculus of competing wills to power, where the greater the contest, the more intense and diversified the community. If we focus on the character of the community articulated through the tensions, however, the sense of contest recedes, and the mutuality of the constituent members is foregrounded. We thus register the continuities, rather than the disjunctions, that make them possible.

In the comparison, Nietzsche's emphasis is on the particular focus: the passion of action and reaction, of contest, conquest, and overcoming:

Every center of force adopts a perspective toward the entire remainder, i.e. its own particular valuation, mode of action, and mode of resistance. The "apparent world," therefore, is reduced to a specific mode of action on the world, emanating from a center. Now there is no other mode of action whatever; and the "world" is only a word for the totality of these actions. Reality consists precisely in this particular action and reaction of every individual part toward the whole—. . . But there is no "other," no "true," no essential being—for this would be the expression of a world *without* action and reaction— (*WP* 567)

Nietzsche's particular focus is a dynamic event in many ways comparable to the notion of virtuality *(de)*. It is unique and devoid of any essentiality. The relationship obtaining among particulars, however, is generally expressed in the disjunctive terms of "contest" and "encroachment" rather than "integration:"

... life itself is *essentially* appropriation, injury, overpowering of what is alien and the weaker; suppression, hardness, imposition of one's own forms, incorporation and at least, at its mildest, exploitation— (*BGE* 259)

For Nietzsche, contest is pursued in two directions. First, the particular extends itself by resisting and overcoming competing centers of power—dominating and absorbing them into its own sphere of influence. Secondly, it is constant competition with itself, seeking to disengage from and overcome what it has created of itself:

What is the greatest experience you can have? It is the hour of the great contempt. The hour in which your happiness, too, arouses your disgust, and even your reason and your virtue. (Z Prologue, 3)

The centers of will to power stand in an antagonistic relationship to one another—a relationship of profound contest. Within the swell of this vast and turbulent sea of contesting magnitudes of power-will, the particular centers are discriminated one *from* the other and conjoined one *with* the other through their mutual tensions. In such a way, these tensions articulate and define the culture.

Unlike virtuality *(de)*, the emphasis is not upon the mutuality and interdependence of these centers, where they enhance and become coextensive with one another by accommodating direction and impulse. Instead, the language is often of one center "consuming" another to express it in its own valuations. The highest transvaluation, then, requires the highest tension and opposition among competing values to fire the intensity of its own overcoming.

Both Nietzsche and the early Chinese tradition are committed to the notion of self-transformation. But whereas the notion of virtuality *(de)* represents a continuous extending that is explicitly conservative as well as innovative, Nietzsche's will to power tends to foreground the discontinuity of self-overcoming. Throughout the Nietzschean corpus, there is repeated reference to the heavy importance of the past—there are *three* metamorphoses of the spirit. Quality necessarily grows out of, and in some sense conserves the meaning of, existing culture. But still, where the emphasis in the Chinese tradition is clearly on the camel (and, appropriately, the dragon) and then the child, Nietzsche—laboring against the enormous weight of "the history of an error"—is perhaps more often the lion and then the child. The difference in emphasis is accommodation versus contest.

XI

There is some common ground in the notion of overcoming ego-self. It is clear that for the classical Chinese tradition, ego-self must be dissolved as a precondition for achieving integration and for extending one's influence in the world. This extension of self naturally requires the dissolution of boundaries, but far from underscoring this deconstruction, the emphasis is on the productive relationship between self and "other" that ensues. While retaining the integrity of one's own impetus, one is able to accommodate and interpret into one's focus those aspects of the environment that one finds most enriching and meaningful. This enables the person of extending *de* to integrate broadly and to be everywhere responsive and efficacious. The political ruler expresses the people in his government by accommodating their natural proclivities and orchestrating an interpretation of culture that is both his and theirs. The artist expresses the clay by accommodating its natural conditions in his construal of it.

Although Nietzsche is also committed to self-overcoming, the project seems to differ in important respects. The particular conjoins with its whole in a calculus of contesting forces. Although Nietzsche's transforming Dionysus is torn to shreds by the Titans, he is constantly remaking himself against the resistance of competing "Dionysi." Coherence lies in the striving of the particular centers of will to power as they exert themselves outward to overcome resistance of other contending centers.

The attitude of the Nietzschean *Übermensch* who engages his world by asserting his will to power against both his environments and himself might be regarded by the person of virtuality as one who squanders his considerable energies by failing to respect the complementarity and synchronicity of things. Energy spent in contest is energy lost to harmony. The person of virtuality celebrates the "enjoyment" of integration and harmony. The Nietzschean *Übermensch*, in the fury of contest, seems to relish personal "joy" rather than a shared "enjoyment."

Abbreviations

All translations from the classical Chinese texts are my own.

A   *Analects*
DDJ *Dao de jing* (or *Lao Zi*)
W   B. Watson, trans., *The Complete Works of Chuang Tzu* (New York, 1968)
ZZ   *Zhuang Zi*

Notes

1. See most recently Alexander Nehamas, *Nietzsche: Life as Literature* (Cambridge, Mass., 1985), "A Thing as the Sum of its Effects," pp. 74–105. Nehamas' use of *The Will to Power* (a portion of the *Nachlass* edited and published by Nietzsche's sister) as almost his single source for interpreting "will to power" as "a thing is the sum of its effects" is, in my opinion, justified by the fact that the passages he cites from *The Will to Power* tend to say only more clearly and more specifically what is already elaborated in works from *Zarathustra* on.

2. For example, see Laurence Lampert's *Nietzsche's Teaching: An Interpretation of Thus Spoke Zarathustra* (New Haven, 1986), pp. 100–20.

3. It is because of *de*'s fundamental importance that the canonical text of this philosophic tradition has come to us as the *"Dao de jing"*—*The Classic of dao and de*—and that the school itself was, at least in the earliest extant record, not called *"Daoism,"* but *"Dao-de-ism."*

4. See Hsiao Kung-chuan, *A History of Chinese Political Thought*, vol. 1, trans. F. W. Mote (Princeton, 1979).

5. J. L. Austin, "A Plea for Excuses," *Philosophical Papers* (Oxford, 1961), p. 149.

6. See, for example, Donald Munro, *The Concept of Man in Ancient China,* (Stanford, 1969), p. 147.

7. Although in modern Chinese these two characters are pronounced differently, they were used interchangeably in the classical language.

8. See Wayne C. Booth, *Modern Dogma and the Rhetoric of Assent* (Notre Dame, 1974), pp. 114, 132, 134.

9. *Grossoktavausgabe*, vol. 15 (Leipzig, 1905), p. 415. Cited in Martin Heidegger, *Nietzsche*, vol. 1, trans. David Farrell Krell (New York, 1961).

10. See, for example, Bernd Magnus, "Nietzsche's Philosophy in 1888: *The Will to Power* and the *Übermensch*," *Journal of the History of Philosophy* 24/1 (1986):79–98. Magnus seems inconsistent. On the one hand, he claims that "put simply, without the *Nachlass* it is virtually impossible to read eternal recurrence and will to power as first-order descriptions of the way the world is in itself, as a description of the world's intelligible character" (p. 83, n. 9). On the

other, Magnus says of Nehamas' decidedly first-order interpretation of will to power—'a thing is the sum of its effects'—that "Nehamas' fine book could have been argued to its conclusions without the *Nachlass* with virtually equal force" (p. 82, n. 6). Magnus seems to believe any account of "will to power" which hints at cosmology or ontology necessarily casts Nietzsche in the mold of the grand systematic philosophers of the tradition—a position that Magnus quite rightly rejects.

11. J. Hillis Miller, "The Disarticulation of the Self in Nietzsche," *The Monist* 64/2 (1981):255.

12. Nehamas, p. 80.

13. Ibid., pp. 49–50. In his analysis of Nietzschean perspectivism, Nehamas moves quickly to develop the needed distinction between Nietzschean perspectivism and relativism.

10

The Highest Chinadom: Nietzsche and the Chinese Mind, 1907–1989

David Kelly

Bizarrely they chanted. "What do we want? Nietzsche! What do we need? Nietzsche!"

—Nicholas Jose, *Avenue of Eternal Peace*[1]

In Alan Bloom's *The Closing of the American Mind*, the spreading influence of Nietzsche is used to stand for the trivialization of the Western intellectual heritage. Nietzsche himself projected a sense of metaphysical terror in the face of the nihilism he saw reproducing itself in the modern world. In the hands of his modern American followers, says Bloom, terror is transformed into mere stress; the tragic dimension disappears. "The new American lifestyle has become a Disneyland version of the Weimar republic for the whole family."[2]

A visit to Beijing in March-June 1988 presented the author with the apparent inversion of Bloom's principle. The opening of the Chinese mind was for the most part, but not exclusively, an Americanization. A vast range of books in translation, improbable only five years before and unthinkable five before that, reproduced the influential American worldview of democracy, individualism, liberalism—from John Rawls to Dale Carnegie; Bloom himself, it was rumored, would join the list soon. Crossing the Pacific with this freight came the steerage passengers of existentialism, phenomenology, and other cultural agents often little in sympathy with liberal democracy. Among China's urban intellectuals, artists, and hangers-on, who were the obvious consumers, it was possible to find all the trivialization, falsification, and sheer vulgarity so

151

painful to Bloom.[3] But equally striking was the way that Chinese social reality reintroduced some of the metaphysical dimensions lost on the initial voyage out over the Atlantic. And the figure of Nietzsche, who had so struck the intellectual leaders of the May Fourth movement seventy years before, once again provided a point of departure for avant-garde intellectuals.

The last two decades have seen the emergence in the West of a vast and influential literature on or inspired by Nietzsche.[4] By no means is all of this registered in China. One connecting thread between the Chinese and Western interpretations is, however, the experience of modernity as a state of continual crisis characterized by nihilism, where

nihilism—the will to ground value in the name of something higher—is the will to ground value in nothingness. When it becomes too difficult to deny this connection between transcendence and nothingness we have the "advent" of nihilism. . . . The modern quest to ward off the experience of nihilism becomes the drive to force everyone and everything into slots provided by a highly ordered system and to pretend the result is self-realization, the achievement of reason, the attainment of the common good.[5]

Despite enormous differences of perspective (Chinese intellectuals are often inclined to see their crisis as one of *getting into* modernity at all), socialist culture has produced a ready understanding of the phenomena to which Connolly refers. While often returning, unfashionably, to the neo-romantic language of the 1920s—taking up China's pre-Marxist intellectual flowering where it left off—Nietzscheanism provides one of the primary resources for intellectuals to register a response to, and very often a rebellion against, the sense of dislocation and disillusionment of the post-Mao era.

Some earlier versions of Nietzschean moral rebellion—principally of Lu Xun (1881–1936) and Li Shicen (1892–1934)—will be described in this study. A sketch of contemporary China, with its cultural crisis and the Nietzsche cult of the 1980s, will then allow us to examine the case of Liu Xiaobo, in 1989 headlined as a hero of the student movement in Tiananmen Square, and so extraordinary a fulfillment of the Lu Xun-Nietzsche tradition. We shall pay selective attention to certain themes, namely the image of the powerful individual, and the power given to such rebellious subjects by truthfulness or authenticity. We shall note the processes of vulgarization and sinification taking place in the development of these themes, and assess their continuing significance in the light of "nihilism with Chinese characteristics."

I

The Chinese intellectual public learned of the philosophy of Nietzsche almost as soon as they became acquainted with Darwin, Rousseau and Mill, that is to say at the turn of the century. The first major thinkers to transmit his ideas in China, Wang Guowei (1877–1927) and Lu Xun (pen-name of Zhou Shuren; 1881–1936), did so as a result of Japanese contacts. Wang saw Nietzsche as little more than a disciple of Schopenhauer, whose philosophical pessimism briefly influenced Wang's search for an aesthetic worldview—a search which notoriously ended in suicide.[6]

Nietzsche's meaning for Lu Xun is a much more contentious issue. There are a multiplicity of perspectives that may be pursued through Lu Xun's work, and these are likely to provide new discoveries and interpretations for many years.[7] It might be noted, for example, that several Russian authors who were heavily influenced by Nietzsche —Artzybashev, Andreev—were themselves influences on Lu Xun, setting up a highly complicated case of "mediated reception." The diffidence Lu Xun sometimes displays about Nietzsche's ideas may owe much to the retreat from Nietzsche noted, once again, among Russians about 1908.[8]

Take the case of *Sanin*, a work by the Russian decadent novelist M.P. Artzybashev (1878–1927). Lu Xun in latter years referred to "the followers of Sanin, who claim they believe in nothing, but who will in fact stop at nothing," as one of the two outcomes of Nietzsche's doctrine of the *Übermensch* (the other was madness). Artzybashev's novel is discussed at length by Edith Clowes as a paradigm of vulgarization. Sanin, a "simple, indeed primitive hedonist," dreams of a time when man will "give himself freely and fearlessly to all pleasures accessible to him." The original concern of the *Übermensch* with subordinating necessity to some higher goal, with self-knowledge and self-perfection, has been disfigured. Sanin and similar heroes, argues Clowes, helped to discredit the German philosopher in the eyes of the broad public, since they were accepted as faithful representations of Nietzsche's thought.[9] Did Lu Xun accept the vulgarization as accurate? Was he, rather, consciously and mockingly pouring scorn on these distortions as echoed in China?

The answer remains elusive. Certainly Lu Xun never attempted to create a Sanin. His Nietzschean motifs are often displayed through antiheroes like Ah Q, who exemplify value delusions akin to Nietzsche's *ressentiment*. Lu Xun illustrates the general principle that hedonism, especially its erotic variations, was unlikely to be taken up as a creed by

Chinese intellectuals. Rather, Nietzsche fortified existentialist strains in Chinese culture, deriving from Daoism and Confucian heterodoxy. In the process of reception, a different cultural substratum was refracted, one in which the sage's inward sincerity had been conceived as a unifying cosmic force. Highly selective and often distorted, Lu Xun's "Nietzschean" attitudes towards the masses and the superman are saved from vulgarization by his cultural and political sensitivity. Itō Toramaru provides support for this assessment in his comparison of Lu Xun's view of Nietzsche with that of the late Meiji literary circles, with which he came in contact in his student days in Japan. For Itō,

In Lu Xun we are totally unable to find the conclusion drawn by Japanese Nietzscheanism that "individualism = instinctivism." In other words, Lu Xun more accurately grasped the essence of the Western understanding of "modernity" than did Japanese literature.[10]

Suggesting that what Lu Xun found in Nietzsche was "a certain welcome pathos," Benjamin Schwartz concludes, "he was not really committed to the whole system of Nietzscheanism as a *Weltanschauung*, nor did he share all of the preoccupations and exasperations of Nietzsche. What seems to have attracted him, above all, was a certain emotion-charged image of the sensitive, spiritual hero confronting a stupid and vicious world, confronting 'the mob'."[11]

The only work Lu Xun is known to have studied in any depth was *Thus Spoke Zarathustra*. Nietzsche wrote, with deliberate emphasis, "Zarathustra is more truthful than any other thinker. His doctrine, and his alone, posits truthfulness as the highest virtue" (*EH* IV, 3). Truth, truthfulness, and deception form an important complex within Nietzsche's thought. This *philaletheia* (passion for truth) is a key to the metaphysical pathos which links Nietzsche and Lu Xun, and which influences Chinese intellectuals down to the present.

Where Western philosophy after Socrates sought to encompass other values under the concept of Truth, Confucian thought has intermittently accorded analogous importance to the concept of Sincerity. "Sincerity," a frequently questioned rendering of the Chinese character *cheng*, is much more a psycho-social value than a logical one. It is rooted in the behavioral norm of truthfulness in the sense of intending not to mislead.[12] It is of interest to Lu Xun scholarship because of his conviction, formed while still a student in Japan, that what the Chinese national character lacked was *cheng* and *ai* (love).[13] The seal carved by the young Lu Xun bearing the motto *cun cheng qu wei* ("preserve sincerity and dispel falsehood") reinforces the impression of a particularly intense concern with *cheng*. The four characters, writes Lu Ge, "express with utmost economy 'the voice of the mind (*xinsheng*)' of the young Lu Xun, and epitomise in the briefest compass his aesthetic thought regarding society, human existence, morality and art."[14] Gálik writes, "it is very probable that a study and reading of certain works, like those of V. Garshin and L. Andreev, and perhaps also of St. Augustine, L. Tolstoy and Jean-Jacques Rousseau, had convinced Lu Xun that the voices of mind have to be sincere, must spring from a pure heart, present reality without either bias or embellishment, admit their own failings and estimate their own capacities without superfluous illusions." In a footnote, Gálik points to yet another source—*Thus Spoke Zarathustra*.[15]

Nietzsche related his view of the mind in new ways to the unfolding drama of modern civilization as a field of cultural and political decadence and renewal. Lu Xun's acceptance of this view of modernity cannot be fully documented in the present work, but as a powerful force in the contemporary Chinese intellectual dynamic it provides important clues for understanding the present cultural crisis.

II

The most explicit of Chinese "Nietzscheans," the philosopher Li Shicen, has many points of similarity to Lu Xun. One scholar maintains that Lu Xun agreed with the rebuttal made by Li Shicen and his associates of the popular view that Nietzsche's ideas were responsible for German militarism and World War I.[16] Li enjoyed a short but brilliant career during the New Culture movement, a period of comparative intellectual openness associated with the student-led demonstrations of May 4, 1919.[17] He was editor of leading journals such as *People's Bell* and *Chinese Educational Review*, as a university professor of philosophy, and as a writer. He claimed that his encounter with Nietzsche (which occurred like Lu Xun's in his student days in Japan) had changed the course of his life.[18]

Marián Gálik finds Li a far more reliable interpreter of Nietzsche's thought than Mao Dun or other May Fourth intellectuals.[19] While the latter often took the theory of the "will to power" literally, as a real power in the socio-political sense,[20] Li Shicen marshals various authorities and his own arguments to set aside this interpretation and to emphasize the ideas of "self-overcoming" and of art as the realm of Nietzsche's greatest contribution. Comparing Nietzsche and Schopenhauer, Li writes in an early article,

Schopenhauer regarded self-consciousness of the Will as a higher consciousness; Nietzsche on the other hand saw it as a higher action. "Drunken ecstasy" (for the latter) is the state when all man's powers of symbolizing reach their full extent. Reaching the ultimate of human existence depends not on language and concepts but on the expression of the symbols of a self which has liberated all its strength. [21]

"Truth" as it is generally conceived is merely ancillary to ascending Life. Li encapsulates the Nietzschean idea of *ressentiment*: "If values are incapable of directing life, propelling life, they become precisely what impedes life. All class hatred, all opposition to the highest types and all violence of the masses stems from this" (*LJ* 39).

Li invokes the authority of Simmel (1858–1918), whose book on Schopenhauer and Nietzsche[22] was a major source of inspiration, to defend Nietzsche against the then current attacks of his ultra-subjectivism. Nietzsche stands for the expression of Life, of the will to power inherent in all selves, and not for the "all things exist for me" of Stirner and the Sophists. Echoing Lu Xun, Li writes,

the victory of the herd instinct is enough to stifle the genuine individual, who is the one who throws off the restraints of social conventions and becomes a totally independent kind of man. Therefore the individual has an inward existence and a decisive, overcoming and creative personality. (*LJ* 39)

Simmel was correct, writes Li, in suggesting that Nietzsche was no mere egoist like Stirner. Human nature is not transcendent, but a "freedom immanent within the genuine individual" (*LJ* 57). The rhetoric here is suggestive of nothing so much as the existentialism of Sartre, but precedent for it may be found as readily in Chinese intellectual culture: Zhuang Zi and Wang Yangming, in their respective periods of pre-Qin and late-Ming China, also attacked conventional *a priori* formulations of human nature which had become hypostatized into unchanging absolutes.

The self which Nietzsche sets in opposition to the collective is not the narrow, egotistical self of Stirner but a cosmic self only realised by the struggle to liberate itself from what constrains it. "I am not an advocate of Nietzsche," Li concludes,

but after close consideration of his thought I can't but admit his real value. We Chinese, due to our phlegmatic disposition, have been despised by the peoples of other countries. Lacking the courage to advance and deficient in creativity, we are docile slaves of custom, merely out of cringing timidity. Bringing up such docile slaves is a waste of the country's money, giving birth to them is a waste of the race's energy. I suggest that we might perhaps find the salvation of these phlegmatic vassals in the thought of Nietzsche, who is so reviled, abused and refuted by our countrymen. (*LJ* 58)

In *Outline of the Superman Philosophy* Li Shicen sets out to apply Nietzsche's attack on decadence to its Chinese manifestations: helplessness, lethargy, vulgar worship of illusions, and greed for comfort and security. He alludes to China's history of ineffectuality from the failed Reform Movement of 1898 up to the time of writing—culminating, it would appear, in the "Jinan outrage" of 1928, when Japanese troops blocked the passage of Guomindang forces of the Northern Expedition under the direct command of Jiang Jieshi.[23]

The thrust of the book is, however, directed at the universal preference for compromise and disengagement which Li senses about him. All sorts of noble ideals such as "dispassion," "action in accordance with the Mean," and the like, express merely the "depravity of hypocrites and slaves." Neo-Confucianism is easily subjected to the critique which Nietzsche had developed against Christianity:

The famous sayings and ancient teachings of China honor reason rather than desire, and regard human desires as subordinate to Heavenly principle, regardless of the fact that there could be no Heavenly principle apart from human desires. The constant preaching of Heavenly principle produces nothing . . . but hypocrites, slaves, inhuman existence and all the poisons of the clan society. So the old values must be forcefully destroyed. (*QS* 2–3)

As Li understands the many shifts of meaning of Nietzsche's famous duality, Dionysus stands for the life-affirming world of Will (*QS* 37ff.). He came to stand also for the acceptance of suffering and the tempering of the personality. Escape into the conceptual world of eternal forms, the Apollonian strategy, was for Nietzsche a demeaning retreat from "authentic" existence. Li's first attack on Chinese culture opens here:

Let us now use Nietzsche's view of human existence to criticize that of the Chinese. They always seek their happiness and security in the conceptual world. In other words, the Chinese always seek the protection of Apollo in search of psychological comfort. If we want to reform this negative and demeaning existence, we must advocate a powerful will. (*QS* 41–42)

Li calls this "raising up a joyful Dionysus," at present "my sole vision, my sole hope" (*QS* 44).

In his "Conclusion," Li strikingly compares Nietzsche and Kierkegaard, who were united in their "passionate praise of life, their use of the methods of creation and overcoming to bring about the elevation of one's own authentic life, and from that to go on to plan the authentic life of all mankind."[24] But whereas Kierkegaard was full of the religious impulse to self-immolation, Nietzsche embodied the spirit of natural science and self-realization.

The Chinese, writes Li, associate individualism with the evil of self-interest. They have no conception of a self-affirmation which is at the same time an affirmation of the whole world, for which one realises one has a responsibility. How can the Chinese realize the dignity of the self and its responsibility when they have been trained to tractability by despotic social mores? It is as if the past had a "special power of fascination" from which it was impossible to awake (QS 92).

Li describes this as "invisible decadence." Dissipation, lack of effort beyond the needs of self-enjoyment, are the signs of visible decadence. In the case of invisible decadence, a person may exert all his strength but still be trapped in a life of inauthenticity:

. . . from rising to resting, sleeping or eating, all the way to speaking or thinking, only knowing how to follow ancient precedent or established convention, passing the time in vulgar mediocrity, never knowing one has a self until death. This then is invisible decadence. (QS 92)

Invisible decadence is hard to detect "because everyone falls in with it and supports it." Without the intervention of a truth-revealing art,

the ineptitude, impotence and pitiable complacency of the Chinese is beyond remedy. . . . The Chinese can only intoxicate themselves with the conceptual illusions of Apollo, not realizing that there is the other world of drunken Dionysian joy . . . or that within the world of Dionysus an Apollonian world is again born forth. Hence the Chinese must have an artistic remoulding also. (QS 93–94)

Li Shicen's views may readily be compared with those of Lu Xun, and he often seems to represent an extension of Lu Xun's (youthful) world-view into academic philosophy. Neither had much time for the kind of vulgarization noticeable in Russian and Japanese Nietzsche cults. Li knew that an ethic of self-realization, understood to be vital to China's political health and indeed survival, imposed a high cost on values supportive of traditional social harmony. The rejection of hypocritical formulations of the good was, on the other hand, offset by appeal to a "religion of humanity" drawn expressly from Feuerbach.[25] Considering Li's subsequent highly publicized conversion to Marxism, a question overhangs both his and Lu Xun's streadfastness in following Nietzsche's demand for apolitical self-realization. Nonetheless they were important voices sounding the note of moral rebellion at crucial moments of the

May Fourth movement. The meaning of this for Chinese culture cannot be treated as settled for once and for all. As secular social thought arose in the cultural dislocation of the 1980s, the modes of discourse of these earlier Nietzscheans were recreated with amazing speed and fidelity to their originals.

III

Chen Quan's writings on Nietzsche for the wartime Kunming journal *Zhanguo Ce* (Warring States) constitute the main trace of his influence between the deaths of Lu Xun and Li Shicen and the Nietzschean revival in the post-Mao reform era. Some distance needs to be kept from the standard Communist position. Such later views of Nietzsche, including that of Yue Daiyun, often look back to Chen and *Zhanguo Ce* as a stereotype of his influence.[26] As Chen (1903–69) was clearly a vulgarizer of a familiar type, there is an injustice here.

In Michael Godley's reconstruction of the intellectual context, the *Zhanguo Ce* group had rather more in common with the Marxists than they could ever admit.[27] Godley's evidence weakens the Communist charge that the group was a simple Guomindang front. Nonetheless Chen was a vulgarizer of the first water, for whom Nietzsche sustained, in Godley's expression, an "insufferable elitism." The careful textual work of Mao Dun and Li Shicen is brushed aside. Nietzsche is worshipped, as Yue Daiyun states, "as an absolute hero," the will to power is understood as literal social and political power and the *Übermensch* as a reborn Oriental despot.

The *Zhanguo Ce* affair no doubt accelerated the "retreat from Nietzsche" by the May Fourth generation of intellectuals. But this seemed to have a dynamic of its own, as Guo Moruo, the Communist cultural authority, explained: "As the tide of revolution rose in the late twenties, our eyes were diverted from looking on high to looking at what was down below, and this brought about a great separation from Nietzsche."[28] The retreat reflected no intrinsic cultural gulf between the Chinese intellectuals and Nietzsche. As we have seen, there was much shared ground, amounting in some cases to a strong affinity. Chinese literary sophistication made it quite possible to make allowance for Nietzsche's patent biases and exaggerations. Nietzsche was in tune with a deeper or at least more general impulse in Chinese thought, running as a subcurrent from the early Daoists and having much in common with what in the West goes under the name of existentialism.

Reappraisal of the May Fourth movement's Nietzschean undertone has been an intriguing and overlooked aspect of the post-Mao period. It took the best part of the ten years from 1976 to 1986 for this to take place, but by the mid-1980s the trend was unmistakable. The sheer volume of work on the "Lu Xun and Nietzsche" problem was an indicator, but the development that was to come went far beyond expectations. A marked shift occurred in 1985 when the facts about *The Will to Power* and the role of Nietzsche's sister in propagating the Nietzsche legend were at last recognized.[29]

The immediate post-Cultural Revolution period saw a brief strengthening of prejudice against Nietzsche. Dai Wenlin typified the belief that the abuses of the Gang of Four could be identified with Nazism.[30] Dai, drawing on the hoary ideas contained in He Dian's "Lu Xun and Nietzsche" of 1939, traced Nazi ideology, and fascism generally, to the writings of Nietzsche.[31] Nietzsche's doctrine of the will to power is the main target of the article. The Gang of Four are accused not only of a blind lust for power, but also of deriving their program directly from Nazism and Nietzsche.

As stock was taken of the intellectual situation in the late 1970s, a more considered and oblique use of "Nietzsche" as a scare-word was noticeable. It was no accident, in the light of central Party policies bound up with reliance on "economic law," that a critique of voluntarism should appear in the flagship journal of the newly established Chinese Academy of Social Science (CASS).[32] Its author associated Nietzsche not so much with fascism as with the more general ideological failing of voluntarism. He claimed that this led the ultra-leftists—and this could be read as including Mao Zedong himself—to disregard the "objective laws" of social and economic development. Many indeed believed that Mao had been the arch-voluntarist. Much Western scholarship has been devoted to the voluntarism of Mao,[33] but none of it has gone so far as to trace it to the direct influence of Nietzsche. Chinese scholars treat it as a serious possibility, but have been reluctant to air their views for obvious reasons. Needless to say this theory, for all its interest, involves at least two misreadings of Nietzsche—one on the part of the young Mao, and one on that of the Chinese Marxists seeking to criticize his "errors." For Nietzsche's thought does not constitute a system which can confidently be tagged as "voluntarism" or as an endorsement of political domination; nor is it clear how such a doctrine, if it indeed existed, might have led Mao to the measures he later adopted.

Significant reappraisals of Nietzsche were to emerge from the Academy of Social Sciences in the 1980s. The director of the Institute of Philosophy and later Vice-President of CASS, Ru Xin, has zigzagged between support for Marxist humanism and the officially sanctioned criticisms of it, saving his position but losing the respect of his peers in the process.[34] Through all this, however, Ru has produced significant scholarly work on Nietzsche, in particular on his aesthetics.[35] His student Zhou Guoping has emerged as perhaps the best known authority on Nietzsche, producing numerous books, articles, and translations, particularly *Nietzsche: At the Turning Point of the Century*.[36] While maintaining the obligatory "Marxist attitude of seeking the truth from facts," Zhou explains in this book that he has accentuated the positive side of Nietzsche in order to correct the traditional attitude of blanket condemnation. He notes the controversy over Lu Xun, regarding the orthodox view of a post-1927 rejection of Nietzsche as "highly questionable."[37] While *Nietzsche* contains little that is new—little that would surprise Li Shicen—it provides for the first time a comprehensive survey of Nietzsche which is alive to the diversity of interpretations in postwar Western circles. Zhou corrects the long-standing misunderstandings of "will to power" as a political voluntarism which we have noted in Mao Dun, Chen Quan, and Chen Cunfu.[38]

Equally significant has been the prominence given to Nietzsche scholarship in the great intellectual debate over culture, the *wenhua re* (cultural fever) of the late 1980s. The first non-official academic institution, the Academy of Chinese Culture, was set up in 1986 and featured in its inaugural, standing-room-only seminars, a paper by the Taiwanese philosopher Chen Guying on the affinities of Zhuang Zi and Nietzsche.[39] As well as Zhou Guoping in CASS, Zhang Rulun and An Yanming of Fudan University have brought Nietzschean cultural criticism to bear on China's contemporary moral crisis.[40]

In addition to their interest in Nietzsche, these scholars share a common thread of interest in neo-Marxism. An Yanming has written on Western Marxism; Zhou Guoping was a contributor to the early 1980s debate on socialist alienation. As Bloom, Stauth, and Turner and others note, Nietzsche has had a decisive impact on Western Marxists and particularly on "critical theorists" like Marcuse and Adorno. As far as contemporary China goes there is no great mystery about this, since Marxism is unavoidably the first school of any educated person. Western or neo-Marxism is one of the avenues of development out of one's early indoctrination.[41]

This conjunction has naturally not been viewed with any warmth by the ideological authorities. They are strongly inclined to regard Nietzsche and cognate thinkers as part of the problem rather than useful diagnosticians. The frequent references in the press to a Nietzsche cult provide fascinating clues to social and intellectual changes extending well past the academic circles so far considered here. A Marxist critic observed:

Not a few young students blindly worshipped Western philosophy. There were "Sartre fans," "Freud fans," "Schopenhauer fans," "Nietzsche fans," etc. Under the influence of the intellectal trend toward "irrationalism" not a few students . . . moved away from any consideration of the social element in human nature as well as the concrete aspects and historical dimension of human existence. They discussed the value of man in relation to other men in an abstract way and sought the enjoyment of sensual desires. They had a one-sided interpretation of "democracy" and "freedom" and they highly prized "self-determination," the "struggle for selfhood" and self-fulfilment."[42]

The official weekly *Liaowang* reinforced this impression on the eve of the upheaval. It divided the reform period into four stages. From 1978 to 1980 was the stage of existentialism; 1981–1984, the stage of enthusiasm for science and technology; 1985–1987, the stage of the "Will to Power"; and 1988 to the present, the stage of pragmatism.[43] Under the stage of the "Will to Power," the authors describe the disillusion with the reforms felt among students in 1985 when many difficulties and "unhealthy trends" (i.e., corruption) reached crisis proportions within the Communist Party:

In their pondering, some students turned negative. . . . Even more pondered on a number of irrational phenomena and attributed them all to a single notion, expressed in the word "power." Power was the one thing necessary, the one thing you could not do without if you wanted to realize the value of human life. For this reason Nietzsche's theory of the "Will to Power" rapidly gained popularity among the students. A "Nietzsche" fever developed. The works of Nietzsche became best sellers. Such sayings as "become yourself," "don't follow me," "the revaluation of all values," "the superman" became favorite slogans often heard on their lips.[44]

If this article went on to look for a silver lining in all this, others were bleaker. In one notorious case, a member of the Youth League murdered his girlfriend and committed suicide. In his residence were found notes showing his devotion to the writings of Nietzsche and Sartre. The Communist Party predictably used these to show that the problem was not of its own making.[45] Intriguingly, more acute defenders of the ideological order have shifted their ground from the traditional class analysis which painted Nietzsche as a reactionary, to a new nativism which seeks to identify with an embattled cultural heritage. For example the rising conservative intellectual star, He Xin, writes:

Amidst the miasma of cultural nihilism, radical anti-traditionalism, as well as among the warped attitudes and extremism of some young intellectuals, if we sit back and consider things calmly and rationally we can discern in their proclamations many familiar shadows of the past. The difference is that the anti-traditionalism and cultural nihilism of those years marched under the banner of Marx and Mao Zedong; today it is hidden under the cloak of Freud and Nietzsche.[46]

The evidence does not support this view. Rather than anti-traditionalism and cultural nihilism seeking the cloak of Maoism, they were the direct and indirect results, respectively, of its policies. The sheer magnitude of the cultural crisis created by the Cultural Revolution took some time to dawn on the Chinese themselves, let alone on foreign observers. Part of the problem was the ideological discourse of Marxism-Leninism, which was constantly invoked to deny the problem's full dimensions. Marxism itself offers very little analysis of power as a human motive. Even the Gang of Four had to be given completely spurious "class backgrounds" for their machinations to be interpretable within the system. While in this study we have stressed that Nietzsche was not the priest of domination by the strong that many have portrayed him to be, it is certainly true that he provides a powerful language for understanding subjective and unconscious factors, including the lust for power.

As I pointed out above, it is often noted that Marxists have had a closet fascination with Nietzsche since the turn of the century at least, precisely because he provides vitamins missing from their intellectual diet. By no means all of his avid young Chinese readers saw him as propounding an alternative ideology. On the other hand, others certainly did. But it was in most ways an *incommensurable* alternative. The moral vacuum following the Cultural Revolution was marked by the existence of several alternative ethical reference points, none of which was able to establish itself securely. In the 1980s many had the tragic sense that while Marxism had helped build a viable nation state, it was powerless to transcend the archaic order—indeed had merely reinforced its most vicious features.

IV

A number of thinkers have become sharply aware of the internalization of ideological conflict within the individual self. This provides the context for Liu Xiaobo's calls for a violent inner break with the superculture of Leninist Confucianism. Liu, regarded by Wang Yihua as the latest in the line of "wholesale Westernisers," was a prominent intellectual supporter of the Beijing democratic movement.[47] He was picked up by the security forces and treated to amazing invective in the official condemnatory literature. His rediscovery of the May Fourth understanding of Nietzsche as a cultural critic provides ammunition for those condemning him as a traitor.[48]

How many of the mass of students converging on Tiananmen square in April 1989 had actually read Liu's *Critique of Choice*, published in 1988, is unknown; it sold out repeatedly and was a collectors item.[49] What is certain is its status as an important document of the antirationalist tendency of younger intellectuals. Drawing on Chinese and European traditions of moral rebellion, they called for the assertion of the subject. Many of them tended to look to Nietzsche and avant-garde aesthetic experience for the keys to the liberation of consciousness. Written in the style of an interminable big-character poster, the *Critique* nonetheless provides fascinating evidence of the continuing importance of a notion of individualism as moral revolt, influential with Chinese intellectuals since Lu Xun. Liu consciously invokes this tradition:

we can then see why Lu Xun so glorified Nietzsche, the theory of evolution, and *Symbols of Suffering*. Nietzsche was the smasher of idols, the symbol of individual freedom; the theory of evolution is the replacement of the the old by the new, the symbol of free competition; and *Symbols of Suffering* is sensual life, the symbol of subconscious distress and the tragedy of existence. . . . In contemporary China Lun Xun-style extremism and ruthlessness is especially needed, especially in dialogue with traditional culture. . . . Summing up the experience of the May Fourth Movement, the result reached should not be an attitude of compromise with the traditional culture, but the start of a long term, thorough-going antifeudal enlightenment movement. . . . The anti-tradition stemming from Lu Xun must be able both profoundly and broadly to transcend the "May Fourth" New Culture movement typified by Lu Xun. (CC 6, 7, 10)

This invocation of Lu Xun accepts his denunciation of the character weaknesses of the Chinese and in particular of the intellectuals. Liu sees them as infected in their very blood with three deep-structural complexes of the traditional culture, namely, antidemocratic populism (*minbenzhuyi*), the Confucian personality (*Kong-Yan renge*),[50] and the harmony of Heaven and Man (*tian ren he yi*). The operation of these deep structures has led even the greatest reformists and revolutionaries back to the embrace of the traditional culture.

These expressions were initially used to epitomize the traditional culture by Li Zehou, a major figure among Chinese social theorists ever since his embroilments over aesthetics in the 1950s. In the post-Mao period Li has written at length on Chinese intellectual history, including the cardinal problems of Western cultural impact in the twentieth century.[51] On the issue of Lu Xun's Nietzschean influences he tended to the orthodox view, holding for instance that while Nietzsche despised the masses, the young Lu Xun's invocation of moral aristocracy was directed only at their false beliefs and values (feudalism), while his own attitude was sympthetically informed by proto-Marxist class solidarity.[52] Li's suggestion of a reversal of the late Qing self-strengtheners' doctrine of *zhongti xiyong* ("Chinese culture as the essence, Western learning as its instrument") to become *xiti zhongyong* ("Western culture with Chinese characteristics") attracted strong criticism. It is not far removed from the ideas promoted in *He Shang*, a documentary television series shown in prime time in 1988 that drew sharp political conclusions from the academic debates on culture. *River Elegy* advances the view that the Communist regime amounted to a traditional autocracy carried on by other means. It had failed to nurture a "maritime" culture equal to the challenge of the world economy. The series defends the Zhaoist policies of coastal development and of the autonomy of scientific and other intellectuals. The cultural chauvinism of the cadre elite, which went hand in hand with anti-intellectualism, comes in for strong criticism. Itself emotionally nationalistic in tone, *River Elegy* indicates that a repressed cultural inferiority complex lay behind the pattern of overt political repression.[53] In the context of a discussion of the aesthetic as the sphere of the truly individual, indeed of utter solitude, Liu goes on to argue that the Confucian "harmony of heaven and man" destroys the capacity for genuine solitude or appreciation of the tragic dimension. Cowardly psychology and slave values are its logical outcomes as the values of feudalism are made psychological and even biological, made into a second nature. Some characteristics: hypocritical modesty which masks back-stabbing, the atomization of people in an anaemic group life lacking in genuine feeling, and the trammeling of the theoretical mind in group-oriented utility, which Liu considers fatal for science.

The specific symptom of the way in which China's ancient culture was rendered utilitarian and pragmatic is the making utilitarian and pragmatic of the lives of the Chinese. It is the form answering to a group personality, a moral personality without individuality, without feeling, it is the outward manifestation of a dependent consciousness, slavishness. Thus, within the cultural tradition specific to China, making utilitarian and pragmatic is to groupify, to politicize, to moralize, to dehumanize. Man is a means, an instrument, not a goal. (CC 192)

Reducing all issues to the absolute criteria of moral perfectionism is the fatal error of Chinese culture. Liu's response to this is total iconoclasm. "I can't see what can be worth hankering after in traditional culture for the Chinese of today" (*CC* 195).

Liu Xiaobo's work is a valuable source of insight into contemporary China's spiritual and social condition. Even if the Events of June 4 had not made him one of the better known Chinese intellectuals, he would have been a major object of study. In large measure this is because of his forthright adherence to the antinomian traditions of Lu Xun and Li Shicen. However, he must be counted as yet another vulgarizer of Nietzsche. His tragic, assertive, forthright individual, though up-dated with many direct borrowings (*en-soi, Dasein*) from the existentialism of Heidegger and Sartre, remains a *fin-de-siècle* caricature. Lacking a sense of irony, Liu sees little but rebellious individualism in Nietzsche. The latter's deep ambivalence about individualism—so often a vulgarized derivative of the nihilist project—would seem to have escaped him. Yet in bringing a wealth of passionately presented material to a metaphysically starved audience, Liu probably would have helped (but for the tragic events of June 1989) to bring about a more profound understanding.

The last writing from Liu Xiaobo's pen before his imprisonment was published in mid-1990, over a year later. It lays to rest the misinterpretation of his position as "wholesale Westernization" and "cultural nihilism." What is of value in the West, writes Liu, is its tradition of critique, but this critique should be applied to Western institutions as much as to Chinese ones. Liu believes this critique is informed by a complete system of transcendental, non-utilitarian values. Nietzsche represents the extreme formulation of these values, which even Lu Xun failed to establish for himself. In a crucial statement Liu writes:

After Lu Xun had transcended Chinese reality and culture by means of critique, he was utterly cut off. Unable to endure the confrontation with the unknown, with the loneliness and terror of the grave by himself, and unwilling to carry on a transcendental dialogue with himself under the gaze of God, the traditional utilitarian personality was reborn within him. Lacking transcendental values, Lu Xun could only fall into decadence. He desired only to "rebel against the darkness" which surrounded him, but was unable to transcend darkness. Although deeply influenced by Nietzsche, Lu Xun's greatest difference from Nietzsche was this: after his disillusionment with humanity, with Western culture and with himself, Nietzsche, fortified by his reference to the *Übermensch* who transcends all, moved toward the elevation of individual life. But after his disillusionment with the Chinese, with Chinese culture and with himself, Lu

Xun never found a frame of reference for transcendental values, turning back instead to the reality he had completely abandoned.[54]

Liu evidently saw himself as completing Lu Xun's *imitatio Nietzschei*, carrying on the critique of Chinese culture by creation of a "frame of reference for transcendental values."

The Chinese assimilation of Nietzsche has much in common with its Russian forerunner, as described in the works of Rosenthal, Clowes, and others. In identifying Nietzschean moral rebellion with a native antinomian tradition, both vulgarization and conscious attempts to correct it are to be found. In China this has to do with the fact that the cultural substratum with which most intellectuals began their careers was not, as in Russia, the Christian faith but a tradition in many ways more naturally in affinity with Nietzsche, namely Daoism and Confucian heterodoxy. The peculiar symbiosis between Marx and Nietzsche, noticed by many writers—Rosenthal and collaborators, Bloom, Stauth and Turner—is of far-reaching significance in China, not least because Chinese assimilate this duality to their own ancient dualism of Confucianists and Daoists.[55] Young Chinese today turn to Nietzsche to obtain an important antidote to ideological alienation, and to recapitulate an ancient alternative culture of moral rebellion. This has been accelerated by a cultural crisis marked by nihilism and widespread perception of normlessness, one in which the Nietzschean emphasis on *truthfulness* as a criterion of individual self-realization developed an irresistible appeal. At work in the 1989 upheaval in China was the phenomenon common to post-totalitarian societies described by the Czech dissident-turned-President Havel, which he describes as "the singular, explosive, incalculable power of living within the truth." This issued forth

in something visible: a real political act or event, a social movement, a sudden explosion of civil unrest, a sharp conflict within an apparently monolithic power structure, or simply an irrepressible transformation in the social and intellectual climate.[56]

This being said, vulgarization of Nietzsche is one of the conspicuous modes of his influence in China. We have seen that this takes different forms. Very common is a crude political interpretation of the will to power. Even where this error is consciously avoided, as in the case of Li Shicen, there is a disappointing blindness to Nietzsche's literary strategies and use of irony. This is true even of Lu Xun, who had by far the deepest natural affinity with the master. It is symptomatic of the post-

Marxist return to the May Fourth in China that Nietzschean motifs are commonly found embedded in romantic metanarratives, as typified in Liu Xiaobo's pathos of the solitary self. One seeks in vain for careful attention to the theme of "disarticulation of the self" which marked Nietzsche's own passionate self-distancing from romanticism.[57]

Although distorted, Nietzsche's abiding influence nevertheless points to extremely significant problems in Chinese culture. One of these is the need for a civil discourse on culture itself. By "civil discourse" I mean an arena in which, despite the existence of a ideological authority, politics and social norms are treated not as givens but as objects of inquiry, dispute, and even rejection.[58] Even where it vulgarizes its model, above all in its naïve politicization of the powerful individual, Chinese Nietzscheanism reveals much about the metaphysical hunger which fuels both dictatorship and dreams of liberation.

Nietzsche dreaded not only nihilism but the dystopian society which would be erected in an attempt to ward off its advent:

On that first road, which can now be completely surveyed, arise adaptation, Higher Chinadom, modesty in the insticts, satisfaction in the dwarfing of mankind—*a kind of stationary level of mankind.* Once we possess that common economic management of the earth that will soon be inevitable, mankind will be able to find its best meaning as a machine in the service of the economy—as a tremendous clockwork, composed of ever smaller, ever more subtly "adapted" gears.[59]

Liu Xiaobo's generation differs from Lu Xun, Li Shicen, and their intellectual fraternity most of all in the level of the "Chinadom" with which they deal. Late Dengist China is indeed the "highest Chinadom" so far encountered. For this generation, it combines all the worst features of modernity and feudalism. Despite undoubted revolutionary achievements—and we should not forget that at one time the regime commanded popular support as a patriotic, liberating force—the daily experience of young Chinese of today has been of the state's apparent "satisfaction in the dwarfing of mankind." That it draws on a past which was known to Nietzsche, in distorted and derivative form, as "Chinadom," is not surprising. Nor is it really surprising that Nietzsche should resume a major role as a source of critical enlightenment.

The Nietzscheanizing of the Chinese mind was, then, as much the recovery of a May Fourth beachhead as a new assimilation. Of course, recovery is not repetition. Now as then, Nietzsche provides both weapon and remedy. But the nature of the malaise has radically altered. Now as then, intellectuals forge an ethos of moral rebellion from the self-critical tools provided by Nietzsche. But indignation against "slave morality," against hypocrisy, *ressentiment*, and levelling now has a different bearing. Our study of the impact of Nietzsche on China in the twentieth century gains its significance, then, from the insights it provides into the nature of the underlying cultural changes which have come with the socialist state. This generation feels that the Nietzschean critique of culture attempted in the May Fourth movement, far from being excessive, did not go far enough. While its contemporary adherents are often critical of Nietzsche and certainly prepared to supplement him with later sources of enlightenment, it is certain that this tradition is far from played out.

Notes

EN—Chinese journals conventionally use the calendar year and month as sole volume and issue identifiers.

1. Nicholas Jose, *Avenue of Eternal Peace* (Harmondsworth and Melbourne, 1989), p. 271. Jose was Cultural Counsellor, Australian Embassy, Beijing, 1986–90.

2. Allan Bloom, *The Closing of the American Mind* (New York, 1987), p. 147.

3. Orvill Schell, *Discos and Democracy: China in the Throes of Reform* (New York, 1988), provides a vivid account of cultural dislocation in the 1980s.

4. For an enthusiastic catalogue of influences, see Georg Stauth and Bryan S. Turner, *Nietzsche's Dance: Resentment, Reciprocity and Resistance in Social Life* (Oxford and New York, 1988).

5. William F. Connolly, "Modernity and Nihilism," in *Political Theory and Modernity* (Oxford and New York, 1988), pp. 12–15, at 13. See also "Nietzsche: Politics and Homesickness," ibid., pp. 137–75. Closely related and useful on Nietzsche is Charles Taylor, *Sources of the Self: The Making of the the Modern Identity* (Cambridge, 1989); and Jürgen Habermas, "The Entry into Postmodernity: Nietzsche as the Turning Point," in *The Philosophical Discourse of Modernity* (Cambridge, 1988), lecture 4, pp. 83–105.

6. Joey Bonner, *Wang Kuo-wei: An Intellectual Biography* (Cambridge, Mass., 1986), pp. 91–96.

7. See Cheung Chiu-yee [Zhang Zhaoyi], *Nicai yu Lu Xun sixiang fazhan* (Nietzsche and Lu Xun's intellectual development) (Hong Kong, 1987), and his more recent "Lu Xun the Chinese Nietzsche," unpublished paper, Sydney University 1990; Yue Daiyun, "Nicai yu zhongguo xiandai wenxue" (Nietzsche and modern Chinese literature), *Beijing daxue xuebao* 1980:3, 20–33; Mabel Lee, "From Chuang-tzu to Nietzsche: On the Individualism of Lu Hsün," in *Austrina*, ed. A. R. Davis and A. D. Stephanowska (Sydney 1985), pp. 140–67.

8. See Bernice G. Rosenthal, ed., *Nietzsche in Russia* (Princeton, 1986); Edith W. Clowes, *The Revolution of Moral Consciousness: Nietzsche in Russian Literature 1890–1914* (DeKalb, 1988). On the "retreat from Nietzsche" see Rosenthal's introduction, p. 5.

9. Edith Clowes, "Literary Reception as Vulgarization: Nietzsche's Idea of the Superman in Neo-Realist Fiction," in Rosenthal, pp. 315–29; on *Sanin* see pp. 324–29. Artzybashev's novel has been translated as *Sanine* (New York, 1926).

10. Itō Toramaru, "Lu Xun zaoqi de Nicaiguan yu Mingzhi wenxue" (Meiji literature and Lu Xun's early outlook on Nietzsche), *Wenxue pinglun* 1990:1 (January):135–47, at 140. See also "Mingzhi sanshi niandai wenxue yu Lu Xun" (Third decade Meiji literature and Lu Xun), *Hebei daxue xuebao* 1982:2 (February):69–80.

11. Benjamin Schwartz, "The Intellectual History of China: Preliminary Reflections," in J. K. Fairbank, *Chinese Thought and Institutions* (Chicago, 1957), p. 17. See also Marián Gálik, "Nietzsche in China," *Nachrichten der Gesellschaft fur Natur- und Völkerkunde Ostasiens* 110 (1974):5–47.

12. David Kelly, "Sincerity and Will: The Existential Voluntarism of Li Shicen (1892–1935)" (Ph.D. diss., University of Sydney, 1981), ch. 2.

13. Xu Shoushang, *Wo suo renshide de Lu Xun* (The Lu Xun I knew) (Beijing, 1952), p. 19.

14. Lu Ge, "Lu Xun yu 'cun cheng qu wei' ji qita," (Lu Xun and 'preserve sincerity and dispel falsehood' etc.) *Lanzhou daxue xuebao* 1982:2, 39–42; repr. in the Zhongguo Renmin Daxue photocopy series *Lu Xun yanjiu* 1982:5, 65–68, at 66.

15. Marián Gálik, "Studies in Chinese Intellectual History III. Young Lu Xun (1902–1909)," *Asian and Oriental Studies* 21 (1985):37–64; see p. 60. See also Gálik's *Milestones in Sino-Western Literary Confrontation (1898–1979)* (Wiesbaden, 1986).

16. Qian Bixiang, "Lu Xun yu Nicai zhexue" (Lu Xun and Nietzsche's philosophy), *Zhongguo shehui kexue* 1982:3, 113–30; English trans. in *Social Sciences in China* 3 (June 1982):142–68.

17. The protests against the passivity of the Beijing government to the Treaty of Versailles (which saw former German interests in China transferred to Japanese control) triggered widespread social and intellectual changes. Although the "New Culture movement" actually got under way some years before, the May Fourth Movement is universally accepted as a watershed in modern Chinese history. See Chow Tse-tsung, *The May Fourth Movement: Intellectual Revolution in Modern China* (Cambridge, Mass., 1960); Lin Yü-sheng, *The Crisis of Chinese Consciousness: Radical Antitraditionalism in the May Fourth Era* (Madison, 1979).

18. Li Shicen, "Wode shenghuo taidu zhi zibai" (An account of my attitude to life), introduction to *Li Shicen jiangyan ji* (Collected lectures of Li Shicen) (Shanghai, 1924), p. 19. Li's career is described in more detail in Kelly, "Sincerity and Will."

19. Gálik gives a useful account of the "Critique" in his article "Nietzsche in China," but fails to mention the *Outline*. There appear to be no other accounts of it in English or Chinese.

20. Gálik, "Nietzsche in China," p. 15, with specific reference to Mao Dun's "Nicaide xueshuo" (Nietzsche's doctrine), in *Xuesheng zazhi* 7 (1919): issues 1:1–12, 2:13–24, 3:25–34, and 4:35–38. Note that this journal is discontinuously paginated.

21. Li Shicen, *Li Shicen lunwen ji* (Collected essays of Li Shicen) (Shanghai, 1924–26); hereafter *LJ*.

22. See Georg Simmel *Schopenhauer and Nietzsche*, trans. with a valuable introduction by Helmut Loiskandl et al. (Amherst, 1986).

23. Li Shicen, *Chaoren zhexue qianshuo* (Outline of the superman philosophy) (Shanghai, 1931), pp. 1–2; hereafter *QS*.

24. *QS* 88–92. Li claims his to be the first discussion of Kierkegaard's thought in Chinese. Lu Xun had earlier mentioned Kierkegaard in one breath with Nietzsche, saying little about him and apparently relying on Brandes; see Lu Xun, *Lu Xun quanji* (Collected works of Lu Xun), 20 vols. (Beijing, 1973), vol. 1, p. 45. Hereafter *LXQJ*.

25. *Li Shicen jiangyan ji*, pp. 29–38.

26. Yue Daiyun, "Nicai yu zhongguo xiandai wenxue" (see note 6); see also Lü Xichen and Wang Yumin, *Zhongguo xiandai zhexue shi 1919–1949* (Modern intellectual history of China 1919–1949) (Changchun, 1984), pp. 424–38.

27. Michael Godley, "Politics from History: Lei Haizong and the *Zhanguo Ce* clique," *Papers in Far Eastern History* 40 (September 1989):95–122.

28. *Guo Moruo wenji* (Collected Writings of Guo Moruo), vol. 8, pp. 261–62. Quoted in Yue Daiyun, p. 22.

29. Li Yuzhong, "Nicai yu Lu Xun guanxi xin tan" (A new discussion of Lu Xun's relationship to Nietzsche), in *Women xinmuzhongde Lu Xun* (Lu Xun in our mind's eye), ed. Guangdong sheng Lu Xun yanjiu xuehui (Guangzhou, 1988), pp. 127–45. See in particular the afterword, p. 145.

30. Dai Wenlin, "Faxisi zhuanzheng zhi sixiang yuanyuan" (The intellectual origins of fascism), *Nanjing daxue xuebao* 3 (1979). Not content to quote Soviet editions of Nietzsche, Dai appeals to Bertrand Russell's *History of Western Philosophy* (New York, 1945) and to its somewhat biased chapter on Nietzsche.

31. He Dian [Wang Yuanhua], "Nicai yu Lu Xun" (Nietzsche and Lu Xun), *Wenyi mantan*, October 1939; repr. in Li Zongying and Zhang Mengxiang, eds., *Liushi nian zai Lu Xun yanjiu lunwen xuan* (Selected essays in Lu Xun studies of the last 60 years) (Beijing, 1981), vol. 1, pp. 231–52. Wang also published this article, under the pen-name Luo Shiwen, in *Lu Xun jiannian teji* (Lu Xun commemorative issue) of the *Zhongguo wenyi congkan* (China arts series), published by Dushu shenghuo chubanshe, 1939.

32. Chen Cunfu, "Weiyizhilun pipan" (Critique of voluntarism), *Zhongguo shehui kexue* 5 (1980):101–21.

33. Maurice Meisner, *Li Ta-chao and the Origins of Chinese Marxism* (Cambridge, Mass., 1967); Frederick Wakeman Jr., *History and Will: Philosophical*

Perspectives on the Thought of Mao Tse-tung (Berkeley, 1973). See discussion in David Kelly, "Sincerity and Will," ch. 1.

34. D. A. Kelly, "The Emergence of Humanism: Wang Ruoshui and the Critique of Socialist Alienation," in *China's Intellectuals and the State: In Search of a New Relationship*, ed. Merle Goldman and Tim Cheek (Cambridge, Mass., 1987), pp. 159–82.

35. Ru Xin, "Lun Nicai beiju lilun de qiyuan" (On the origins of Nietzsche's theory of tragedy), *Waiguo meixue* (Beijing, 1985), vol. 1, pp. 183–205.

36. Zhou Guoping, *Nicai: zai shijide zhuanzhedian shang* (Nietzsche: At the turning point of the century) (Shanghai, 1986). See also *Nicai shiji* (Poems of Nietzsche) (Beijing, 1986).

37. Ibid., pp. 251–52.

38. Ibid., pp. 70ff.

39. Chen Guying, "Nicai zhexue yu Zhuangzi zhexue de bijiao yanjiu" (Comparison of the philosophies of Nietzsche and Zhuangzi), *Zhongbao yuekan* (Taibei) 1986, no. 2:66–72; no. 3:65–70; no. 4:78–83.

40. Zhang Rulun, "Nicai meixue sixiang chutan" (Nietzsche's Aesthetics), *Qingnian luntan* 6 (May 1985):74–87; An Yanming, "Lun Nicaide wenhua pipan" (On Nietzsche's Cultural Criticism), in *Duanlie yu jicheng* (Rupture and continuity), ed. Fudan Xuebao (Shanghai, 1987), pp. 334–57, 393–413. An Yanming translated Georg Brandes' *Nietzsche* for the "World master thinkers series": *Nicai* (Beijing, 1985).

41. An Yanming, "Guanyu Makesizhuyi zherue jichu wenti de lishi chensi" (Historical considerations on the fundamental question in Marxist philosophy: Plekhanov, Stalin, and Lukacs on the foundations of Marxist philosophy), *Fudan Xuebao* 1985:3 (March); Zhou Guoping and Jia Zelin, "Sulian zhexue zhong de ren he rendaozhuyi wenti" (Problems of man and humanism in Soviet philosophy), in *Ren shi Makesizhuyi de chufadian* (Man is the starting point of Marxism), ed. Wang Ruoshui (Beijing, 1981).

42. "Western thought from Marxist View," *Inside China Mainland* 1987:11 (November):6–7; translation of "Makesizhuyi yanjiangtuan zai Hangzhou daxuesheng zhong" (Marxist lecture team among Hangzhou university students), *Banyuetan* 1987:12 (25 June):15–17.

43. "Trends in Student Thought: How Much Western Influence?" *Inside China Mainland* 1989 (July):23–25; translation of "Fansi yu xuanze: Xifang wenhua dui dangdai xuesheng de yinxiang" (Reflection and choice: The influence of Western culture on today's students), *Liaowang Zhoukan* (overseas ed.) 1989:18 (1 May):18–20.

44. Ibid., p. 24.

45. Yin Huimin, "Nicai, ni hai ren buqian" (Nietzsche, you really cause damage), *Jiushi niandai* 7 (July 1987):78–80.

46. He Xin, "Wode kunhuo yu youlü" (My perplexities and concerns), *Xuexi yuekan*, 1988:12, 34–38. Quoted in He Xin, "A Word of Advice to the Politburo," translated, annotated, and introduced by Geremie Barmé, *Australian Journal of Chinese Affairs* 23 (January 1990):49–76.

47. Geremie Barmé, "Confession, Redemption and Death: Liu Xiaobo and the Protest Movement of 1989," in *The Broken Mirror: China After Tiananmen*, ed. George Hicks (Oxford and Hong Kong, 1990). See also Wang Yihua, "Reflections on Contemporary China's 'culture fever'," *Ming bao yuekan* (Hong Kong) 4 (April 1989):35–39, at 37.

48. Wen Ping, "From national nihilism to national betrayal: a comment on Liu Xiaobo's fallacy of bourgeois liberalization," *Renmin ribao* (overseas edition), November 7, 1989; trans. in BBC, *Survey of World Broadcasts*, 10 November 1989, B2/1–4. See "The Purge Begins," *Asiaweek*, 23 June 1989, 22–30, for a description of Liu's arrest; for the official view see Wang Zhao, "Seize the Vicious Manipulator—Liu Xiaobo," *Beijing Review*, 10–16 July 1989, 22–25. For a sympathetic account of Liu's motives, see Bei Ling, "Bie wu xuanze: ji wode pengyou Liu Xiaobo" (No other choice: a memoir of my friend Liu Xiaobo), *Ming bao yuekan* 1989:4 (April):32–34.

49. Liu Xiaobo, *Xuanze de pipan* (Critique of choice) (Shanghai, 1988); hereafter *CC*. On the book's popularity, see Bei Ling, "Bie wu xuanze."

50. Literally "the personality of Confucius and Yan Hui." Yan Hui was Confucius' favorite disciple, famous for his self-effacing docility.

51. See Hsiung Tzu-chien, "Li Zehou dui Rujia sixiang shi de xilun" (Li Zehou's analysis of Confucian thought), *Zhongguo dalu yanjiu* 31:4 (October 1988):67–74; He Xin, "Li Zehou yu dangdai Zhongguo sichao" (Li Zehou and contemporary Chinese intellectual trends), *Guangming Ribao*, 16 May 1988; Du Yaoming, "Li Zehou zenyang zou shang duli sikao zhi lu?" (How did Li Zehou start on the road to independent thought?), *Ming bao yuekan* (Hong Kong) 1987:9 (September):12–16.

52. Li Zehou, "Luelun Lu Xun sixiangde fazhan" (Outline of Lu Xun's intellectual development), *Zhongguo jindai sixiang shi lun* (Essays on modern Chinese intellectual history) (Beijing, 1979), pp. 439–71; discussion at 448ff.

53. See, for a full text, Su Xiaokang and Wang Luxiang, eds., *He shang* (Beijing: Xiandai chubanshe, 1988). A full translation appears in *Joint Publication Research Service Report: China*, CAR-88–002–L (6 December 1988):1–42. See also "TV Series Runs into Flak," *Inside China Mainland* 11:1 (January 1989):1–10 (includes translations from Hong Kong journals); Frederick Wakeman, Jr., "All the Rage in China," *New York Review of Books* 36:3 (March 2, 1989):19–21.

54. Liu Xiaobo, "Yige fan chuantongzhuyizhede fanxing" (Reflections of an anti-traditionalist), *Ming bao yuekan* (Hong Kong) 1990:7 (July):13–16.

55. On the continuing relevance of this duality see Lucian Pye, *The Mandarin and the Cadre: China's Political Cultures*, Michigan Monographs in Chinese Studies, no. 59 (Ann Arbor, 1988).

56. Vaclav Havel et al., *The Power of the Powerless* (London, 1985), p. 42.

57. See J. Hillis Miller, "The Disarticulation of the Self in Nietzsche," *The Monist* 64 (April 1981):247–61.

58. David Kelly, "Chinese Intellectuals in the 1989 Democracy Movement,"

in *The Broken Mirror*, pp. 24–81. Christopher Buckley (Sydney University) has applied the idea of "civil discourse" to the recent Chinese fascination with science as an ideological solvent.

59. WP 866. See the discussion in Connolly, *Political Theory and Modernity*.

IV

JAPAN

11

The Early Reception of Nietzsche's Philosophy in Japan

Graham Parkes

The enormous impact of Nietzsche's thought on the intellectual life of Japan, which registered while he was still alive and persists with increasing strength to this day, is a phenomenon that may seem to stand in need of explanation. Many things representative of Japanese culture—from the gem-like brilliance of *haiku* to the limpid clarity of the modern novel, from the incomparable Maitreya statuary of the Nara period to the meaning-charged slow movements of Noh drama, from the studied simplicity of the tea ceremony to the hieratic dignity of the films of Ozu—exude an Apollonian measure and serenity that contrast vividly with the Dionysian excess that informs Nietzsche's most powerful work. The firm grounding of Japanese culture in the Confucian conception of the self as a matrix of familial and social relationships rather than as something appurtenant to the autonomous individual would appear to render it unreceptive ground for Nietzsche's particular genus of healthy "selfishness." It may therefore be helpful to begin by conveying a sense of the assumptions and concerns that informed the scene upon which the figure of the German philosopher burst within months of his death, after several years of hovering, as it were, in the wings. The story of his initial impact on Japanese thought is long and complex, and only a partial and selective account can be given here.[1] But Nietzsche is such a multifaceted figure that even a brief characterization of the response to his work on the part of a truly alien tradition stands to illuminate some additional aspects of his achievement.

It was during Nietzsche's student days, in the mid-1860s, that West-

ern philosophy was first introduced to Japan. While Nietzsche was neglecting his theology studies at the University of Bonn in favor of independent philosophical research, a brilliant young Japanese by the
name of Nishi was reading widely in European philosophy while a post-
graduate student at the University of Leyden, not far to the North.[2]
Nishi Amane was one of the hundreds of Japanese intellectuals who had
been sent by the government to study in Europe following the opening
of Japan a decade earlier, after a two-hundred-and-fifty-year period of
self-imposed isolation from the rest of the world. Beginning with the
appearance of American warships in Tokyo Bay in 1853, a number of
events had impressed upon the Japanese the scientific and technological
superiority of the Western nations, and as part of a program to attain
parity they had embarked on the energetic endeavor to understand and
assimilate the mind and spirit that lay behind European preeminence in
things material.

Although he had been sent to Holland to study law and political science, the main areas of Nishi's study there (which he continued in Paris)
appear to have been the logic and social philosophy of John Stuart Mill
on the one hand, and the positivism of August Comte on the other. On
his return to Japan Nishi wrote and lectured widely on British and
French philosophy, and went on to become the major translator of Western philosophical terminology into Japanese. (He enjoys the appellation
"father of modern Japanese philosophy" in part for having coined the
term *tetsugaku* as a translation of *philosophia* and its modern cognates.)

One of the most important consequences of the dissolution of the
feudal Tokugawa regime and the beginning of the Meiji Restoration in
1868 was the lifting of the prohibition of Christianity which had been
in effect for several centuries. The actual numbers of Japanese who became Christians in the decades after the de-proscription of the religion
in 1873 were small, but many of the converts were prominent intellectuals whose ideas were to exert a disproportionately large effect on the
political and cultural changes of the next several years.[3] Christian ideas
were behind many of the calls for social reform during the early Meiji
period, but more important was the idea of the significance of the "inner
life" for the development of the individual and, by extension, of the
society.[4] It is appropriately ironic, in view of Nietzsche's radical polemics
against Christianity, that the prior prevalence of the Christian idea of
interiority helped prepare the ground for the reception of his ideas in
Japan toward the turn of the century.

Around 1882, the time Nietzsche was writing the first part of *Thus
Spoke Zarathustra*, an important shift began to take place in Japanese

intellectual life. Up until this point the most powerful currents of Western thought had been positivism, utilitarianism, and various forms of social Darwinism. (Along with Comte and Mill, Herbert Spencer was a major figure, and the ethics of T. H. Green remarkably popular. Rousseau was also acquiring a large following, as indicated by the publication of a Japanese translation of *The Social Contract* that same year.) But now there began a decisive swing in the direction of German *Bildung,* a move toward the philosophy in particular but also to German achievements in the sciences as well as in literature and music. Although Nishi had extolled the merits of Kant's "Essay on Eternal Peace" and had read and discussed the German Idealists, the field of Kant studies now broadened rapidly, and the works of Fichte, Schelling, Hegel, and even Schopenhauer began to be read and written about with the consummate assiduousness that typified the Japanese assimilation of this period.[5]

Nietzsche's first appearance on the intellectual scene in Japan is shrouded in (some might say: appropriate) obscurity. The earliest trace of his influence went undiscovered until 1977: it is to be found in an article comparing the ethical ideas of "Mr. Friedrich Nietzsche and Count Leo Tolstoy" which appeared in the Christian literary journal *Shinkai* in 1893.[6] The piece was published anonymously—a not uncommon practice at the time—but attempts to identify the author, which often succeed in such cases, have in this instance failed.[7] The essay is however quite pedestrian and of merely historical interest, as evidenced by its evoking no response whatsoever on publication.

I

In 1888, Nietzsche wrote:

I am no human being, I am dynamite. . . . I am necessarily also the man of calamity. For when truth enters into a fight with the lies of millennia, we shall have upheavals, a convulsion of earthquakes, a moving of mountains and valleys . . . there will be wars the like of which have never yet been seen on earth. (*EH* IV, 1)

It was only a few months later that the psychical explosion took place that was to plunge the author into an eleven-year night of the soul. As if to confirm the ancient Greeks' sense of the closeness of the manic and the mantic, the detonations of the first of the predicted series of wars burst forth in 1894—though not yet so close to home—with the outbreak of the Sino-Japanese War. Strong nationalist sentiment had been fermenting in Japan since the "unequal treaties settlement" forced upon the country by the Western powers seven years earlier. Victory in the war against China, which was in part a response to aggressive Western colonialism there, was the first successful assertion of Japan as a world power. Several of the components of this nationalism—such as the Confucian-derived ideas of the "family state" (*kazoku kokka*) and "national morality" (*kokumin dōtoku*), as well as the divinity of the Emperor as father of the nation-family—being diametrically opposed to any form of individualism, were important conditions of the debate over Nietzsche that was soon to take place. The Triple Intervention on the part of Russia, France, and Germany, which forced Japan to return the newly won Liaotung Peninsula to China, served further to stimulate nationalist and expansionist sentiments and to exacerbate anti-Christian and anti-Western feeling in general.

It was into this charged atmosphere that Nietzsche was first introduced at the level of the university. The rapid building up of the school and university systems had been of central importance for the Japanese process of modernization, and education an indispensable means of social integration and inculcation of "national morality." The Imperial University of Tokyo had assumed an important position at the peak of this educational system, with the task of educating the ruling class in the latest developments in science and technology in Europe and America. But it also gave the new Japanese intellectual elite access to the cultural self-consciousness of Europe—thereby generating a certain tension. Modern European individualism provided a standpoint from which to criticize the backwardness of those aspects contemporary Japan that were still tightly bound to tradition. Yet in an atmosphere of burgeoning nationalism this kind of individualism did not become popular, and the intellectuals thus found themselves in a position of "aesthetic distance" from the process of modernization.

One of the leading philosophers at The Imperial University, Inoue Tetsujirō, had gone to Germany in 1884 and studied philosophy with such luminaries as Kuno Fischer, Eduard Zeller, Wilhelm Wundt, and Eduard von Hartmann.[8] After returning to a professorship at Tokyo in 1890 (the first such chair at the Imperial University), he was instrumental in bringing there a Russian scholar of German-Swedish extraction by the name of Raphael von Koeber. Koeber, who had been recommended by Hartmann, had studied music with Tchaikovsky in Moscow before going on to philosophy and literature at Jena and Heidelberg. His primary interest was Schopenhauer, and he soon developed into a charismatic teacher who was to influence a whole generation of Japanese thinkers.[9] It was around 1894–95 that Koeber began to mention in his lectures a German philosopher by the name of Friedrich Nietzsche: he apparently said that although Nietzsche's style was magnificent, "his teachings must be forcefully rejected as the most extreme form of egoism."[10]

In 1897 Inoue went to Paris to deliver a paper at the 11th International Congress of Orientalists. Stopping in Germany on his way back, he was amazed to find intellectual life there consumed by a fascination for the writings of Nietzsche. Out of curiosity Inoue bought the philosopher's complete works to take back to Japan with him. Although he did then introduce the author to his students it was in the mode of disrecommendation, with the warning that Nietzsche's thinking would "cause considerable harm to the intellectual world." In an essay published a few years later, Inoue writes: "Nietzsche was a poet rather than a systematic thinker. . . . As a philosopher one finds in him self-contradiction and unhealthiness in the highest degree." Inoue later became a vociferous opponent of Christian ideas and a vigorous promoter of right-wing nationalist ideology.[11]

The first essay exclusively devoted to Nietzsche to appear in Japan was "Nīche shisō no yunyū to bukkyō" (The reception of Nietzsche's thought in relation to Buddhism), which was published in the journal *Taiyō* (*The Sun*—an appropriately Zarathustrian title) in March of 1898. This essay, too, appeared anonymously, but there is general agreement that the author was Anesaki Masaharu, a young Schopenhauer scholar and recent graduate from Tokyo in philosophy of religion.[12] Rather than being a consideration of parallels between Nietzsche's ideas and Buddhism, the essay is primarily an exhortation to Buddhists in Japan to respond positively to the influx of German philosophy by becoming more philosophical. The author urges the study of Nietzsche as a way of strengthening the philosophical foundations of Japanese Buddhism and of defending against encroachments by Christian ideas.

Anesaki goes on to make some perceptive remarks concerning possible resonances between Nietzsche's and Buddhist thought: "Even though Nietzsche himself did not exactly greet Buddhism with enthusiasm, one can say that in the ideal of the *Übermensch* he comes close to the idea of the Buddha."[13] As for the apparent contradiction between the denial of the ego practiced by Buddhism and the apotheosis of it in the figure of the *Übermensch*, Anesaki claims that it obtains only with respect to early, Hinayana Buddhism and not to the later Mahayana with its doctrine of "the identity of the not-I and the great I" (*muga suna-*

wachi daiga setsu).[14] The essay concludes with another expression of the hope that young Buddhists will rise to the occasion and appropriate the impulses imparted to Buddhism by the advent of Nietzsche's ideas. This challenge was not to be taken up for some time—even though Nietzsche's name was soon to become a household word in Japan.[15]

Before the curtain rises on the major drama of the "aesthetic life debate," a brief prelude, in the mode of farce, is played out in the 1899 issues of the periodical *Waseda gakuhō*. The protagonist is an aspiring litterateur of tender years by the name of Hasegawa Tenkei, but an important supporting role is played—unexpectedly—by contributors to the July 1899 issue of a philosophy journal published in Chicago. Tenkei had been introduced to Nietzsche by Raphael von Koeber, who had also brought his attention to an issue of *The Monist* containing two essays on Nietzsche: one a nine-page hatchet job jointly authored by Heinrich Goebel and Ernest Antrim, the other a forty-four page tract by the editor himself, Paul Carus.[16] Both articles are informed by a superficial reading of what appears to be a relatively small portion of Nietzsche's published works, and they fulfill all one's worst fears of how beginning readers will misunderstand him. Whereas Carus discerns something of value here and there in Nietzsche's work, the heavy sarcasm of the Goebel and Antrim piece allows no glimmer of worth to escape. But these misconstruals are mild in comparison with the constructions put upon them by the young Tenkei, whose hyperbolic rehashings could simply be dismissed if they and their author were not to become a strong anti-Nietzschean force in the debate to follow.[17]

Tenkei begins by admitting with disarming candor that his essay is based on articles that appeared in the previous month's *Monist*. But in what follows there is no indication of what are simply translations from Goebel and Antrim or from Carus, and what are interpolations from the author—though Tenkei's contributions are consistently shriller and more extravagant. A representative passage:

Nietzsche thinks that . . . there is no authority higher than what we desire, and to follow this [principle] is proper behavior. So, whoever wants to commit adultery may do so; whoever wants to murder may do so. Whoever has the need to steal may take another's property. For the ego [*jiga*] is the sole and highest master. . . .[18]

While one can find a basis for most of the extravagances of Tenkei's essay in the *Monist* articles, the points have in every case been rendered more lurid, coalescing in a picture of Nietzsche as the extremest advocate of nihilism, immorality, egotism, and glorification of brute instinct.

II

Although Nietzsche the philosopher had been dead since 1889, the life that remained expired in August of 1900. The next few months saw the appearance in Japan of three memorial essays, by Yoshida Seichi, Tobari Chikufū, and Ueda Bin (this last being a translation of an article "Friedrich Nietzsche" by the French philosopher Henri Lichtenberger which had appeared in France only a few months earlier).

In January 1901 an essay entitled "Bunmei hihyōka toshite no bungakusha" (The litterateur as culture-critic) appeared in the journal *Taiyō*, authored by the literary critic Takayama Chogyū, a good friend of Tobari Chikufū's. Chogyū (his literary name) was a prolific and brilliant writer who exerted an unprecedented influence over his generation. He was to die of tuberculosis at the end of the next year at the age of thirty-one, leaving behind seven volumes of collected works. For some years previously Chogyū had been an ardent proponent of "Japanism" (*Nihonshugi*), but the appearance of this latest essay marked a turn away from nationalism to a sharp critique of Japanese culture and contained the beginnings of a pronounced individualism.

The essay begins with the author's admitting that he has only recently found time to read "a few of Nietzsche's writings," but that he finds their unusual perspectives to be eye-opening.[19] Remarking that Nietzsche is "a fine poet rather than a philosopher," Chogyū proclaims his true greatness to reside in his being a *Kulturkritiker*. He then launches into a scathing critique of modern Japanese society, applying Nietzsche's critique of the decadence of nineteenth-century European culture (as articulated in the *Untimely Meditations*) to the case of Japan.[20] The parallels are extensive, and Chogyū's substitution of targets works uncommonly well—as evidenced by the howls of protest and torrents of invective that greeted the publication of his diatribe. A further cause for outrage was that not only did Chogyū hail Nietzsche as "a friend of youth," thus injecting a revolutionary element into the challenge, but he also commended his "extreme individualism," which he styled in addition "mysterious and fiery." This was indeed inflammatory stuff to drop on a society where the forces of reaction were working to build Japan into a world power on the basis of a radically *anti*-individualist national morality. But however inflamed the rhetoric of the responses to Chogyū's essay, they were directed at its author and the name of Nietzsche was hardly mentioned—yet.

A fuller picture of Nietzsche's thought is given by Tobari Chikufū in a series of four essays which appeared throughout the year 1901 in the journal *Teikoku bungaku* (Literature of the Empire). Chikufū drew on a wider range of secondary sources than his friend had done: in addition to Ziegler's work he leaned heavily on an essay by the Danish scholar Georg Brandes entitled "Aristokratischer Radikalismus."[21] In this series of essays, Chikufū took Chogyū's application of Nietzsche's critique of European culture to the contemporary Japanese situation and not only intensified it through even more provocative language than his friend had employed, but extended it to all aspects of Japanese cultural life, directing especially scathing barbs at the sterility of contemporary academics. But whereas Chogyū had devoted less than a fifth of his article to Nietzsche (he had gone on to extol other such "culture critics" as Tolstoy, Ibsen, Whitman, and Zola), Chikufū's essays fulfilled the expectations of their collective title "On Friedrich Nietzsche" by making him the primary and sustained focus. And to make matters worse, he praised in even more glowing terms and at greater length Nietzsche's "extreme individualism."

In August 1901, while Chifukū's series was still appearing, Takayama Chogyū published the essay that served as the fuse for the "aesthetic life" debate and which propelled Nietzsche into general public awareness in Japan: "Biteki seikatsu o ronzu" (On the aesthetic life). It is an irony that would have amused Nietzsche that in this crucial text he was "dishonored in the breach"—that he burst upon the scene in the mode of absence—since nowhere in the essay is there a mention of the name "Nietzsche." Chogyū asserts that the life of morality and the life of knowledge are worthless in comparison with the value of "instinct" (*honnō*). So far so Nietzschean. But then, making a connection that remains obscure, Chogyū asserts that "what has the purest aesthetic value is the satisfaction of the instincts." (The etymological link between "aesthetic" and "the senses" does not operate between the Japanese terms: the *bi* of *biteki* means simply "beautiful.") While Chogyū's thesis could be seen as compatible with Nietzsche's statement in *The Birth of Tragedy* that "the world is justified only as an aesthetic phenomenon," his emphasis on the immediate satisfaction of instinct and the implicit denigration of self-control takes his thinking in a direction different from Nietzsche's. Chogyū goes on to assert that "the utmost happiness in life is the satisfaction of sexual desire"—the first direct statement of that proposition in Japanese literature. To make the whole thing more provocative, the author intersperses his lyrical outpourings about love and desire with quotations from and allusions to the Bible.

In the latter part of August, Hasegawa Tenkei published a two-part rejoinder to Chogyū's essay in the *Yomiuri shinbun*, a leading news-paper. Chifukū then published a response to Hasegawa in *Teikoku bungaku* under the title "Biteki seikatsuron to Nīche" (Nietzsche and the theory of aesthetic life), interpolating it into his series "On Friedrich Nietzsche." Chikufū suggests that Chogyū's ideas came from Nietzsche, and that the "instinct" he was talking about was the "instinct for free-dom" discussed in *On the Genealogy of Morals* (II, 17). In order further to inflame public opinion, Chifukū highlights the hedonistic and indi-vidualistic features of the "aesthetic life" advocated by Chogyū/Nietz-sche. In combination with the essays in Chikufū's series on Nietzsche, the most recent of which had just given the unfortunate example of a child-murderer whose single-minded purposiveness in murdering a small child is cited as an example of will to power geared toward the "aesthetic life," this assimilation of Nietzsche and Chogyū prompted the letting loose of all hell.

It made little difference that Chogyū immediately repudiated the claim that he was a "follower of Nietzsche" and asserted that the ideas in his aesthetic life essay were arrived at quite independently. He did admit that he found the *man* Nietzsche, his personality, to be an inspi-ration, but denied to the end (justifiably, it seems) that Nietzsche's ideas had influenced his own thesis. The debate that followed, which involved most of the major literary figures of the day and brought the name of Nietzsche—if only a few of his ideas—to the attention of the majority of literate Japanese, raged for the next two years. Since the arguments that ensued are not very instructive philosophically, they may be passed over here—with the remark that a characterization of the period as one of "the brutalization of literary politics" seems if anything under-stated.[22]

It is hard to understand just why Chikufū's linking of Nietzsche's name with Chogyū's "aesthetic life" thesis should have provoked such a volume of vituperation directed against *Nietzsche*. A number of factors appear to have contributed, not the least of which was a mood of increas-ing xenophobia in the aftermath of the Sino-Japanese War. Not that there was any lack of animosity toward Chogyū and Chikufū personally (ninety percent of the ensuing arguments were blatantly *ad hominem*), but it was a convenient way of fueling public resentment to portray them as besotted by *foreign* immoralism and individualism. Also, there was nothing to counterbalance Chikufū's lurid rhetoric and irresponsibly chosen examples, since hardly any of the anti-Nietzsche faction had ac-tually read a word of his texts. And whereas the Nietzsche supporters (who were mostly graduates from the University of Tokyo) were reading for the most part the French and German secondary literature, their antagonists (who were primarily from Waseda University) were almost totally dependent on the secondary literature in English, which at that time was markedly biased against him—in some cases hysterically so.

Insofar as it is possible to compare degrees of initial misunderstanding of Nietzsche's ideas, if it was greater in Japan than elsewhere (and some of the early Anglo-American misinterpretations were quite egregious) this is largely because they were not grounded in a reading of the texts. The Japanese debate was certainly the most destructive initially— Chikufū was later fired from his teaching post by the government on the grounds that his Nietzschean views were "incompatible with the Emperor system."[23]

III

The one participant in the debate who is distinguished by having a respectable understanding of Nietzsche's ideas is Anesaki Masaharu (literary name Chōfū), whose essay on Nietzsche and Buddhism was discussed earlier. Chōfū was one of Chogyū's closest friends, and he had gone to Germany to study philosophy and religion before the aesthetic life debate broke out. He was one of the few people aside from Chikufū to support Chogyū, which he did by way of three "Open Letters" to him which were published in *Taiyō*.

Chōfū had the advantage of having some closely mediated sense of Nietzsche's life and personality, through his studying with two men who had been good friends of Nietzsche's. He first went to Kiel to work with Paul Deussen, who had known Nietzsche since their schooldays at Schulpforta—though there had been a cooling in their relations since Nietzsche had renounced the philosophy of Schopenhauer, whom Deussen continued to admire. Chōfū later went on to Leipzig to study with the Professor of Indology there, Ernst Windisch, who had been a graduate student with Nietzsche in Leipzig and who had introduced him personally to Wagner. It was presumably to some extent the association with Windisch that inspired in Chōfū a great love of Wagner: he made several pilgrimages to Bayreuth during his stay in Germany, and was eventually to come out in favor of the Wagnerian ideal of universal love as opposed to Nietzsche's less "spiritual" philosophy.

Shortly after Chōfū's arrival in Kiel in July 1900, Kaiser Wilhelm made his famous speech warning of the dangers of "the yellow peril," as warships were dispatched to smite the fractious Chinese. This show of rhetoric made the new visitor feel less than welcome in the state of Prussia, a feeling exacerbated by the prevailing anti-Asian feeling on the part of the general populace. However, the sense of being in an alien society served to sharpen Chōfū's culture-critical eye, so that the first open letter to Chogyū contains some insightful criticisms of the Reich from an avowedly Nietzschean perspective, which the author then explicitly applies to the contemporary Japanese situation, buttressing in retrospect the critique made by Chogyū in his "Litterateur as Culture-Critic" essay. In the context of the enthusiasm on the part of people like Inoue Tetsujirō for the wholesale importing of the authoritarian political system of Prussia as a model for Japan, Chōfū warned against the extreme nationalism and militarism that had grown out of the Reich's essentially "soulless" basis in material prosperity. He expresses a quite Nietzschean horror at the way "patriotic self-adulation" means "the extinction of the worth of the individual."[24] A prophetic warning in view of the rise of fascism in both Germany and Japan over the ensuing few decades.

In his third open letter, Chōfū relates how he was drinking a glass of wine on the veranda of Deussen's house one evening in the summer of 1900 when a telegram came announcing Nietzsche's death. Deussen was silent for a while, as tears welled up in his eyes. He then said that since Nietzsche had for the previous ten years lived only as a physical frame, the demise of that frame was of no great significance. The anti-Nietzsche faction in Japan had argued that he was a sociopathic solitary and, by implication, a bad man. Chōfū's anecdote may have served to convey a different picture of Nietzsche the human being.

One of the major themes of this last letter of Chōfū's—which he composed in London, having left Germany by this time (May 1902)—is the relationship between the thinking of Schopenhauer, Wagner, and Nietzsche on the topic of the will. His comments help to situate Nietzsche's thought with respect to two of the most powerful influences on it, although the author's love for Wagner prevents him from seeing either what it was about Wagner's understanding of the will that Nietzsche found unsatisfactory or the ways in which he went beyond the Wagnerian *Weltanschauung*.[25] Although Chōfū makes it clear that he considers the early, Wagnerian Nietzsche to be the best one, he does see in what respects Nietzsche's ideas were an advance on Schopenhauer's, expressing this again by way of a comparison with Buddhism. He believes that Schopenhauer himself came to realize that there were shortcomings in his notion of nirvana as the extinction of the will, and suggests that this idea corresponds to the early Buddhist notion of "blissful dissolution of the I" (*muga-jakumetsu*); what Schopenhauer needed was to progress to the Mahayana idea of "prolonged existence of the great I" (*daiga-kyūjū*). Chōfū goes on to say that this development was in fact achieved a generation later in the philosophy of Nietzsche.

Two other features of the aesthetic life debate are worth mentioning in view of the chapters in the present volume dealing with Nietzsche in relation to Chinese thought. The first is that the writer Lu Xun, who was to play a major role in introducing Nietzsche's ideas into China, came to Tokyo to study in 1902, at the height (or nadir) of the debate. While the terms in which the controversy was being conducted at this point must surely have given him a misleading first impression of Nietzsche's philosophy, at least he would have been gained a sense of the philosopher's importance and his possible relevance for East Asian culture.

The previous year the Nietzsche-Tolstoy comparison had been revived through the translation of an article that had appeared in the *International Journal of Ethics*.[26] Later in the year the philosopher Nakajima Tokuzō gave a lecture entitled "Nīche tai Torusutoishugi" ("Nietzsche against Tolstoyism") which dealt with the relationship between Tolstoy and Nietzsche against the background of Schopenhauer, Christianity, and Buddhism. In the course of a discussion of the problem of morality in relation to what is natural, the author claims that for Nietzsche virtue must be based in the "instincts" of the body and also be "free and unconstrained" (*shōyō semarazu*). The term *shōyō* is a key term in the Daoist philosophy of Zhuang Zi—and indeed Nakajima goes on to quote from the *Dao de jing* of Lao Zi and to suggest that on the issue of the natural "Lao Zi and Zhuang Zi are in agreement with Nietzsche."[27]

A few months later a sinologist by the name of Kubo Tenzui entered the debate with a piece entitled "Waga iwayuru 'Biteki seikatsu'" (Our 'Aesthetic Life') which appeared in September 1901. The author expresses some support for Chogyū but criticizes him for leaving the content of the aesthetic life so vague. He goes on to remark that Chogyū's thesis appears to have been anticipated some two thousand years earlier in the work of Zhuang Zi.[28] In support of his claim Kubo goes on to cite three passages from the *Zhuang Zi* which reinforce the point alluded to earlier by Nakajima.

For our present interests it will be sufficient to look at just the first passage, since the other two simply reinforce the same points. It comes from the end of the "Webbed Toes" chapter, and deals with the issue of human "nature" or "character" (*xing*, Jpn. *sei*—both terms being closely derived from the word for "life," *sheng/shō*):

When I call someone a fine human being, it is not benevolence or righteousness that I am talking about, but simply the quality of his powers . . . [and] a trust in the essentials of our character and destiny.[29]

The "powers" referred to here is the person's *de*, his *virtus* in the original sense of the word, his potential—which depends for Zhuang Zi on the workings of the natural forces of Heaven through him.[30] "Benevolence" (*ren*) and "righteousness" (*yi*) are the two primary "virtues" in Confucian ethics, and so Zhuang Zi's idea is an effective tool for undermining the authoritarian national morality espoused by the anti-Nietzsche faction in the debate. The *Zhuang Zi's* concern with "fathoming" and "nurturing" one's *nature* has a significant parallel in Nietzsche's concern with *life* and the way certain moralities turn life against itself and lead to decadence. Correspondingly, the Daoist interest in conditions of our existence (*ming*; traditionally rendered as "destiny") are echoed in Nietzsche's attempts to cultivate *amor fati*, or "love of fate."[31]

One further voice in the debate—though still small in this particular context—deserves mention: that of the novelist Mori Ōgai. Together with Natsume Sōseki, Ōgai was the most important writer of the Meiji period, and the influence of these two figures on the subsequent reception of Nietzsche was considerable, even though they did not themselves write much about him. Ōgai had spent four years in Germany studying medicine, from 1884–88 (there was even a period during which both he and Nietzsche were in Munich at the same time), but thanks to his literary interests and abilities he was becoming well known as a writer and an expert on German literature. Although he does not appear to have come across Nietzsche's name while he was in Germany, Ōgai may have been one of the first people in Japan to know of him, since in 1894 a friend who had just returned from Germany lent him several of Nietzsche's texts. Ōgai writes in a letter of his borrowing some recent works in German philosophy: "Above all a Friedrich Nietzsche, who seems to me to be quite an extraordinary philosopher."[32]

Ōgai's first published mention of Nietzsche occurs in the introduction to a collection of essays which appeared under the title *Tsukikusa* at the end of 1896. There he is critical of Nietzsche's "immoralism" (*hidō*), though his barbs are directed more at Nietzsche's followers than at the man himself. On the other hand Nietzsche's individualism is regarded as a possible antidote to the Naturalist movement that was prevalent in the Japanese literature of the time. Ōgai appears to have gleaned most of his knowledge of Nietzsche from secondary sources—though this was to change after 1907, when he began to study the *Collected Works* in the original.[33] Ōgai's contribution to the aesthetic life debate was minimal, taking the form of a short critique of Takayama Chogyū in a newspaper article in October 1901. He writes:

If one compares the "theory of aesthetic life" with the writings of its source, Nietzsche, which give the impression that their author has escaped from the cage of a bird or beast of prey, it comes off as gentle and mild. For me that theory still portrays a Nietzsche without claws or fangs. . . .[34]

In Ōgai's first full-length novel *Seinen* (*Youth*), published in 1911, which can be seen as a kind of *Bildungsroman*, there is a criticism of the Japanese adoption of Western ideas in the following terms:

Everything we bring to Japan becomes diminished. It's the same with Nietzsche and the same with Tolstoy. I am reminded of a passage from Nietzsche: "The earth has become small, and on it hops the last man, who makes everything small. . . . 'We have invented happiness,' say the last men, and they blink." We Japanese have imported all sorts of beliefs and isms which we play around with and blink.[35]

Direct contact with the primary source appears to have opened Ōgai's eyes to some of the positive aspects of Nietzsche's thought, but an ambivalence still remains which seems to come from a somewhat literal reading of will to power in its relation to individualism. In another part of *Seinen* he implies a criticism of Nietzsche by having one of the characters represent, in opposition to the "egoistic individualism" of Nietzschean "will to power," a kind of "altruistic individualism" that maintains an intellectual and spiritual freedom while at the same time observing conventional mores.[36] In spite of this ambivalence, however, Ōgai's interest in Nietzsche persisted over the years.

Sōseki, whose main field was English literature, taught at Tokyo Imperial University after spending several years in England, and soon became the most influential writer of the period. While the debate over Nietzsche's individualism was raging, these two writers were independently working on the problem of individualism especially as it concerned the ethical orientation of intellectuals. While the modernization of Japan had liberated many thinkers of the period from the bonds of tradition, it was impossible for them to advocate a European individualism without being exposed to the accusation of egoism—as the debate over Nietzsche so clearly demonstrated. But Ōgai and Sōseki, even though they were consummately familiar with European ideas, had undergone too thorough an education in classical Chinese literature to be as naively enthusiastic about Nietzsche as Chogyū and Chifukū were.[37]

In contrast to Ōgai, Sōseki knew Nietzsche primarily through his reading of the English translation of *Zarathustra*, which appears to have left him with the impression that Nietzsche's ideas of the *Übermensch* and "the eternal recurrence of the same" made little sense. His marginal notes to the 1899 translation by Alexander Tille have been preserved, and are interesting in their ambivalence. Comments such as "mere jargon" and "foolish rhapsody" are balanced by notes reading "very true" and "good." It is interesting that Sōseki sees a number of parallels between passages from *Zarathustra* and ideas from the Buddhist and Confucian traditions. At one point he writes: "This is oriental. Strange to find such an idea in the writings of a European."

In his novels Sōseki was more concerned than Ōgai with the problem of egoism in the modern period, and his solution was a more traditional (if idiosyncratic) one, involving recourse to a quasi-Buddhist-Daoist ethics of selfless life in accordance with nature—his favorite catch-phrase for which was *sokuten kyoshi* ("follow Heaven and eliminate the self"). Ethics involving some kind of transcendence of the individual ego was to become a major theme in the next phase of the reception of Nietzsche, at the hands of Watsuji Tetsurō and Abe Jirō, two philosophers who were devotees of Sōseki and frequent visitors to his home.[38] Ōgai and Sōseki prepared the way for a new phase of Nietzsche's reception in another respect, insofar as they encouraged Ikuta Chōkō to translate *Thus Spoke Zarathustra*—a daunting task, in which Ōgai willingly offered his assistance. Appearing in 1911, this was the first Japanese translation of a complete work of Nietzsche's.

IV

After the aesthetic life debate finally subsided at the end of 1903, there was something of a cooling-off (understandably, in view of the prolonged heat of the strife) in the Japanese interest in Nietzsche. The Russo-Japanese War of 1905 (another war "the like of which had never been seen") fully diverted the national energies, and its successful outcome for Japan constituted a major event in world history—the first defeat of a (quasi-) European power by an Asian nation. The series of translations of Nietzsche's works begun by Ikuta Chōkō in 1911 continued steadily, with the result that a Japanese edition of the complete works was published between 1916 and 1929. The publication of this edition was to exert a great influence on subsequent Japanese literature—and especially on such figures as Akutagawa Ryūnosuke and, later, Mishima Yukio. It took longer, however, for Nietzsche's works to be admitted into the canon of philosophical research that was developing in Japan, the major components of which had come to be the epistemologies of German Idealism and neo-Kantianism. The person who did most the change this situation was Watsuji Tetsurō, who ranks among the two or three greatest figures in modern Japanese philosophy.[39]

After enjoying the benefit of a first-class education which exposed him to a wide range of European culture, Watsuji entered the Philosophy Department at Tokyo Imperial University in 1909. Unsure for a while whether to study philosophy or literature, he was soon writing stories and plays and editing a literary magazine with his friend Tanizaki Jun'-ichirō, who went on to become one of Japan's foremost novelists. Watsuji's passion for literature no doubt influenced his decision to devote himself to the study of Nietzsche, and he was also encouraged in this by his mentor Raphael von Koeber. But when the young graduate student wrote a dissertation on Nietzsche for the faculty of philosophy at Tokyo the topic was deemed unacceptable. Inoue Tetsujirō was still the Head of the Department and refused to countenance a dissertation on such a non-philosopher. Watsuji was instructed to write on Schopenhauer instead, and he hastily put together a dissertation on "Schopenhauer's Pessimism and Theory of Salvation." But two years later, in 1913, he published a four-hundred page tome entitled *Nīche-kenkyū* (A study of Nietzsche), in which Schopenhauer's name is hardly mentioned.

Watsuji's *Study of Nietzsche* distinguished itself not only by its monumental scope, but also through being the first attempt to engage the idea of "will to power" seriously. Watsuji patterned his book after the table of contents of Elizabeth Förster-Nietzsche's edition of *Der Wille zur Macht*, and tried to reconstruct the entirety of Nietzsche's thought around this framework. While this youthful work (published when the author was only twenty-four) is a landmark in Japanese Nietzsche studies, it was also a very personal one. (In the preface the author writes: "The Nietzsche who appears in this study is strictly my Nietzsche. I have tried to express myself through Nietzsche.") The work also shows influences from the *Lebensphilosophien* of Georg Simmel and Henri Bergson, and it sometimes seems that Watsuji may be reading into Nietzsche some ethical ideas from Sōseki and the Kyoto philosopher Nishida Kitarō. These latter influences may have helped to lead Watsuji to his conception of the cosmic dimensions of will to power, and to the idea that one can identify with these dimensions by transcending the individual self.

Watsuji was a prolific writer, and a number of works appeared in the course of the next decade which show the influence of Nietzsche to a greater or lesser extent. The year 1915 saw the publication of a substantial monograph on Kierkegaard, which was responsible for introducing that thinker to the Japanese intellectual world. This was followed in 1918 by a collection of essays under the title *Gūzō saikō* (Revival of idols), in the preface to which the author announced a "turn" (*tenkō*) in his thinking away from "individualism." This turn was to a large extent conditioned by Watsuji's friendship with Sōseki, to whom he had been introduced in 1913. Sōseki was moving at that time away from a kind of aesthetic individualism to the Way of *sokuten kyoshi*.[40] But the turn also involved a change in subject matter. Up until 1917 Watsuji's interests had been almost exclusively in Western culture, but now he was beginning to study the East Asian traditions. Of particular interest in this period is his claim that there are distinctly "Dionysian" components in ancient Japanese culture.

The next decade saw the publication of a series of works inspired by this turn, the first among which were: "Nihon bunka no jūsōsei" (The stadial character of Japanese culture) in 1918, *Koji junrei* (Pilgrimages to ancient temples) in 1919, and *Nihon kodai bunka* (Ancient Japanese culture) in 1920. Just as Nietzsche had complemented trenchant criticisms of European decadence (as in the *Untimely Meditations*) with commendations of the spirit of Greek antiquity (as in *Philosophy in the Tragic Age of the Greeks* and *The Birth of Tragedy*), so Watsuji accompanied his critique of contemporary culture with a call for a revaluation of the cultural achievements of Japan's ancient past. As Dilworth points out, this may signal an awareness on Watsuji's part of Nietzsche's repudiation of "Romantic individualism" (a repudiation that appears to have gone unnoticed by the aesthetic life debaters) and a correspondingly greater appreciation of Nietzsche's classicism. It can also be argued that the influence of Nietzsche the philologist persists throughout many of Watsuji's subsequent works—even those postdating his remark in 1926 that he had gone beyond his "Nietzschean phase."[41]

It may be appropriate to conclude with a brief overview of the salient points of Nietzsche's subsequent influence on Japanese philosophy. As social problems began to arise in the wake of Japan's rapid industrialization, the ethical ideas of such "culture humanists" as Watsuji and Abe were unable to offer much in the way of a solution. The advent of Marxism in the 1920s, which arrived glowing with the aura of the Russian

Revolution, totally transformed the Japanese intellectual scene. After a brief flowering, however, the Marxist movement was brutally suppressed by the government. The consequent feeling of impotence on the part of the intellectuals grew as the militarist factions in the government became more powerful. As the militarists expanded the war of conquest in China, they became ever more expert at employing conventional norms for ideological purposes and at using the Emperor cult as a means of social control. During this period, intellectual activity became increasingly crippled, whether through political persecution or inner resignation, and the only significant developments in Nietzsche scholarship were at the hands of Miki Kiyoshi, who was the first to situate Nietzsche's critique of reason and his engagement with nihilism in the context of the history of Western philosophy.[42]

Miki grew up under the influence of the culture humanists, but went to the Imperial University of Kyoto—a rather unusual choice at that time—to study philosophy under Nishida Kitarō. From 1922 to 1924 he continued his study of philosophy in Germany, primarily with Heidegger in Marburg. After a short stay in Paris he returned to Japan, whereupon he set himself the task of overcoming the "romantic" concern with the individual self which he found in the culture humanists and of opening up the intellectual world to Marxism and the social-historical dimension of thinking in general.

The intellectuals' feeling of powerlessness in the face of the continuing military expansion of Japan struck Miki as having much in common with the mood of *Angst* that pervaded Germany in the 1920s, where he thought that Nietzsche's critique of reason had contributed to the collapse of the picture of humans as rational beings. When the news reached Japan that Heidegger had joined the National Socialist Party, Miki claimed that this was evidence that only the anti-enlightenment side of Nietzsche had broken through in Heidegger, and he called for a ground-level confrontation with Nietzsche in order to restore reason to its rightful place. In an essay from 1935 entitled "Nietzsche and the Thinking of the Present," he tried to articulate the world of Nietzsche's thought in terms of his original interest in philology, and to show that the tension in Nietzsche between "philologue" (understood as love of *reason*) and "misologue" was at the root of the contemporary intellectual crisis. Another of Miki's contributions was to show the extent to which Nietzsche can be understood as a precursor of philosophical hermeneutics—an especially perspicacious reading in view of the interpretation later developed by Karl Jaspers.

For the most part, however, the growing militarism and increasingly fascistic nature of the Japanese government during the thirties more or less killed overt interest in Nietzsche. There is a striking contrast between the utter indifference toward Nietzsche on the part of the Japanese fascists and the zeal with which their counterparts in Germany and Italy were appropriating—and willfully distorting—his ideas to their own political ends. A beneficent aspect of this neglect, however, was that there was no taboo on Nietzsche's name in Japan after the Second World War. On the contrary, a general disorientation and a desire to understand the post-War situation served to create a receptive atmosphere for a more developed interest in his work—all the more so because Existentialism in general was rapidly becoming popular in intellectual circles. There was also a greater acceptance of Nietzsche's ideas in the universities, in part as a result of a large increase in the number of academic positions that were created in Germanistik and philosophy. The volume of secondary literature on Nietzsche began to burgeon, and some of his writings were translated many times over.

A major factor in this "Nietzsche renaissance" was the publication in 1949 of *The Self-Overcoming of Nihilism* by Nishitani Keiji, which by its careful reading of the original texts marked the beginning of a new era in Japanese Nietzsche studies. Among other things, this work displays an acute sensitivity to the unique problems of nihilism and modernism in post-War Japan—as evidenced in a chapter called "The Meaning of Nihilism for Japan."

Overall, the pattern of the initial reception of Nietzsche's ideas in Japan is not all that different from those of the receptions in Europe, the most salient common feature being the extreme polarization of the reactions. The polarization—in part a consequence of the size and multifaceted nature of the Nietzschean *oeuvre*—was greater in Japan because the language barrier rendered the initial interpretations even wilder than usual. Another common feature is an appreciation of Nietzsche's practice of *Kulturkritik*, which translated remarkably well into the Japanese context. The significance of Nietzsche's putative individualism was more exaggerated in Japan than elsewhere simply because the relation of the individual to society was such a sensitive issue in the middle years of the Meiji period. There are indeed strong strains of individualism in Nietzsche's thought; but when commentators accuse some of his Japanese supporters of reading into his texts ideas from the Buddhist and Daoist traditions, they are overlooking a strong counter-tendency in Nietzsche's thinking that has been generally ignored even by Western commentators who are sympathetic. This counter-strain involves the themes of the ego as an utterly fictional construct, the radical multiplicity of the "I," and the Dionysian dissolution of the boundaries of the self—all of which find their fullest and most powerful expression in *Zarathustra*. The critical distance provided by a standpoint based in the East Asian tradition allowed some of the early Japanese commentators to recognize the importance of these themes—an awareness of which persists in contemporary Japanese scholarship, as the following three chapters of the present volume show.

A final note to balance the Apollonian images which the opening paragraph associated with the Japanese tradition. The Dionysian has been there all along, as Watsuji pointed out: it is just that the Apollonian overlay has been so brilliant as to blind us to its presence. Noh drama exemplifies the duality beautifully with its synthesis of both powers. And indeed no more forceful evocation of the Dionysian can be found in the West than the frenzied dances to flute and drum of the daemonic demon-figures of some of the best plays—dynamic images, surely, of the kind of god in whom Zarathustra himself could believe.

Notes

1. The only major study in English is the monumental doctoral dissertation by R. S. Petralia, which runs to no fewer than 811 pages: "Nietzsche in Meiji Japan: Culture Criticism, Individualism and Reaction in the 'Aesthetic Life' Debate of 1901–1903" (Washington University [Saint Louis], 1981). The only book on the topic to have been published in a Western language is Hans-Joachim Becker, *Die frühe Nietzsche-Rezeption in Japan (1893–1903): Ein Beitrag zur Individualismusproblematik im Modernisierungsprozess* (Wiesbaden, 1983). Both studies are excellent.

2. For a brief account of Nishi's career and ideas, see Gino K. Piovesana, S.J., *Contemporary Japanese Philosophical Thought* (New York, 1969), pp. 5–18.

3. See Irwin Scheiner, *Christian Converts and Social Protest in Meiji Japan* (Berkeley, 1974).

4. The major figure here is Kitamura Tōkoku, a good account of whose ideas and their effect is to be found in H. D. Harootunian, "Between Politics and Culture: Authority and the Ambiguities of Intellectual Choice in Imperial Japan," in *Japan in Crisis*, ed. Bernard S. Silberman and H. D. Harootunian (Princeton, 1974).

5. Ernest Fenellosa, best known as an expert on Oriental art and associate of Ezra Pound's, spent much of his twelve years in Japan (1878–90) teaching the history of philosophy from Descartes to Hegel.

6. "Ōshū ni okeru tokugi shisō no ni daihyōsha Furiderihi Nitsushe-shi to Reo Torusutoi-haku to no iken kikaku" (A comparison of the views of Friedrich Nietzsche and Count Leo Tolstoy, the two representatives of ethical thought in Europe), *Shinkai* 4 (December 1893).

7. The article would appear to be a translation-cum-paraphrase of an essay by the German-Russian author Nikolaus Grot, which was subsequently published under the title "Nietzsche und Tolstoj" in *Die Zukunft* (Berlin) 21 (1897):414–24. See Becker, ch. 1.

8. See Piovesana, pp. 37–42.

9. See Piovesana, pp. 48–52.

10. According to the report of the philosopher Kuwaki Gen'yoku, cited in Becker, p. 42.

11. The quotations from Inoue are cited in Petralia, p. 213 and Becker, p. 43.

12. Anesaki went on to pursue a distinguished career as a professor of philosophy of religion at Tokyo, with visiting appointments later at Harvard and the Collège de France. He is the author of *A History of Japanese Religions*.

13. Cited in Becker, p. 47.

14. While Petralia brands this suggestion of Anesaki's as "one of the most *sui generis* of the myriad erratic interpretations of Nietzsche on record" (p. 220), it strikes the present author as in certain respects quite prescient.

15. While the philosopher Watsuji Tetsurō, whom we shall be discussing shortly, was to write the first major study on Nietzsche in 1911 and then go on to become a serious student of the Japanese Buddhist tradition, he did not make explicit the connections between the two. Becker cites as the classic work in the field Sonoda Kōkun, *Nīche to bukkyō* (Nietzsche and Buddhism) (Kyoto, 1931). In 1949 Nishitani Keiji takes up the question of what impulses Japanese Buddhism can fruitfully absorb from Nietzsche in *The Self-Overcoming of Nihilism* (ch. 9 and Appendix).

16. Heinrich Goebel and Ernest Antrim, "Friedrich Nietzsche's Uebermensch"; Paul Carus, "Immorality as a Philosophic Principle," *The Monist* 9 (1899). This same issue also contains, by a nice coincidence, a paraphrase by Carus of the paper delivered by Inoue at the Congress of Orientalists in Paris. Although Japanese names are being given in the East Asian manner, with the family name first, most of the writers involved in the aesthetic life debate were known by their adopted, literary names, which come after the family name. Thus in the context of the debate Hasegawa is usually referred to as "Tenkei."

17. Petralia points out that Tenkei's introduction would be the first intimation for Japanese readers of "the international scope of the debate [about Nietzsche]" as well as their first exposure "to Western interpretations of Nietzsche's thought" (p. 224).

18. Cited in Becker, p. 65.

19. Becker provides a translation of the section of the first part of the essay, which deals with Nietzsche, in an appendix. Petralia argues convincingly, on the basis of recent Japanese scholarship on the question, that it is unlikely that Chogyū had read much Nietzsche at all by the time he wrote this essay. His understanding appears to have come from a reading of Theobald Ziegler's *Die geistigen und sozialen Strömungen des neunzehnten Jahrhunderts* (Intellectual and social currents of the Nineteenth Century), a work first published in 1899 which devotes two chapters to a discussion of Nietzsche's ideas.

20. Based as it is on a cursory reading (if that) of a tiny portion of Nietzsche's *oeuvre*, the essay conveys a somewhat misleading sense of Nietzsche's philosophy. Chogyū conflates the ideas of the genius and the *Übermensch*, for example, and suggests that Nietzsche rejects history and tradition outright. He does, however, see that the paradigm of the *Übermensch* is "the artist and creator."

21. Georg Brandes, "Aristokratischer Radikalismus: Eine Abhandlung über Friedrich Nietzsche," *Deutsche Rundschau* 63 (1890). This is a German translation of the original Danish version which appeared the previous year. An English translation of the original constitutes Part I of George [*sic*] Brandes, *Friedrich Nietzsche* (London, 1914). The foremost Japanese researcher in this field, Sugita Hiroko, has shown that Chikufū also drew on Theobald Ziegler's *Friedrich Nietzsche* (Berlin, 1900) in the latter essays of his series.

22. The term is Petralia's; see his chapter 4.

23. A later entrant into the debate, the philosopher Nakajima Tokuzō, was another casualty: he was fired from his teaching positions in 1902 for promoting ideas that were "incompatible with the national polity."

24. First open letter to Chogyū, published in *Taiyō*, February/March 1902 (cited in Becker, p. 173).

25. Of the accounts of the philosophical differences between Wagner and Nietzsche, the best—because the most attentive to the details of their respective works—is that given by Roger Hollinrake in *Nietzsche, Wagner and the Philosophy of Pessimism* (London, 1982).

26. Maurice Adams, "The Ethics of Tolstoy and Nietzsche," *International Journal of Ethics* (Philadelphia) 11 (October 1900).

27. Cited in Becker, p. 72. The first chapter of the *Zhuang Zi* is entitled *Xiao yao you*, which means something like "Free and Easy Wandering."

28. Cited in Becker, pp. 133–35.

29. *Zhuang Zi*, ch. 8; cited in Becker, p. 133. Becker cites the translation by Richard Wilhelm from 1912, *Dschuang Dsï: Das wahre Buch vom südlichen Blütenland*. This is a pioneering version of the Zhuang Zi, but the Christianity-inspired tone of it tends to obscure the resonances with Nietzsche. The philosophically more sophisticated English translation by A. C. Graham, *Chuang Tzu: The Inner Chapters* (London, 1981), has been used here (modified with the help of Roger Ames). The other two passages quoted by Tenzui come from the introduction to chapter 11 and the end of chapter 16.

30. The reader may want to refer back to the essay by Roger Ames to see how the idea of *de* could be understood in relation to Nietzsche's will to power.

31. The parallel works well as long as one understands both *ming* and Nietzsche's *fatum* as coming as much from within as from outside the self. An illuminating discussion of *amor fati* (from a perspective informed by the Daoist and Buddhist traditions) is to be found in Nishitani's *The Self-Overcoming of Nihilism*.

32. Cited in Becker, p. 51. The month and year are not given in the date of the letter, but it has been convincingly argued that the date is March 31, 1894.

33. Among the works Ōgai read are: Brandes's "Aristocratic Radicalism" essay; Ola Hansson, *Der Materialismus in der Literatur* (Stuttgart, 1892); Johan-

nes Volkelt, *Ästhetische Zeitfragen* (München, 1895); and, later, Julius Zeitler, *Nietzsche's Ästhetik* (Leipzig, 1900).

34. Cited in Becker, p. 130.

35. Cited in Richard John Bowring, *Mori Ōgai and the Modernization of Japanese Culture* (Cambridge, 1979), p. 142. The Nietzsche quote is from *Zarathustra*, Prologue 5.

36. See Bowring, pp. 145–48. In the semi-autobiographical novel *Mōsō* (Daydreams), written in 1911, a character who sounds a lot like Ōgai speaks of "Nietzsche's philosophy of the overman [as] . . . an intoxicating wine rather than a satisfying food."

37. This was another factor that conditioned the reception of Nietzsche: the classical education in Chinese literature—or the lack of it. The earliest Nietzsche enthusiasts came from the first generation of intellectuals *not* to have received such an education.

38. Abe Jirō was another major figure in Japanese Nietzsche scholarship during the teens and twenties. His reading of Nietzsche in his study of 1919, *Nīche no Tsaratsustora kaishaku narabi ni hihyō* (Nietzsche's "Zarathustra": Interpretation and Critique), is informed by the ethical ideal of a move from the conscious ego to a universal self. But because of his concern with ethics, Abe's presentation of Nietzsche tends to etiolate the latter's critique of morality, rendering his ideas harmless by assimilating them to a humanitarian love of one's neighbor.

39. There is sadly little in English on Watsuji's work. Two interestingly different perspectives are offered by Robert N. Bellah, "Japan's Cultural Identity: Some Reflections on the Work of Watsuji Tetsurō," *Journal of Asian Studies* 24/4 (1965):573–94, and David Dilworth, "Watsuji Tetsurō (1889–1960): Cultural Phenomenologist and Ethician," *Philosophy East and West* 24/1 (1974):3–22. Piovesana's brief treatment, "The Ethical System of Watsuji Tetsurō," is worthwhile; a longer, though largely anecdotal, discussion is Furukawa Tetsushi's "Watsuji Tetsurō, the Man and his Work," which is appended to the only English translation that has been made of one of Watsuji's books: *A Climate: A Philosophical Study*, trans. Geoffrey Bownas (Tokyo, 1962).

40. Dilworth provides a helpful account of the profound influence of Sōseki's ideas on the subsequent development of Watsuji's thinking in the second section of his "Watsuji Tetsurō" article, "The Influence of Natsume Sōseki."

41. The hermeneutics of Dilthey came to be another major influence on Watsuji's many writings in the field of what Dilworth calls his "cultural phenomenology," as did the work of Scheler, Husserl, and Heidegger.

42. I am indebted for the following account of Miki's role in the Japanese Nietzsche reception to an unpublished paper by K. Ōishi of Tokyo University.

12

Nietzsche's Conception of Nature from an East-Asian Point of View

Ōkōchi Ryōgi, *translated by Graham Parkes*

I

In one of Nietzsche's posthumously published notes from the year 1881 we find the following noteworthy fragment:

My task: The dehumanization of nature and then the naturalization of humanity, after it has attained the pure concept of "nature." (*KSA* 9, 11[211])

Similar remarks are scattered throughout the notebooks from this period, such as the following:

Toward "A Sketch of a New Way of Living": *First book* in the style of the first movement of [Beethoven's] Ninth Symphony. *Chaos sive natura*: "on the dehumanization of nature." (*KSA* 9, 11[197])

The modern scientific counterpart to belief in God is belief in the universe as an *organism*: this disgusts me. This is to make what is quite rare and extremely derivative, the organic, which we perceive only on the surface of the earth, into something essential, universal, and eternal! This is still an anthropomorphizing of nature! (*KSA* 9, 11[201])

The naturalizing of humanity demands that one be ready for what is absolutely sudden and thwarting. (*KSA* 9, 11[228])

Human beings and philosophers have in the past projected the human *into nature*—let us dehumanize nature! (*KSA* 9, 11[238])

What did Nietzsche mean by such locutions as "the dehumanizing of nature," "the naturalizing of the human," or "the pure concept of nature"?

200

If we try to understand these fragments with respect to their possible interrelations, the path of Nietzsche's thinking will gradually become visible. The overall meaning of these notes can be discerned in an earlier fragment:

Principle idea: It is not that nature deceives us as individuals and furthers its purposes by such deception: it is rather that individuals interpret all existence according to individual—which is to say false—standards; and since we wish to justify this procedure, "nature" must appear as a deceiver. In fact there are no *individual truths*, but only individual *errors*—the *individual* is itself an *error*. Everthing that goes on in us is in itself something *other*, which is unknown to us: it is we who project intention and deception and morality on to nature. I am concerned to distinguish two things that are generally conflated: imaginary individuals and the actual "life- systems" of which each of us is an instance. The "individual" is merely the sum of conscious sensations and judgements and errors, a *belief*, a tiny piece of the actual life-system, or else many pieces of it that have been synthesized or phantasized together [*zusammengefabelt*], a "unity" that doesn't stand up. We are buds on a single tree—what do we know about what can become of us in the interests of the whole tree! But we have consciousness, as if we would and should be *everything*, a phantasm of the "I" and all "not-I." Let us stop feeling ourselves to be such phantastic egos! Let us gradually learn to throw off the imaginary individual! Discover the errors of the ego! Realize egoism as an error! And not understand altruism as its opposite! *That* would be love for other imaginary individuals! No! Let us go beyond "me" and "you"! Feel cosmically! (*KSA* 9, 11[7])

Nietzsche is here branding the deeply entrenched modern European idea that human being consists in individuality as an "error" and "phantasm," maintaining that the "imaginary" individual is in fact merely a piece of the greater "life-system," a bud on the great tree of nature. He is trying to go beyond the imaginary "me" and "you" to be one with the "cosmic" life-system as nature. This is nothing other than the "naturalization of the human," while the "pure concept of nature" refers to the "cosmic" "life-system."

The situation in the world today is in fact just the reverse: the imaginary individual uses his so-called "consciousness" to apprehend nature and thereby anthropomorphizes it through the willful imposition of human standards. One should, according to Nietzsche, restore to this falsified nature its own authenticity and "dehumanize" it; and from the human side one should re-"naturalize" oneself. To bring about these reversals is what Nietzsche sees as "[his] task."

Such reflections on "nature" are not, however, restricted to the year 1881, which was so decisive for his thinking, but they rather stretch throughout his career. Already in the unfinished but very important early essay "On Truth and Lie in the Extra-Moral Sense" (from 1878) we find the beginnings of this kind of thinking:

Once upon a time, in some out of the way corner of that universe which is dispersed into numberless twinkling solar systems, there was a star upon which clever beasts invented knowing. That was the most arrogant and mendacious minute of "world history," but nevertheless, it was only a minute. After nature had drawn a few breaths, the star cooled and congealed, and the clever beasts had to die.—One might invent such a fable, and yet he still would not have adequately illustrated how miserable, how shadowy and transient, how aimless and arbitrary the human intellect looks within nature. There were eternities during which it did not exist. And when it is all over with the human intellect, nothing will have happened. For this intellect has no additional mission which would lead it beyond human life. Rather, it is human, and only its possessor and begetter takes it so solemnly—as though the world's axis turned within it. But if we could communicate with the gnat, we would learn that he likewise flies through the air with the same solemnity, that he feels the flying center of the universe within himself. There is nothing so reprehensible and unimportant in nature that it would not immediately swell up like a balloon at the slightest puff of this power of knowing.[1]

We find many related remarks about nature in the writings of Nietzsche's later period, too. It will be instructive to cite several of them here:

Philosophers have sought to resolve the world into: 1) images (appearances) or 2) concepts or else into 3) the will—in short into something familiar to us from human beings—or else to assimilate it to the soul (as "God").

People have projected "cause and effect" as a relationship known to be valued for human activity into nature. . . .

The science of mathematics dissolves the world into *formulas*. . . .

Against this one must assert what concepts and formulas can only be: means of comprehension and calculability, *practical applicability* is the goal: that human beings may make use of nature, the reasonable limit.

Science: the appropriation of nature for human purposes— (*KSA* 11, 25[308])

to "humanize" the world means to feel ourselves more and more as masters in it— (*KSA* 11, 25[312])

"Science" (as it is pursued today) is the attempt to create a common sign-language for all phenomena, for the purpose of easier *calculability* and hence mastery of nature. However, this sign-language, which brings together all observed *laws, explains nothing*—it is simply a kind of shorthand *description* of what happens. (*KSA* 11, 26[227])

Extreme positions are not replaced by moderate ones, but by other extreme— but reversed—positions. And so belief in the absolute immorality of nature, in its lack of purpose or meaning, is the psychologically necessary *affect* when belief in God and an essentially moral order is no longer tenable. (*KSA* 12, 5[71] 4; *WP* 55)

Such reflections of Nietzsche's on nature, although fragmentary, were not any kind of "sideline" but were rather thought out with respect to his masterwork *Thus Spoke Zarathustra*, and consequently also in relation to his "most abyssal thought" of the eternal recurrence of the same. And from his final period of creative activity there comes the following reflection on the theme of nature:

I too speak of a "return to nature," though it is really not a going back but a *coming up*—up to a high, free, even terrible nature and naturalness, one that plays with great tasks. . . . (*TI*, IX 48)

All these reflections on nature and the natural surely demand a still more precise and careful interpretation. Nevertheless, we may draw from the passages quoted above the following provisional conclusions:

1) Nietzsche's thoughts on nature are not merely of incidental value and are by no means casual or peripheral; they are, on the contrary, essential and stand in clear and significant relationship to his major works.

2) They are consistently related to the objects of his passionate and polemical critiques—namely, to the topics of "faith" and "morality," and above all of "science" in the modern sense. We shall return to this issue later.

3) Nietzsche's thinking about "nature" and "the natural" no longer moves within the framework of modern scientific thinking after Descartes. His radical critique of the Western tradition is intended to break through this framework. This is not to say, however, that he no longer stands within the great and many-layered tradition of the West. This is evidenced by, among other things, his ambiguous and complex relationship to Spinoza, and also by his relationship to Goethe's view of nature, even though Nietzsche does not explicitly acknowledge these relationships.[2] One could therefore say that in his thinking about nature Nietzsche moves along the borders of Western thought. This "bordering" allows us to pose from our side a parallel question with respect to nature—namely, how in the East "nature" is to be understood.

II

In Japanese, the general term used for "nature" and its equivalents in other European languages is *shizen* (or *jinen*). In translating from these languages into Japanese, and also in the reverse direction, the two concepts are more or less automatically assumed to be equivalent in meaning. This is in a certain sense justified, especially when it is a question of nature in the modern scientific sense. In another sense, however, the two concepts are radically different in meaning. The European concept "nature," coming as it does from the Greek notion of *physis* by way of the Latin *natura*, has behind it a long history of changes in meaning. The range and depth of this concept are extremely complex, even though the objective and objectivized conception of nature as determined by the natural-scientific way of thinking is in our time the dominant one. It is this conception that Nietzsche opposes with such sharp criticism, and his aim is to regain a deeper and more primordial sense of this conception of nature.

The East Asian idea of *shizen* did not undergo a comparable historical development, since this kind of developmental-historical thinking has always been foreign to the Japanese, and to East Asians in general. Originally this concept does not mean anything objective or objectified that takes place in front of or outside of human beings, but is rather an expression of the spontaneous way of being of all things (it is written with the Chinese characters *zi ran*). In its original usage it does not take on a substantival but only an adjectival or adverbial form. In this respect it is essentially different from the objective, substantive nature-concept of modern Europe, although it *is* related to the notion expressed in the locutions "naturally" or "by nature." Through contact with modern European civilization, however, the Japanese concept underwent a considerable extension of its meaning, and it acquired thereby a twofold and double-layered sense. The Japanese word "nature" (*shizen*) became a substantive and, used in this way, came to mean the same as the objective, natural-scientific concept of modern Europe. In spite of this, the original sense of the word at the deeper level of meaning remained unchanged. But this circumstance is not one of which everyday Japanese life is sufficiently aware, and indeed it seems to have sunk deep into the unconscious. This is why the Japanese conception of nature is so ambiguous; both conceptions are for the most part obscured, while at the same time they are widely used as being roughly equivalent.

If we now introduce Nietzsche's conception of nature, as we cursorily sketched it above, into the sphere of this problem, it may work as a mediating factor between the not quite congruent levels of meaning of the two Japanese concepts. It is not possible to articulate the nature of this bridging in detail here, but the interested reader of Japanese may wish to consult the relevant literature on the topic.[3] For the time being we shall take, as a working hypothesis so to speak, the concepts of "nature" in the European sense and *shizen* in the Japanese sense as being roughly equivalent.

If in thinking about the Asian conception of nature as *shizen* we go back to the ancient Chinese worldview, a familiar passage from Lao Zi immediately comes to mind:

> There is a thing confusedly formed,
> Born before heaven and earth.
> Silent and void
> It stands alone and does not change,
> Goes round and does not weary.
> It is capable of being the mother of the world.
> I know not its name
> So I style it "the way."
> I give it the makeshift name of "the great."
> Being great, it is further described as receding,
> Receding, it is described as far away,
> Being far away, it is described as turning back.
> Hence the way is great; heaven is great; earth is great; and the king
> is also great. Within the realm there are four things that are great,
> and the king counts as one.
> Man models himself on earth,
> Earth on heaven,
> Heaven on the way,
> And the way on that which is naturally so.[1]

According to Lao Zi's "cosmological-mythical" thinking as expressed in these last four lines, to live in accordance with nature is the best, most ethical, highest, and in this sense "most natural" way of life. Such a way of life is for Lao zi at the same time a kind of "non-acting" (*mui*; Chinese: *wu wei*), a "non-interfering self-so-ing" (*mui shizen*; Chinese: *wu wei zi ran*). This is expressed in chapter 63 of the same text:

Do that which consists in taking no action; pursue that which is not meddlesome; savour that which has no flavour.

Make the small big and the few many; do good to him who has done you an injury.

Lay plans for the accomplishment of the difficult before it becomes difficult; make something big by starting with it when small.

Difficult things in the world must needs have their beginnings in the easy; big things must needs have their beginnings in the small.

It is extremely difficult for us "moderns" properly to understand such paradoxical utterances of ancient Chinese wisdom as "living according

to nature" and "practicing non-interfering activity" as they were originally intended. From the perspective of the modern scientific, active
(and even activist) way of thinking, such an understanding is open to
the criticism that precisely this kind of "idle" and passive attitude is
what brought about the quietistic resignation that has for centuries held
the whole of Asia in a state of "Asiatic standstill." Such a criticism may
even be to some extent justified. However, anyone who sees the nineteenth century in Europe as a bygone era of "happiness" in contrast to
the unhappiness and the "abyssal" nature of our own century—in other
words, anyone who has encountered Friedrich Nietzsche—will not find
this criticism to be of great moment, and will probably regard the "practice of non-interfering activity" in a very different light.

"Practicing inaction" does not, of course, mean detached contemplation in the sense of "doing nothing"; it signifies rather that all human
activity, even subjective and willed activity, is—as long as it is "according to nature," which is to say "spontaneous" and therefore "natural"—
proper and true activity. A Korean philosopher has written about this as
follows:

That paradoxical principle of "inaction" (wu wei) by no means signifies a complete suspension of activity. As passive activity in the sense of letting-be, instead
of artificial fabrication, it constitutes the methodical moment in a higher ethical
mode of life, the meaning of which—insofar as it consists in a sublimity that
supersedes everything concrete—is nevertheless without ideality, and thus does
not come into conflict with the substantiality of prosaic existence.[5]

The expression "*passive* activity in the sense of letting-be" is a function
of the limited expressive capabilities of the Indo-European languages.
"Practicing inactivity" is neither passive nor active, but rather transcends the dichotomy between active and passive and is precisely "natural" activity. It is between such an active and willed activity and an
apparently passive letting-be that the dimension of a "higher" mode of
life than the "prosaic"—that is, merely intellectual or quotidian—way
of being is opened up.

In this context it may be instructive to adduce some ideas from the
sphere of medieval Japanese thought, and specifically from a text that is
still widely read today, the *Tannishō* by Shinran (1173–1262):

Birth is attained through Amida's compassionate means, when Faith is firmly
established; hence, our own contrivance is not to be involved. If we look up to
the Vow-Power all the more as we realize our evilness, the feeling of tenderness
and forbearance will arise in us as a course of nature.

In anything related to Birth, we should, without clever thought, always remind ourselves fondly of our deep indebtedness to Amida's Benevolence. Then the Nembutsu is uttered. This is the natural outcome. Non-contrivance on our side is called "naturalness." This, indeed, is the Other-Power.[6]

And in one of his last letters Shinran writes about nature as follows:

We say "nature" (*jinen*): *ji* means "of itself," having nothing to do with the doing and saying of human beings, it means "letting be" or "letting do"; *nen* means the same thing. . . . *Jinen* originally means letting be and letting say. The vow of Amida Buddha has from the very start nothing to do with human doing and saying. Trust in Amida Buddha's accepting human beings [into the Pure Land] occurs naturally, and has nothing to do with whether the person thinks himself good or evil. Precisely this is "natural"; so I have heard [from my teacher Hōnen]. The vow consists in letting us human beings become the highest Buddhas. The highest Buddha has neither form nor color. Because he has no form he is called "nature" [*jinen*]. If he shows himself in a form, he is no longer a highest Buddha, and so there is no highest Nirvana. In order to let us recognize this formlessness the Master taught me Amida Buddha in this way. Amida Buddha is the means to let us know how nature really works.[7]

We see here that all the basic ideas of Pure Land (*Jōdo*) Buddhism— Amida-Buddha (infinity), Nembutsu (the chanting of his name), "the power of the Other" (*tariki*), nirvana, and so forth—ultimately converge upon the idea of "nature" (*jinen*). However many ways there may be of understanding these ideas, the important thing for our present purposes is simply that a single idea of "nature" should constitute such a crucial focal point in the thinking of one of Japan's greatest religious figures.

Let us now turn to the way nature is understood in modern Japanese thought, which has been "baptized by science," as it were. The philosopher Nishida Kitarō (1870–1945) has written about nature as follows:

There is only one reality, although it presents itself in various ways when seen from different perspectives. One tends to think of nature [*shizen*] as an objective reality quite independent of our subjectivity, but strictly speaking this kind of nature is not a true reality but merely an abstract concept. The essence of nature consists in an event of immediate experience in which subject and object are not yet separated. What we think of as the real plant, for example, is the living plant with all its shapes and colors, the actually perceived fact. It is only when we reflect on this, abstracting the moment of subjective activity from this concrete reality, that it appears as if it were purely objective nature. And what the natural scientists call nature, in the strictest sense of the word, is an extreme case of this kind of "objective" thinking; it is nature at its most abstract, at the farthest remove from true reality. . . .

The aim of science these days is to become as objective as possible. Accordingly, psychological phenomena must be explained physiologically, physiological phenomena chemically, chemical phenomena physically, and physical phenomena mechanically. But what is this purely mechanical explanation which underlies all these other modes of explanation? What is called pure matter is something that we can never actually experience, and anything that is in any way experienceable must enter consciousness as a phenomenon of consciousness. But everything that appears as a fact of consciousness is wholly subjective, and not any kind of purely objective matter. What is called pure matter possesses no graspable, positive characteristics whatsover, but only quantitative ones that have to do with space, time, and motion; it is a purely abstract concept like a concept in mathematics.[8]

What then is this "spirit" which we usually think of in opposition to nature? . . . One usually thinks of spirit as an independent reality separate from objective nature. But just as purely objective nature separated from the unifying subject is an abstraction, so too is purely subjective spirit separated from objective nature an abstraction. . . .

One usually thinks of spirit as a unifying function of reality, and as a particular mode of reality opposed to nature. But there is actually no unifying function that would be separate from that which is being unified, just as there is no subjective spirit that would be separate from objective nature. To say that we know something means simply that we become one with this something. When we look at a flower, we become one with the flower. (*A Study of Good*, ch. 9)

It is interesting that Vincent Van Gogh had some similar things to say about Japanese art in a letter he wrote to his brother Theo in 1888:

In looking at Japanese art we encounter people who are apparently wise, intelligent, and even philosophical. How do they spend their time? Do they try to calculate the distance between the earth and the moon? No! Do they study the policies of Bismarck? Not that either. They study a single blade of grass.

But this blade of grass gradually allows them to draw and paint plants of all kinds, all seasons, landscapes with all kinds of mountains and fields, and eventually even animals and human beings. This is how they spend their lives. But life is too short for us to be able to paint everything.

Believe me, they live amidst nature as if they were themselves flowers. Isn't what these Japanese teach us in fact true and genuine religion?[9]

There are remarkable parallels here with the ideas of Nishida which we have just cited. It is no coincidence that Van Gogh intuited in the work of Japanese painters—while we do not know, unfortunately, just whose works he was familiar with, he is surely referring to some Japanese wood-block prints (*ukiyo-e*)—such a *natural* wisdom and way of life. It may have been precisely because he was not a philosopher, not someone compelled to think in language, but rather a painter capable of thinking in form and color, that Van Gogh was able to attain intuitive and empathetic insight into the nature of art, religion, and life itself.

III

In the course of the preceding reflections on the East Asian conception of nature as *shizen* a number of apparently paradoxical ideas came to light: that "inaction" is the highest mode of a life that takes its lead from nature; that becoming-Buddha is a natural process that takes place without the contributions of human activity and ideas; that contemplating a flower is becoming one with the flower; and so forth. All these expressions are attempts to overcome the dualistic thinking that is indispensable for analytical reflection by the intellect. They are all trying to go beyond doing and letting, self- and other-power, subject and object, in order to reach the totality that is the true naturalness of things. Similar attempts have been made in the West in, for example, the existential philosophies of Kierkegaard and Heidegger, Hegel's dialectic of the Concept, Spinoza's idea of *deus sive natura*, and the *unio mystica* of the medieval thinkers, corresponding to the philosophies of totality that have been (and are being) developed in the East, where intuitive experience is primary.

It is thus understandable why natural-scientific thinking and the technological mode of thought that developed from it in the modern age, as well as the concomitant idea of developmental progress, did not evolve in the East. So-called natural-scientific thinking is a thinking that objectivizes everything and is to this extent a mechanistic, materialistic, and anthropocentric mode of thought. Another Japanese philosopher, Nishitani Keiji, has addressed this issue in the following terms:

Since the advent of modern times, the world view of natural science has been tied up with the question of atheism. The rejection of the existence of a personal God arose as a consequence of the rejection of a teleological view of the world. Generally speaking this atheism has taken the standpoint of scientific rationalism. Its contents boil down to a form of materialism. And its spirit is "progress."

The element of materialism in modern atheism relates to the fact that it has taken the essence of the things of the world to be matter. The element of scientific rationalism stems from an assertion of the power and right of human reason to control such a world. In contrast to the standpoint of an earlier metaphysical rationality that considered itself constituted by and made subject to the divine order of creation, the new rationalism has represented human reason as coming forth to dismantle the framework of divine order. The world has been seen as materialistic and mechanistic because its order lost the sense of dependence on the *personal* will of God it once had under the teleological scheme. The character of the world came to be divorced form the personal character of God. This meant, in turn, that the world was considered to be completely accessible to human reason, inasmuch as the materialistic world view implied that the stuff of the world is absolutely passive to the control of man. Conversely put, in conformity with the notion that all things in the world are essentially reducible to matter, and from the perspective of the one who controls the world, man arrived at an awareness of his own reason as something absolutely active and absolutely free. Human reason was thus transferred to a field on which it seemed to enjoy absolute authority, where it no longer had the need, nor even the opportunity, to see itself as belonging to a divine order or as subordinate to the will of God. [10]

Japan, however, had to adopt and "imitate" this natural-scientific way of thinking, and above all its "practical applicability," out of a national necessity and with a "naive and uncritical" zeal, at a time when in the West itself there were already some major figures such as Baudelaire and Nietzsche who had seen through the nature of the scientific way of thinking and experienced fear and anxiety in the face of it. [11] Although Nietzsche was not able to gauge the full and frightening extent of scientific "achievement" as exemplified in atomic weapons, the destruction of the environment, organ transplants, and so on, he was nevertheless prophetic in writing the following:

Science today has absolutely *no* belief in itself, let alone an ideal above it. . . .

Today there are plenty of modest and worthy laborers among scholars, too, who are happy in their little nooks; and because they are happy there, they sometimes demand rather immodestly that one ought to be content with things today, generally—especially in the domain of science, where so much that is useful remains to be done. I am not denying that; the last thing I want is to destroy the pleasure these honest workers take in their craft: for I approve of their work. But that one works rigorously in the sciences and that there are contented workers certainly does *not* prove that science as a whole possesses a goal, a will, an ideal, or the passion of a great faith. The opposite is the case:
. . . science today is a *hiding place* for every kind of discontent, disbelief, gnawing worm, *despectio sui*, bad conscience—it is the unrest of the *lack* of ideals, the suffering from the *lack* of any great love, the discontent in the face of involuntary contentment.

Oh, what does science not conceal today! how much, at any rate, is it *meant* to conceal! The proficiency of our finest scholars, their heedless industry, their heads smoking day and night, their very craftsmanship—how often the real meaning of all this lies in the desire to keep something hidden from oneself! Science as a means of self-narcosis: *do you have experience of that?*

Whoever associates with scholars knows that one occasionally wounds them to the marrow with some harmless word; one incenses one's scholarly friends just when one means to honor them, one can drive them beside themselves merely because one has been too coarse to realize with whom one was really dealing—with *sufferers* who refuse to admit to themselves what they are, with drugged and heedless men who fear only one thing: *regaining consciousness.* (*GM* III, 23)

Nietzsche realized that thinking that is merely scientific is an "abyss" and in this sense one of the "great nihilistic movements," among which Nietzsche counted such religions as Christianity and Buddhism. Unless its practitioners—in this case scientists—are sufficiently self-aware, this mode of thinking can become a narcotic, "opium for the scholars" as it were. Nietzsche's critique of science, in his own words, "the questionability of science" in the dual sense, can be traced from his earliest through his latest writings. And it is only from this broad horizon that his reflections on the "pure concept of nature," as well as on the "naturalization of the human" and the "dehumanization of nature," can be properly understood.

There have been some attempts recently to synthesize the predominant Western and Eastern ways of thinking as a way of coming to terms with the current global crisis,[12] although such attempts, whether they acknowledge it or not, are simply drawing the ultimate conclusions from what Nietzsche was writing in the early eighteen-seventies. For example:

It is not a matter of getting rid of science but rather of *mastering* it. For science is in all its aims and methods utterly dependent on philosophical ideas, *though it easily forgets this. The dominant philosophy has to consider the problem of the extent to which science is allowed to grow: it must determine its* value! (*KSA* 7, 19[24])

Nietzsche was of course unable to foresee the transformation modern physics was to undergo after Einstein, nor did he have much acquantance with "Eastern mysticism." In fact he came "too early," like the madman in *The Gay Science* (aph. 125). This is perhaps the reason his attempt to think through and overcome "modernity" could not succeed, and why his radical critique of the entire Western tradition ended up in a cul-de-sac, or led to such difficult ideas as the "eternal recurrence of the same" or the "will to power." But does his greatness as a thinker not lie also in the fact that even before the end of the last century he clearly foresaw the great danger of the scientific mode of thought that was purely Cartesian and Newtonian, and sought to overcome it?

With respect to the recent attempts to engage this issue from a comparative perspective, one has to ask whether it is advisable to subsume such different ways of thinking as Hinduism, Buddhism, Daoism, and Zen under as global a concept as "Eastern mysticism," as some of these attempts have tended to do. One might also question the wisdom of neglecting Western mysticism, which constitutes an important part of Christianity. At any rate everything seems to indicate that the question of nature—or, more precisely, new reflection on the concept "nature"— has become one of the most important issues in the West as well as the East. Without scientific thinking and its various achievements, the world of today would be unable to subsist; on the other hand this kind of thinking is no longer capable of dealing with the problems that currently beset us. This has by now become clear to everyone, at least in the so-called "developed countries." The kind of scientific thinking that objectifies everything, as well as its "practical applicability" and technological mode of thought directed toward "utility," must all be restricted, "mastered," and understood in context—or else the human species will stand little chance of surviving. The question then arises: how and where can we find a standpoint from which scientific-technological activity can be overseen and, if necessary, overcome? Is it perhaps to be found in Nietzsche's attempts at a "pure concept of nature"? Or else in the ancient Asian tradition with its "inaction-practicing naturalness"? Or in the attempt at a possible synthesis of both in the "transition to the solar age"? We simply do not know. While we cannot simply transpose ourselves back into the past, it might be possible to return to the tradition in order to reappropriate its ancient wisdom—to "incorporate" it, as Nietzsche says—for the sake of the future. This might even be a necessity [Notwendigkeit] in the Nietzschean sense—in the sense of a "turn of adversity" [Wende der Not].[13]

Notes

1. *Philosophy and Truth: Selections from Nietzsche's Notebooks of the Early 1870s*, ed. and trans. Daniel Breazeale (Atlantic Highlands, 1979), p. 79 (translation slightly modified).

2. The phrase quoted above, *chaos sive natura*, is of course reminiscent of Spinoza's *deus sive natura* and his distinction between *natura naturans* and *natura naturata*. Even the "ultimate formula" of Nietzsche's thought, *amor fati*, recalls Spinoza's *amor dei intellectualis*.

3. Kokusai-Kyōdō-Tōgi (International Colloquium), *Shizen towa nani ka* (What is nature?) (Kyoto, 1984); Ōkōchi Ryōgi, *Jinen no fukken: Nīche no kagaku-hihan to Shinran no jinen hōni* (The restoration of nature: Nietzsche's

critique of science and Shinran's idea of natural spontaneity) (Tokyo, 1985); Yabu Akira, *Honyaku no shisō—shizen to nature* (Thoughts on the translation of "shizen" and "nature") (Tokyo, 1977).

4. Lao Tzu, *Tao Te Ching*, trans. D. C. Lau (Hong Kong, 1982).

5. Cho Kah Kyung, "The Significance of Nature in the Chinese World of Thought" (Dissertation, Heidelberg University, 1956).

6. Shinran, *Tannishō*, trans. Fujiwara Ryosetsu (Kyoto, 1966), p. 68.

7. Shinran, *Mattōshōo*, trans. Ueda Yoshifumi (Kyoto, 1978), sec. V.

8. Nishida Kitarō, *A Study of Good*, trans. Valdo Viglielmo (Tokyo, 1969), ch. 8 (translation modified in collaboration with the original translator).

9. This passage, in a slightly different translation, can be found in Irving Stone, ed., *Dear Theo: The Autobiography of Vincent Van Gogh* (New York, 1969), p. 389.

10. Nishitani Keiji, *Religion and Nothingness*, trans. Jan Van Bragt (Berkeley and Los Angeles, 1982), p. 53.

11. EN—This is a major theme in an earlier text of Nishitani's, *The Self-Overcoming of Nihilism*, where many of the author's reflections are based on essays on this topic by Karl Löwith.

12. See, for example, Fritjof Capra, *The Turning Point* (New York, 1985).

13. EN—This idea of Nietzsche's (expressed in the play between *Notwendigkeit* and *Wende der Not* in *Thus Spoke Zarathustra*) is another major theme in Nishitani's *The Self Overcoming of Nihilism*.

13

The Problem of the Body in
Nietzsche and Dōgen

Arifuku Kōgaku, *translated by Graham Parkes*

As is well known, Nietzsche characterized the body as a "great reason" and the spirit as "small reason" (Z I, 4). In so doing he not only assigned a priority to body-reason over intellect-reason, but also suggested that the latter is a mere "tool or toy" of the former. Dōgen, one of the greatest Japanese Zen masters of the Kamakura period (1200–1253), similarly emphasized the priority of somatic practice over spiritual-intellectual training, although he held that both were important. A comparison of the ideas of these two thinkers concerning the body is best introuced by a consideration of the Nietzschean and Buddhist critiques of the idea of the "I," or ego. I shall then give an account of Dōgen's idea of "somatic practice" in Zen, and of Nietzsche's assertion of the primacy of body over soul, or spirit. We shall conclude with a consideration of the body's relation to "great nature," which will provide a context for summing up the major points of correspondence and difference between the two thinkers.

I

According to the well-known dictum of Pascal, the human being is "a reed, the weakest thing in nature, but a thinking reed" (*Pensées* 347). It was above all Descartes and Kant who conceived of the human subject as the thinking I, as intellect or reason, insofar as they took thought (*pensée, cogitatio*) to be the essence of the human I, and privileged the thinking I as the most excellent of all finite beings. For Descartes the

214

proposition "cogito, ergo sum" is the first principle of philosophy, and for Kant the basic proposition of the synthetic unity of apperception—"I think"—is the "highest principle of all operation of the understanding."[1] This view distinguishes the rational human being as superior to animals and plants, which function on instinct. On the other hand, however, the emphasis of the superiority of the thinking I over nature and the body has two attendant disadvantages. In the first place, the more emphasis is placed on the rationality of the thinking I, the more one tends to forget the importance of the senses as natural human capabilities. The human being, *qua* embodied, stands in direct contact with the environment and the natural world, while reason and understanding deal with the things of nature in only an indirect way. Nietzsche warns of the danger of absolutizing the intellect in a passage from *Twilight of the Idols*:

"Reason" is the cause of our falsification of the evidence of the senses. Insofar as the senses show becoming, passing away, change, they do not lie. . . . But Heraclitus will always be right in this, that being is an empty fiction. The "apparent" world is the only one: the "real" world has only been lyingly added. (*TI* III, 2)

The second danger lies in the finite nature of the thinking I, insofar as it unable to attain complete objectivity in its knowledge. The thinking I, which proceeds according to concepts and rules, is a pivot upon and from which the individual empirical I receives its transcendental universality (consciousness in general, reason, and understanding), and conversely the transcendental supra-individual universality can be concretized and actualized through the empirical I-subject. But if one were to carry out the self-projection of reason and the self-legislation of the understanding in the realm of nature without sober reflection and critique, one would end up with a merely dogmatic subjectivism in accord with the dictum of Protagoras: "the human being is the measure of all things"—which would be an expression of the worst anthropocentrism.

Our "I" is then "the only being in accordance with which we make or understand all being. . ." (*KSA* 12, 2[91]). The value, truth, and significance of the world would all then lie "in our interpretation" (*WP* 616). If "all other beings are made" in the image of the thinking I, then "ultimately the belief in the 'I' stands or falls with belief in logic, i.e., in the metaphysical truth of the categories of reason" (*KSA* 12, 7[55]). It would appear, then, that all objects of knowledge are in a sense projections of the reason of the thinking I, posited in advance by the human understanding. These categories of reason operate by means of distinctions and oppositions such as those between substance and accident, cause and effect, and action and agent. The first of what Nietzsche calls in *Twilight of the Idols* "The Four Great Errors" is that of "mistaking the consequence for the cause," which he also refers to as "reason's intrinsic form of corruption" (*TI* VI, 1). He sees such "basic errors of reason," which (mis)understand all activity as being produced by an agent, by a subject, as having become petrified in language, which accounts for their tenacity. One of the many striking examples of this kind of "seduction by language" is to be found in *On the Genealogy of Morals*:

[It] is as if there were a neutral substratum behind the strong man, which was *free* to express strength or not to do so. But there is no such substratum; there is no "being" behind doing, effecting, becoming; "the doer" is merely a fiction added to the deed—the deed is everything. (*GM* I, 13)

If, moreover, the thinking I, which as reason has been considered by many philosophers in the tradition as being capable of attaining eternal truths, is only—as Nietzsche claims—something in the process of becoming, one phenomenon among many, our attitude toward previous theories of knowledge will be radically altered. If one takes "becoming"—as both Nietzsche and the Buddhists do—as the only reality, one can no longer expect the categories of reason to work at all in the struggle to attain truth.

Buddhism maintains the principle of I-lessness from the ontological-metaphysical standpoint as well as from the ethical-religious standpoint. With respect to the former, the basic contention is that all entities and activities are ephemeral and pass away in constant flux. Everything constantly arises, passes away, and disappears. There is therefore no eternal substance, but rather everything is characterized by "emptiness" (*śūnyāta*). Buddhism introduces a principle here of "codependent arising" (*pratītyasamutpāda*), according to which there are no things independent or self-sufficient, but rather everything is dependent on something else, which leads to an "absolute relativity" of everything that happens. Thus the way of being of everything is characterized by the Buddhists as "I-less" or "empty." In calling the world "empty," however, Buddhism is far from assuming the existence of some heavenly world beyond this world. On this point it is far from Platonism and Christianity—and indeed quite close to Nietzsche's "active" nihilism.

The ethical-religious standpoint is expressed in the following passage from the "Genjōkōan" chapter of Dōgen's major work, the *Shōbōgenzō*:

To learn the Buddha Way is to learn the self. To learn the self is to forget the self. To forget the self is to be enlightened by all things. To be enlightened by all things is to liberate one's own body-mind as well as other body-minds from the bondage of the small "I."

Buddhism calls for human beings to act I-lessly because it holds that the source of all evils and errors lies in the egotistical I. The first move Buddhism makes, therefore, is to try to go beyond the standpoint of the I. Dōgen has the following to say about the relationship between the Buddha Law [the Dharma] and the self: "It is an error to seek the Dharma through the self. But when the Dharma has been received through the right transmission, one's real self is immediately illuminated" ("Genjōkōan").

Zen Buddhism also emphasizes along with I-lessness the idea of "not-thinking." It is less a case of suspending human thought altogether than of effecting a liberation from egoistic attitudes. As formulated by Descartes and Kant, thinking is a function of the I, without which it would be impossible. Not-thinking is possible only insofar as the individual becomes a purely somatic "subject." In ordinary thinking, one does not concentrate on the actualization of the object of thought, or at least the object is not itself actualized. Even if I say the word "fire" a thousand times my tongue will not get burned. There is always a distance, then, between thinking and being, concept and object. Buddhism is concerned to abolish the dualities created by such distancings, and emphasizes the harmonious correspondence between the terms of such separations as well as the nonduality of all contraries.

In the second place, not-thinking means a concentration on the activity itself, which is above all effected by the body. However much one thinks of the good, one does not produce any good merely by thinking about it. Every activity demands that the human being return to and become body and thing, which is ultimately a return to nature. Although there may be thinking at the source of an action, it is necessary to move out of thinking and come back to things and to nature in order for activity to be consummated.

II

Zen Buddhism has an eminently practical philosophy, on account of which it is called a "religion of practice." It always emphasizes the nonduality of body (*Leib*) and mind, spirit and body (*Körper*). As a result, orthodox Buddhism does not acknowledge an immortality of the soul. Within Buddhist practice a distinction is nevertheless made between spiritual practice and somatic practice. As Dōgen puts it in a chapter of the *Shōbōgenzō* entitled "Shinjingakudō" ("Body-Soul-Practice"):

There are two methods of learning the Buddha Way: learning with the mind and learning with the body. Spiritual practice means learning with all the capabilities of the mind. . . . Somatic practice means learning with the body, and practicing especially with the body of flesh and blood. The Buddha-body emerges only out of the practice of the Buddha Way, and what emerges out of the practice of the Buddha Way is called the Buddha-body.

In this chapter, Dōgen first deals with the soul and then subsequently with the body, although it is clear that he assigns priority to the latter. A basic tenet of Buddhist practice is that the body is more important than the mind, which is a reversal of the everyday understanding of the mind as being superior to the body.[2]

There are in fact three aspects to Buddhist practice, corresponding to three methods of learning the Buddha Way: precepts (law), meditation, and wisdom. This last naturally has to do with spiritual practice, while precepts and meditation concern somatic practice—the former external practice and the latter internal.

The precepts, which belong to the first level of Buddhist study, have to do mostly with the regulations governing everyday life, with how one is to behave as a good human being and a proper Buddhist. Zen is especially concerned with rules of conduct in the monastery, which regulate the activities of washing oneself, eating, drinking, and working. Dōgen even takes up the topic of the evacuation of the bowels, describing in some detail the proper way for the Zen adept to proceed in such matters. The Zen idea that one is to direct the spirit mediately, by means of direct mastery of somatic behavior, is manifested especially concretely at this level of practice, in contrast to everyday life in which such rigor and precision is generally neglected.

In any case the first task for the student of Zen is to accommodate his own body to the forms and principles of behavior and praxis. It is significant that aside from Zen Buddhism, all the traditional "ways" [dō] of art in Japan—the tea ceremony, the art of the sword, the Noh drama—lay special value on the beauty of the physical form and have developed sophisticated aesthetics of those respective forms. This is a manifestation of the conviction that the human being can gain control of the spirit or intellect only through the consummation of physical form by way of mastery of the body. In the beginning, considerable effort is required to make all actions and passions of the self conform to a definite concrete pattern; but by shackling oneself with such a form, it is possible to shape the body, which otherwise remains one-sidedly instinctual in its nature, into a proper and appropriate agent. The everyday attitude attempts to master the body by means of the mind, on the premise that the subject of consciousness, the I, is able to control to some extent what goes on with the brain, the mouth, and other movements of the body. Dōgen's approach to the mind-body relationship reverses this everyday attitude, insofar as he advocates the mastery of the mind by means of the body.

It is especially at the second stage, which is called *jo* (Skt. *dhyana*: meditation), that the body comes to assume a quite different role in the body-mind relationship. In devoting oneself exclusively to the practice of *zazen* (sitting meditation) it is necessary to give up all activity in the form of acting upon the external world, to cut off deliberately and artificially all theoretical concern and practical dealings with the rest of the world. According to Dōgen: "One must abandon all opportunities for intercourse with other people and things, and discontinue every form of letting or doing." It is a case from the very start of reversing the usual mode of being of the self as I-subject.

Zazen practice is the self-projection of the body into the "great nature" as cosmos. For this one needs a kind of *epoché*, an absolute checking or restraining of all thinking and acting. But this is more than an *epoché* as a theoretical procedure as practiced in contemporary phenomenology; it is an utterly practical procedure by means of which the self is able to transform itself into the pure body-self. In zazen no intrusion of the mind is permitted. The formation of the Buddha-body is undertaken by the body alone. Zazen is the formation of an "overhuman" (*übermenschlich*) body by means of the human body. Dōgen describes the techniques employed in zazen as follows:

One thinks neither of the good nor of the bad. One may call upon neither the mind or consciousness nor on judging or thinking. One should especially not intend to become a Buddha. One is to detach oneself completely from others and the world.[3]

In zazen one is to sit immobile, like a huge mountain. From this there emerges "not-thinking," which means the suspension of all mental activity and willing. It is nothing other than the human being's becoming through the body a thing of nature. It is in this that "the mysterious art of zazen practice" consists.

An expression from everyday Japanese may help to illuminate the somatic nature of zazen. One conveys the idea of dedicating oneself to-tally to something by saying *karadagoto*. This means, literally, to do something with the strength of one's whole body, but it also carries the connotation of having one's heart in it—perhaps something like the En-glish "body and soul." Dōgen poses the following question: "Does one attain the Buddha Way through the mind or through the body?" He goes on to answer as follows:

In Buddhism one can naturally learn the Buddha Way both through the body and through the mind. But if one strives with the mind alone, one will never in all eternity attain the Buddha Way. It can be attained only if one gives up all egoistical knowing, thinking, interpreting, and understanding, only if one gives up one's mind in the sense of the small I as subject of consciousness. A great Zen master (Kyōgen; Chinese: Xiangyan) attained enlightenment upon hearing a pebble strike bamboo. Another master (Reiun; Chinese: Lingyun) upon seeing a peach tree in blossom. These are cases of attaining enlightenment through the body and mastering the Buddha-Dharma. One can approach the Buddha Way closer and closer the more one frees oneself from egoistical thinking, knowing, and perceiving, and devotes oneself entirely to zazen practice through the body. The Buddha Way is therefore to be attained above all through the body.[4]

Zen Buddhism's strong emphasis on somatic practice can be further explained, perhaps, by considering the Japanese words for body (*Leib*): *mi* and *karada*. As well as the literal meaning "body," *mi* also means "self," or "I," or one's "own." There is a saying in Japanese: "*Mi o sutete koso, ukabu se mo are*," which means something like: "One can help oneself only when one leaves one's body—that is, gives up the small, egoistical I." This is why Dōgen says, "The Dharma is of far more value than our small body. Abandon the world and follow the Way. If we think we are of more value than the Dharma it will never be transmitted, received, or attained."[5]

We saw earlier that, for Nietzsche, to hold to the rationality of the thinking I at any price was accompanied by two dangers: on the one hand, that of neglecting or denigrating the roles of the senses and the body, and on the other, of forgetting the finite nature of human reason and of absolutizing the thinking I. Nietzsche calls the proponents of this kind of position "despisers of the body," about whom he has Zarathustra say the following:

Let them not learn differently nor teach differently, but only bid farewell to their own bodies—and thus become dumb.

"Body am I and soul"—so speaks the child. And why should one not speak like children?

But the awakened, the enlightened man says: I am body entirely, and nothing beside; and soul is only a word for something about the body.

The body is a great reason, a multiplicity with *one* sense, a war and a peace, a herd and a herdsman.

Your small reason, my brother, which you call "spirit," is also an instrument of your body, a little instrument and toy of your great reason.

You say "I" and are proud of this word. But greater than this—although you will not believe in it—is your body and its great reason, which does not say "I" but does "I." (Z I, 4)

The Western philosophical tradition prior to Nietzsche had for the most part despised the body and the earth, having invented a pure spirit equipped with reason as the knowing subject of eternal truth. Not only did most previous thinkers ignore the body, they even regarded it as an enemy. "Their insanity," writes Nietzsche in a note from 1888, "was to believe that one could carry around a 'beautiful soul' in a misbegotten corpse" (*KSA* 13, 14[96]). In the Preface to *The Gay Science* he proposes a radical characterization of the relation of traditional philosophy to the body:

The unconscious disguise of philosophical needs under the cloaks of the objective, ideal, purely spiritual goes to frightening lengths—and often I have asked myself whether, taking a large view, philosophy has not been merely an interpretation of the body and a *misunderstanding of the body*. Behind the highest value judgments that have hitherto guided the history of thought, there are concealed misunderstandings of the physical constitution—of individuals or classes or even whole races. (*GS* Preface 2)

This oblivion of the primacy of the body with respect to the soul and spirit is all the more surprising when one considers that, although the form of the body is mutable—a major reason for its having been denigrated metaphysically—it is at least concrete, in contrast to the invisibility of the soul or spirit. On the grounds that we can know next to nothing concretely about the soul, Nietzsche maintains that the body is "by far the richer phenomenon, affording much clearer observation" (*KSA* 11, 40[15]). "It is therefore methodologically permissible," he says, "to take the *richer* phenomenon as a key to the understanding of the poorer" (*KSA* 12, 2[91]). This statement provides a major clue to Nietzsche's way of inquiring into the human condition.

The "soul" was, Nietzsche admits, a seductive and mysterious idea, to which the philosophical idealists and rationalists of the tradition were firmly attached. But, when one thinks about it, the idea of the body is surely more seductive and mysterious:

The human body, in which the whole of the farthest and nearest past of all organic becoming again becomes vitally incarnate, through which and way beyond which an enormous inaudible river seems to flow: the body is a far more amazing idea than the old "soul." (*KSA* 11, 36[35])

At the same time, this history of the body has a future:

The entire development of the spirit is perhaps a matter of the *body*: it is the story—now becoming perceptible—of a *higher body's shaping itself*. The organic climbs up still higher levels. Our desire for knowledge of nature is a means by which the body wants to consummate itself. . . . *Ultimately it is not a matter of human beings at all: the human must be overcome.* (*KSA* 10, 24[20])

This is reminiscent of the aim in Zen to practice with the human body in order to realize an "overhuman" body.

In speaking of the body, Nietzsche makes a distinction that has a counterpart in Zen thought: namely, between the "I" and the "Self," giving priority to the latter as the more primordial phenomenon.

Sense and spirit are instruments and toys: behind them still lies the Self.
It rules and is also the I's ruler.
Behind your thoughts and feelings, my brother, stands a mighty commander, an unknown sage—he is called Self. He lives in your body, he is your body. (Z I, 3)

One reason why Nietzsche identifies the Self with the body is that they both *do* rather than say, they act without the need for reflection. This is again an idea that is found in Zen: the idea that the body is a more powerful "self" than the mind or spirit.

For any of the activities of the spirit to become actualized, as we said earlier, they have to be concretized through the body. The locus of this concretization is the earth, the world of nature that is the medium in which the body lives its life. As is particularly clear from Part One of *Zarathustra*, the problem of the body is exemplary of the larger issue of "the sense of the earth" (*der Sinn der Erde*). "You are not bridges to the *Übermensch*," says Zarathustra to the despisers of the body. The way to the *Übermensch* consists in developing a "higher body," which is equivalent, in the broader context of Nietzsche's philosophy, to a cultivating of a "sense of the earth," a realization of the world of nature. But let us see how this move through the body into the larger cosmos is effected in Zen Buddhism.[6]

III

In order fully to appreciate why Zen Buddhism lays so much emphasis on somatic practice, we must look at how it conceives the human being's relationship to nature, or what Nietzsche calls "the sense of the earth." The human body is itself a part of nature, and it is through the body that the human world and the natural world, the microcosm and the macrocosm, are connected with one another. As discussed earlier, the problem of I-lessness in human action leads to the problem of embodiment, and this in turn leads to the problem of nature, since bodily activity takes place in and is dependent on the world of nature. In Zen, the aim is to give up the small, egoistical I, which through reflection and thought tends to separate itself from the natural world, and realize oneself as the "great I" which is inseparable from the great world of nature. The way to this realization is through the "gate," so to speak, of the human body.

Dōgen attributes the following characterization of the relationship between the self and the earth to "an ancient Buddha":

The whole earth is the true body of the Buddha, the whole earth is the gateway to liberation, the whole earth is the eye of Vairochana Buddha, and the whole earth is the *dharmakāya* of the Buddhist self.[7]

At every moment the self lives as the body in relationship with the entire universe, but for the most part we tend to forget this and lose awareness of our constant relationship to the whole. When Gautama Buddha reached his great enlightenment, he is said to have said, "I and the earth have attained the Buddha Way simultaneously, and all things—mountains, rivers, plants, and trees—have become Buddhas [enlightened beings]." It was not the egoistical I of the Buddha that became enlightened, but rather a self-transcending, self-forgetting I, a great "I-less" I equivalent to a cosmic self. It is in this sense that Dōgen writes: "The term *jindaichi* [the whole earth] is intimately familiar to us. Infinite and unbounded we call the whole earth."[8]

The equivalence of the greater self and the whole earth means that the self's authentic activity takes place with awareness of the greater context. This kind of activity is exemplified in the bodhisattva ideal of Mahayana Buddhism, the bodhisattva being one who vows to work toward the salvation of all sentient beings prior to his own salvation. To appropriate this attitude of the bodhisattva is to experience oneself as born simultaneously with mountains, rivers, and the wide earth, and as acting in harmony with the Buddha. Zazen practice is designed to lead to just such a realization. As Dōgen explains it:

The activity of the Buddha always takes place simultaneously with the whole earth and with all sentient beings. If an activity does not take place with the whole earth it is not an activity of the Buddha's. All Buddhist practice necessarily takes place from start to finish with the whole earth and with all sentient beings.[9]

In spite of the differences between the traditions out of which Dōgen and Nietzsche grew and against which they reacted, we have seen that their views concerning the nature of the thinking I are remarkably similar. Although Dōgen is not, like Nietzsche, arguing against a tradition of subjectivity that radically separates the mind from the body, it is significant that they both adopt a position that emphasizes the body over the mind, soul, or spirit. While Dōgen advocates the somatic practice of zazen as a way of going beyond the egoistical self to a greater, I-less self, Nietzsche encourages a realization of the body as a "great reason" which does "I" rather than says "I."

The major difference between the two positions is that the body, for Nietzsche, still retains certain features of individuality, and indeed an individuality that confers a sense upon the earth while remaining to some extent separate from it, whereas Dōgen more or less identifies the I-less self and body with the earth and nature. While Nietzsche's ideas about the body appear to be based in considerations of evolutionary biology, Dōgen's ideas about somatic practice are grounded in an experience of religious awakening—even though they are subsequently elaborated through philosophical reflection. There is a correspondence again, however, in the fact that Nietzsche's condemnation of the traditional exaltation of rational spirit led him to develop a remarkable "metaphysics" of the body (even though he was denied the opportunity to publish a full elaboration of these ideas), while Dōgen's high esteem for somatic practice led him to develop (if not altogether consciously and explicitly) some ideas about the human body that were unusually profound.

Notes

1. Descartes, *Discourse on Method*, part 4; Kant, *Critique of Pure Reason*, 17, B 136.

2. See the chapter on Dōgen in Yuasa Yasuo, *The Body*, ed. Thomas P. Kasulis, trans. Nagatomo Shigenori and Thomas P. Kasulis (Albany, 1987), pp. 111–24.

3. *Shōbōgenzō*, "Zazengi."

4. Dōgen, *Zuimonki* II, 26.

5. *Shōbōgenzō*, "Raihaitokuzui."

6. EN—The original version of Professor Arifuku's paper contained a section which developed Nietzsche's views on nature and the natural; but since this is the topic of Professor Ōkōchi's contribution to the present volume, it has been omitted in this translation.

7. *Shōbōgenzō*, "Yuibutsu Yobutsu." The *dharmakāya* is the highest body— ineffable and non-substantiated—of the Buddha in his identity with the universe. The name "Vairochana" means, literally, "sun Buddha"; this deity represents the illuminating that exists everywhere.

8. *Shōbōgenzō*, "Yuibutsu Yobutsu."

9. Ibid.

14

The Eloquent Silence of Zarathustra

Sonoda Muneto, translated by *Graham Parkes* and
Setsuko Aihara

I

When Shakyamuni, sitting under the bodhi tree by the river Nairanjana, attained the highest level of enlightenment, he enjoyed the happiness of liberation while still meditating and thought to himself as follows: "The Dharma that I have finally attained is extremely profound, difficult, and subtle, and is beyond all thinking. Most people, however, are attached to the senses and worldly things; they are ensnared by greed and hatred, and so they may never understand the Dharma that I have attained. I shall therefore live quietly in this state of nirvana, without trying to preach the Dharma to others." When Brahma, Lord of the universe, realized that Shakyamuni was thinking along these lines, he quickly came down to him and implored him as follows: "Great Lord, please preach your teaching to the world. There are also people whose defilement of mind is minor. If they do not hear the teaching of the Dharma, they will become completely corrupted; but if they hear your teaching they may be able to attain enlightenment." Since Shakyamuni remained motionless, Brahma repeated his entreaty three times. Then Shakyamuni surveyed the world with his Buddha Eye. In the lotus pond there are blue lotuses and red lotuses and white lotuses. Some of them grow in the mud, remaining submerged beneath the surface of the water; others grow in the mud and reach the surface of the water; yet others grow in the mud and break through the surface of the water without being defiled by the muddiness. Thus there are some sentient beings with much defilement and some with less defilement, some who are dull and prone to evil doings and some who are brighter and inclined toward good deeds, and there are some who are difficult to preach to successfully and some who are easy to teach. After seeing that this was the situation in the world, Shakyamuni said to Brahma: "The Gate of Immortality is open to those who have ears," and thereupon announced his resolution to preach the Dharma. Thus he made the first turn of the Dharma wheel at Deer Park, and the highest Dharma came to be disseminated throughout the world.

During the summer and autumn of 1884 Nietzsche read *Das System des Vedanta* by his friend Paul Deussen and also Oldenberg's *Buddha: Sein Leben, seine Lehre, seine Gemeinde*.[1] In the *Nachlass* from that period one can find here and there excerpts and reading notes from both books, but it is difficult to determine with what kind of care Nietzsche was reading these texts. Part Three of *Thus Spoke Zarathustra* had been published in April of that year, and Nietzsche thought that with the appearance of this third part the work was complete. However, while he was pondering over a plan for a new work, it eventually came to take the form of Part Four of *Zarathustra*. His reading of the books mentioned above coincided with the time he was contemplating the further additions to *Zarathustra*.

The second part of Oldenberg's book recounts the life of the Buddha, and the story of the Buddha's attainment of enlightenment leading to the first turn of the Dharma wheel is told almost exactly as it first appears in the *Mahāvagga* [I.5.2]. Brahma kneels down before the Buddha and says humbly: "Indeed the world will collapse. Indeed, if your majesty resides in tranquility and does not preach the Dharma the world will be ruined." It seems that Nietzsche may be overlapping Zarathustra and the Buddha on the point of preaching the Dharma. A note from the *Nachlass* reads as follows: "Zarathustra 1. terrible tension: Zarathustra must *come* or else everything on earth is *lost*."[2] Needless to say, Zarathustra's going under (*Untergang*) begins as early as the Prologue of the work, and this "Zarathustra 1" might allude to a new Zarathustra book. But in any case it is clear that Nietzsche was constantly connecting the figure of Zarathustra with the mission of the announcement of the highest teaching of the Dharma, and so to examine *Zarathustra* in the context of the announcement or transmission of the truth will probably yield something of significance.

Great delusion prevailed until the Buddha resolved to disseminate the teaching of the Dharma. His resolve had to overcome doubts concerning the abilities of the people who would receive the Dharma as well as suspicion regarding language as a means of communication. However, as a spring that comes out of a high place has reason to fill up and overflow, the Buddha's love for sentient beings overcame his doubts concerning communication, and this is the source of the bodhisattva ideal in Mahayana Buddhism. While the story of the Buddha is concerned with the issue of the communication of the truth by way of language, Zarathustra's first descent from the mountain is prompted by the desire to "give [his wisdom] away and distribute it . . . to outstretched hands" and is informed by his self-awareness and self-confidence as the herald (Z Prologue, 1). Nevertheless, the issue of the communication of the truth in *Zarathustra* is already signalled by the fact that the thoughts to be told here are not to be spoken directly from the thinker's mouth but rather through the mask, so to speak, of Zarathustra. The composition of this book, the primary action in which is Zarathustra's *speaking*, is in itself an expression of Nietzsche's attitude toward the issues of the communication of truth through language and of language itself, and at the same time it suggests the uniqueness of the thoughts to be communicated here. While a direct comparison of Zarathustra's descent from the mountain with the Buddha's first turning of the Dharma wheel may not itself be significant,[3] it is worthwhile to inquire into Nietzsche's conception of language and to contrast it with oriental or Buddhist views, invoking these two cases as clues.

We must examine the view of language that is behind Nietzsche's being able to communicate only through the mask of Zarathustra. We should further ask what it is that Nietzsche was able to say in *Thus Spoke Zarathustra*, or, where he was unable to speak, what it is that he was able to communicate through his silence.

II

Although Nietzsche does not say a great deal concerning the essential nature of language, some of his most interesting and coherent observations occur in the short essay "On Truth and Lie in the Extra-Moral Sense," which he wrote in 1873 but left unpublished. This essay was strongly influenced by Schopenhauer's theory of understanding, but at the same time it importantly anticipates all of Nietzsche's views on language up until his late years. The piece begins with an account of the origin and meaning of language for humankind in the style of a fable. Nietzsche then asks whether there is such a thing as absolute truth, pure truth that is true in all cases, and proceeds to inquire into the origins of the "drive for truth." It is here that language, which supports the activity of acquiring knowledge, becomes an issue. But it does not become an issue merely as a means; rather, the point is that "the legislation of language also gives the first laws of truth: for it is here that the contrast between truth and lie first arises."[4] It is not that truth makes language possible, but rather that language is the basis for truth and for the ability to differentiate truth from lies. Through "the legislation of language" the chaotic world of becoming is for the first time given a certain order, and on the basis of the relations thus established the individual attains the goal of self-preservation. Things such as language, truth, and knowledge are after all simply devices created by the intellect for the sake of the preservation of the individual.

According to Nietzsche, language expresses nothing more than the relations of things to human beings, and is never able to grasp the essence of things. When the world is fastened and fixed within language, the truth of the world of becoming has already escaped this network. Language merely constructs a fictitious world of "Being." The arbitrariness of language appears most clearly in the formation of concepts: "Every concept arises through the equation of unequal things" (83/880). For example, in the real world there never exist two leaves that are identical. But the concept of "leaf" is formed as if "leaf," the *Ur-form* of a leaf, exists separately from any actual living thing, entirely disregarding individual differences. When we say the leaf is "red," this does not mean that we know "redness" itself. We simply call the neural stimulus that the object gives us "red," without there being any causal relationship between the stimulus from the object and the judgment "red" on the part of the subject. However, language goes on creating its own unique world of concepts, the world of grammar, regardless of the actual world. Nietzsche does not make explicit in this essay his mistrust of the subject-predicate structure that is the basis of all forms of judgment—and indeed of grammar in general—but it may be inferred from the above argument. The later works often point up the restrictions imposed by linguistic structure, and his criticisms are reflected in the fact that his style gradually becomes richer in substantives. In any case Nietzsche holds that language establishes a pyramidal order of grades and classes and creates a new world consisting of rules, priorities, subordinations, and definitions of boundaries, such that this world eventually comes to regulate the actual world.

In an aphorism from *Human, All Too Human* he writes about the "new world" created by language:

The significance of language for the evolution of culture lies in this, that human beings set up in language a separate world beside the other world, a place they took to be so firmly set that, standing upon it, they could lift the rest of the world off its hinges and make themselves master of it. To the extent that human beings have for long ages believed in the concepts and names of things as in *aeternae veritates* they have appropriated to themselves that pride by which they raised themselves above the animal: they really thought that in language they possessed knowledge of the world. . . . Here [in science], too, it is from the *belief that the truth has been discovered* that the mightiest sources of energy have flowed. A great deal later—only now—it dawns on people that with their faith in language they have propagated a tremendous error. Happily, it is too late for the evolution of reason, which depends on this faith, to be again put back. (*HA* I, 11)

Nietzsche also says that human beings "have fantasized" that they possess in language not just inscriptions but the highest knowledge about things, but that this world of language is an error and a fabrication. His saying that the realization of this error "fortunately" came too late, is a manifestation of the strong positivistic attitude and "Enlightenment"-character of his middle period. The nuance of these statements is slightly different from the tone of "On Truth and Lie," but the basic attitude of suspicion toward language as a means to the attainment and communication of truth remains even after *Human, All Too Human.*

There are also passages in "On Truth and Lie," however, where Nietzsche adopts a somewhat different viewpoint when talking about language. He argues that the world of becoming is first given as a neural stimulus, which is then transformed into an image and fixed. This is the first stage of metaphor. The image is then transformed into a sound, and thus the word is born. Language thus comes about through an extremely bold leap, a metastasis into an entirely different realm. In the business of speaking language a profound human pleasure finds expression. Nietzsche even thinks that "to dispense with (*wegrechnen*) the fundamental drive to the formation of metaphors" would be tantamount to "dispensing with humanity" (89/887). In the activity of expressing certain phenomena through language, human beings participate in the fundamental process of life and in the wonderful power of creative fantasy. Indeed, when the primordial world of metaphor is forgotten, spoken words necessarily become rigidified into "concepts" and incorporated into the systematic framework of truth. On the other hand, in the activity of speaking in metaphor the vital pleasure of life is always directly manifested.

In this essay Nietzsche argues, on the one hand, that language is a mere tool invented by the intellect for the sake of self-preservation, and he offers a sober critique of the drive for truth and of the kind of "truth" fabricated by language. On the other hand, he remains fully cognizant of the principle of creative life which lurks not in words spoken but in the activity of speaking words: "This drive to the formation of metaphors, the fundamental human drive . . . is not in fact vanquished and is scarcely subdued by the fact that from its own most ephemeral products, the concepts, a regular and rigid new world is constructed as its prison" (88–89/887). He goes on to elaborate a figure of the intellect as an artist engaged in the creative employment of language:

[The intellect] is never more luxuriant, richer, prouder, more clever and more daring. With creative pleasure it throws metaphors into confusion and displaces the stones of abstractions, so that, for example, it designates the stream as the moving path that carries human beings where they would otherwise walk. It has now thrown the token of bondage from itself: at other times it endeavors, with gloomy officiousness, to show the way and to demonstrate the tools to a poor individual who covets existence, and like a servant who goes in search of booty and prey for his master it has now become the master and dares to wipe from its face the expression of indigence. . . . That framework and planking of concepts to which the needy human being clings his whole life long in order to preserve himself, has become for the liberated intellect nothing but a scaffolding and toy for its most audacious feats: and when it smashes this framework to pieces, throws it into confusion, and puts it back together in an ironic fashion, pairing the most alien things and separating the closest, it is demonstrating that it has no need of these makeshifts of indigence and that it will now be guided by intuitions rather than concepts. (90/888)

Language for this kind of artist is not a tool for the purpose of self-expression, but is rather an expression of the life-force itself. Nature's fundamental creative force itself overflows through the mouths of human beings. The figure of the artist depicted here is similar to the figure of the lyric poet which Nietzsche describes in *The Birth of Tragedy* as a model of the process by which tragedy is born. In the musical ecstasy of the Dionysiac artist, the lyric poet fuses himself with the Primal Unity, which is filled with agony and contradiction. This is a state in which subjectivity has already been abandoned. This musical condition is now projected as an image under the operation of the Apollinian drive that is the second fundamental drive of nature. After undergoing a mystical loss of self, the lyric poet sings "I!" referring to his self which has been further heightened as an Apollinian image. But this "I" is not identical with the "I" in the world of conditioned reality.

To escape in ecstasy from the empirical ego and to unite with nature itself is, for Nietzsche, the basis of the lyric and of poetic language in general. But in *The Birth of Tragedy* he suggests that the seeds of *all* dramatic art lie here. In this condition one becomes aware of the ease with which the self can be transformed into an other. For Nietzsche lyric and drama are similar insofar as they both have musical ecstasy as their womb. The difference is that while the lyric poet says "I" as usual, even in ecstasy, the dramatist speaks as the person into whom he has transformed himself. The words of the poet who creates in ecstasy are close to an undifferentiated cry, and are music and gesture themselves. In either case the language uttered is not the language of communication in which rigid concepts are constituted, but rather the expression and overflow of the life-force itself: it functions as intuitive communication only among those who are experiencing together the ecstasy and metamorphosis in ecstasy.

This fundamental creative activity of language is also related to the view of language embodied in Nietzsche's praise of Wagner's "poetic nature" in the essay "Richard Wagner in Bayreuth": "Wagner forced language back into its primal condition, where it hardly thinks anything in concepts, but is still itself poetry, image, and feeling" (*UM* IV, 9). But except where Nietzsche later talks about the process of writing *Zarathustra*, these kinds of statement about language are restricted to this early period. By contrast, the other view of language to be found in "On Truth and Lie," which points up the fragmentary and fictitious nature of language as a means to the cognition and communication of truth, endures throughout Nietzsche's work. Given such an ambivalent view of language, even though he harbors a deep mistrust of language in certain respects, Nietzsche, nevertheless, continues to attempt to communicate through language. Sometimes he plunges himself into lyrical ecstasy and sings as if he himself were transformed into a Dionysiac figure. But when he tries to communicate ideas that are difficult to express in concepts, his favorite strategy is to speak through a created persona—to speak deliberately through a mask. In *The Gay Science* he puts the first intimation of the thought of eternal recurrence into the mouth of a demon [*GS* 341], and the "death of God" is first proclaimed by a madman who runs through the streets carrying a lantern in broad daylight [*GS* 125]. Shortly thereafter, Nietzsche attempts to communicate these ideas by speaking through the mask of the character Zarathustra.

III

In the section of *Ecce Homo* that deals with *Thus Spoke Zarathustra*, Nietzsche writes that "the fundamental conception of the work, the idea of eternal recurrence, this highest formula of affirmation that is at all attainable" dates from August of 1881. He wrote *Zarathustra* in order to communicate the idea of eternal recurrence, which he considered "the heaviest thought," the one most difficult to understand and the heaviest weight in the overcoming of nihilism. In "The Convalescent" in Part Three, his animals call Zarathustra the "teacher of eternal recurrence." In spite of this, however, the idea is hardly ever spoken of directly by Zarathustra himself.

The major themes announced in the Prologue are the death of God and the *Übermensch*, while the idea of eternal recurrence is merely alluded to by the image of Zarathustra's eagle and serpent who appear circling high above his head at the end of the Prologue. The major themes of Parts One and Two are the self-overcoming that is necessary for the attainment of the condition of the *Übermensch*, the images of the virtues appropriate to this task, and the idea of the liberation of the will. When, in Part Three, the idea of recurrence finally begins to figure importantly, it is treated as a vague "vision and enigma" which Zarathustra recounts to a crew of sailors, or it is spoken through the mouths of the animals, or else sung in a mood of ecstasy. Part Four ends with Zarathustra's finally resolving to announce the idea of recurrence, at the point where he is about to "go under" for the third time. The fundamental idea of the book is not, then, really spoken about directly until the end.

The first published mention of the idea of recurrence is aphorism 341 of *The Gay Science*—but even here it is framed by the question: "What if, some day or night a demon were to steal after you in your loneliest loneliness, and were to say to you . . . ?" The thought is adumbrated in terms that are deliberately vague and allusive, couched in layers of conditional and interrogative sentences. It seems as if the idea is in constant fear of being spoken of explicitly.

We often say things like "the content of a certain thought takes a certain form of expression." However, genuine thoughts, for Nietzsche, are not the kinds of thing that can be separated into content and form. In order for a thought to be communicated fully, the questions of when, by whom, how, and to whom the thought is expressed are of crucial importance. In Buddhist sutras one usually finds in the opening section a statement of when, where, by whom, and to whom the "content" is recounted, as well as how it was heard and how it was believed (belief/ *shin*, hearing/*mon*, time/*ji*, speaker/*shu*, place/*sho*, audience/*shû*). To have all six elements properly in place is called "*rokuji jōju*" (Fulfillment of the Six Elements) and is regarded as a necessary condition for the communication of truth. Something akin to this *rokuji jōju* would seem to be an integral part of the thought of recurrence, insofar as it cannot fully be what it is as long as it is merely expressed abstractly and conceptually. In this sense we could say that Nietzsche had to compose *Zarathustra* in order to provide a unique site in which to communicate this most difficult of thoughts.

The idea of eternal recurrence is first presented in Part Three, "On the Vision and Enigma," and the scene makes clear that the identity of the audience is of great importance. The audience addressed by Zarathustra after a silence of two days consists of a crew of "bold sailors." He begins his speech by saying:

To you, the bold venturers and adventurers, and whoever has embarked with cunning sails on dreadful seas,
    to you who are intoxicated by riddles, who take pleasure in twilight, whose soul is lured by flutes to every treacherous abyss,
    for you do not want to feel for a thread with cowardly hand; and where you can *guess* you hate to *calculate*—
    to you alone do I tell this riddle that I *saw* . . . (Z III, 2 1)[5]

Zarathustra tries to present the idea of recurrence as a vision and a riddle to an audience of sailors who prefer to "guess" intuitively rather than to "perform logical deductions." The idea is not to be communicated by way of a ladder of concepts or logic, nor is it presented as something complete in itself. It wants to be perceived intuitively and guessed both in the process as it gradually arises and also at the moment when it "flashes." Zarathustra must himself mature as the teacher of eternal recurrence, and at the same time he must wait for a suitable audience of disciples to emerge. *Thus Spoke Zarathustra* is then the story of Zarathustra's silence if we look at it with respect to the idea of eternal recurrence. But now the question is what this silence of Zarathustra's is saying about eternal recurrence. Zarathustra's eloquence is formidable, but there are many scenes in which it is his silence that implies something deeply impressive. I should like now to explore the meaning of that silence by selecting some of those scenes.

The Prologue begins with Zarathustra's addressing the sun, and his speech introduces a theme that runs throughout the entire work.

Great star! What would your happiness be, if you had not those for whom you shine!
    You have come up here to my cave for ten years: you would have grown weary of your light and of this journey, without me, my eagle, and my serpent.
    But we waited for you every morning, took from you your overflow and blessed you for it. (Z Prologue, 1)

As far as the relations between one who gives with endless generosity and one who receives are concerned, the happiness of the one who gives is provided precisely by the existence of the one who gladly receives, and it is this condition that motivates Zarathustra's descent from the mountaintop. He realizes that he needs "hands outstretched to receive." This is the background to "Zarathustra's Prologue," which he delivers to an audience of townspeople who have gathered in a marketplace to watch a performance by a tightrope walker. After speaking for a while about the *Übermensch*, Zarathustra suddenly falls silent:

When Zarathustra had spoken these words he looked again at the people and fell silent. There they stand (he said to his heart), there they laugh: they do not understand me, I am not the mouth for these ears. (Z Prologue, 5)

After picking up his spirits, Zarathustra goes to talk about the "last human," but realizes that, after all, his words are not having the desired effect. He then speaks to his heart as follows:

They do not understand me: I am not the mouth for these ears.
    Perhaps I have lived too long in the mountains, listened too much to the trees and the streams. . . .

Through delivering these first speeches Zarathustra comes to understand that he should first seek a suitable audience, and that the maturing of the listening ear is a presupposition for the communication of truth. His silence here is one compelled by the circumstances.

In Part One, Zarathustra stays in the town called "The Motley Cow," acquires some trustworthy disciples, and speaks to them of the sense of the great earth, of the body, and of the creation of new values. But after a while he bids his disciples farewell and returns to his mountaintop retreat. On his departure, his disciples present Zarathustra with a staff. Leaning on this staff, he speaks to them of "the bestowing virtue" and of love for the great earth—but in the middle of his speech he suddenly breaks off: "When Zarathustra had said these words, he fell silent, like one who has not said his last word; long he balanced his staff doubtfully in his hand" (Z I, 22 §3). The staff has a golden handle on which a serpent is curled around a sun. Taking notice of this golden handle, Zarathustra praises the virtue of gold and the sun which give light with endless generosity: "a golden sun and around it the serpent of knowledge." The image of the serpent wound around the sun suggests that the highest knowledge is the idea of eternal recurrence. The gift of the staff happens to remind him of his mission as the teacher of eternal recurrence, but he is not yet able to resolve to announce the idea. When

Zarathustra eventually speaks again, it is to say that the disciples should
not simply seek a teacher but should first seek themselves and find
themselves: they have not yet matured sufficiently to be able to assimilate the thought of eternal recurrence. Zarathustra's silence here is an
indication of his internal struggle, and suggests the need for a ripening
of the time for the communication of truth.

Part Two of the book contains hardly any reference to the thought of
eternal recurrence. Nevertheless, the tension between Zarathustra's mission to communicate the thought and the time's not being ripe for it is
heightened, and reaches its climax in the conversation between Zarathustra and the "voice without voice" in the last chapter, "The Stillest
Hour" (Z III, 22). But before examining this conversation I should like
to consider some passages from "On Redemption," which prefigure the
theme of the later chapter. There Zarathustra speaks of "the will," and
of redemption of the past by way of will, before an audience of cripples
and beggars:

To redeem the past and to transform every "It was" into an "I wanted it
thus!"—that alone do I call redemption!
    Will—that is the great liberator and bringer of joy: thus I have taught
you, my friends! But now learn this as well: the will itself is still a prisoner.
(Z II, 20)

Will liberates, but it cannot will backward: "That time does not run
backwards, that is [the will's] wrath; 'That which was'—that is the stone
which it cannot roll away." And yet Zarathustra does not, as Schopenhauer does, teach a way of emancipating oneself from the will and of
making desire into non-desire. The creative will must say, "But I will it
thus! Thus shall I will it!" to the very end.

    But has it ever spoken thus? And when will this take place? Has the will yet
been unharnessed from its own folly?
    Has the will become its own redeemer and bringer of joy? Has it unlearned
the spirit of revenge and all teeth-gnashing?
    And who has taught it to be reconciled with time, and higher things than
reconciliation?
    The will that is the will to power must will something higher than all rec-
onciliation—but how shall that happen? Who has taught it to will backwards,
too?

But then Zarathustra suddenly falls silent:

At this point of his speech Zarathustra suddenly stopped and looked exactly like
a man seized by extremest terror. With a terrified gaze he looked at his disciples;

his gaze transpierced their thoughts and the thoughts behind their thoughts as if with arrows.

What is implied behind this silence is again the idea of eternal recurrence. Will cannot will backward. But if all things are to return eternally, to will forward means to will the past as it is; the idea of eternal recurrence is itself what teaches the will to be reconciled with time. And yet Zarathustra is still unable to give voice to the idea. A hunchback in the audience sees through the meaning of this silence, realizing that Zarathustra has not yet said what he should be saying: ". . . and with pupils one may well tell tales out of school. But why does Zarathustra speak to his pupils differently—than to himself?"

In the conversation in "The Stillest Hour" the "voiceless voice" orders Zarathustra to speak his last words soon. "Yes, I know it," he replies, "but I do not want to say it." His excuse is that he has not yet sufficiently ripened to speak of "it." Here is another indication that the book that has the thought of recurrence as its core is less concerned with the thought itself than with the issue of how to elaborate the appropriate site, or situation, for the successful communication of the thought. The thought wants to be communicated not as something fully formed, but as something in the process of arising gradually and in the moment of being opened up.

IV

In the middle of Part Three of *Zarathustra*, the protagonist gives up trying to proclaim the idea of eternal recurrence and returns to his solitude up in the mountains. He no longer talks to people or to any disciples: he converses only with his animals and with his own heart. (In Part Four as well he does not address people in the "world below," but speaks only to the "higher humans" who have come up to the mountaintop in order to find him.) When he returns to his cave, his solitude welcomes him gently, saying to him, "Here all things come caressingly to your discourse and flatter you: for they want to ride upon your back. Upon every image you here ride to every truth" (Z III, 9). In his solitude language is freed from the task of communication and can transform the world as it is into sound and image with gay abandon. In solitude language can go back to that primordial "joy in creation." Thinking back to his experiences in the world below from the standpoint of his solitude, Zarathustra says:

Here, the words and word-chests of all being spring open for me: all being here wants to become words, all becoming here wants to learn from me how to speak.

Down there, however—all speech is in vain! There, the best wisdom is to forget and to pass by: I have learned *that*—now! . . .
But down there, everything speaks, everything is unheard. . . .
Everything among them speaks, no one knows any longer how to understand. (Z III, 9)

The chapter entitled "The Convalescent" tells of how Zarathustra overcomes the greatest nausea, which has been caused by the dark and terrifying aspect of the idea of recurrence: "Man returns eternally! The small man returns eternally!" (Z III, 13 §2). His animals comfort him with gentle conversation as he recuperates from his nausea. In reply he says to them:

Oh my animals, go on talking and let me listen! Your talking is such refreshment: where there is talking the world is like a garden to me.
How sweet it is, that words and tones are there: are words and tones not rainbows and seeming-bridges between what is eternally separated?

Words cannot capture the essence of things as they are. At the moment when they might succeed in doing so, the world constructed by language has already become something different from the actual world. Words are merely "rainbows and seeming-bridges"—although for the convalescent the pleasure of constructing bridges of illusion is the pleasure of fresh life and creation.

Are things not given names and tones so that human beings may refresh themselves with things? Speaking is a beautiful foolery: with it human beings dance over all things.
How sweet is all speech and all the lies of music! With tones our love dances upon many-colored rainbows.

At the urging of his animals, Zarathustra resolves upon his mission to be the teacher of the eternal recurrence, but he is no longer going to try to teach by speaking, but rather by *singing*—which is the way words eternally return to the joy of the moment when they arise as rainbow-bridges. After the conversation with his animals Zarathustra falls into a profound silence which lasts a long time. The world of tranquility and silence afforded by solitude is where truth may arise and new words emerge. Silence here is not silence as the negation of speech, as it has been up to this point in the text: it is rather the silence in which a kind of truth may emerge. Zarathustra then conducts a private conversation with his own soul in silence, and sings songs to praise life and life's eternal recurrence.
Karl Jaspers touches on the issue of the "communication" of existen-

tial truth in his book *Vernunft und Existenz*, saying that truth itself must be in the process of "becoming" (*werdend*) in order for genuine communication to be possible.[6] Truth has to be the kind of truth that is itself communication, and when it is formalized as a dogma it is transformed into mere "knowledge of something." This means that truth experienced existentially is able to manifest its true depths at the point where one runs up against the limits of communication by language. Jaspers is not talking exclusively about the essence of language here, but is rather saying that in any case "truth" is fulfillable only "existentially and historically," and is something that can be not spoken "of" (*von*) but only "out of" (*aus*). Finally he concludes: "The ultimate in thinking, as in communication, is remaining silent."

Nietzsche is not, however, trying to describe the world of silence itself in *Thus Spoke Zarathustra*; he is rather concerned to show that when spoken language exhausts itself by tracing the relations that concepts weave—by becoming metaphysical language—the resultant silence, tranquility itself, becomes after all a kind of language and may gradually emerge as truth. He tries to open up a world in which it is not the language of understanding or of individual feelings that emerges, but where language itself arises as a primordial force that desires to manifest itself. In Part Four of *Zarathustra*, the sound of the bell which comes up from the deep valley to the ears of all those who have wandered outside Zarathustra's cave at midnight, after the farcical performances of the "higher humans" are over, can be said to symbolize a truth arising out of silence. Zarathustra then teaches the meaning of each stroke of the bell by singing the "Nightwanderer-Song" (IV, 19), which embodies the heart of the thought of recurrence. The absence of any phrase corresponding to the twelfth stroke of the bell may suggest a truth that is beyond all language.

We have examined several scenes from *Thus Spoke Zarathustra*, focusing on Zarathustra's silence, which was sometimes due to the lack of a suitable audience, sometimes to the audience's not being mature enough for what was to be said, sometimes to the immaturity of the speaker himself or to nausea at the implications of the thought—all instances of the "impossibility of verbal communication." On the other hand, Zarathustra's silence in the solitude of the mountains is silence as a place in which truth may itself speak. In this silence he experiences the force of truth itself becoming language and emerging. The next morning Zarathustra prepares to go down again, as at the beginning of the Prologue, in order to seek a new site for the communication of the thought, encouraged by the appearance of the sign of the "laughing lion." He moves repeatedly from speech to silence and back, and indeed the entire work has the structure of an endless cycling between speech and silence.

In a note from the *Nachlass* from the 1880s (one that the editor of *The Will to Power* placed at the beginning of the book), Nietzsche writes: "Great things demand that one remain silent about them . . ." (*WP* Preface, 1). The "great things" referred to here include such things as European nihilism, the establishment of new values, and the idea of eternal recurrence. These great things, which have to do with two thousand years of Europe's history and its future, would rather not be spoken of at all than be spoken of only half-way. For the site of confrontation with great things, it is silence that is appropriate. However, Nietzsche goes on to say ". . . or else speak greatly: greatly, meaning cynically and innocently." Once again he reverts, after all, to saying things.

V

The *Vimalakīrtinirdeśa* is one of the earlier Mahayana sutras, and is distinguished not only by its dramatic construction but also by the fact that it does not, like most sutras, recount the speeches and deeds of Shakyamuni, but rather has as its protagonist a rich and worldly sage by the name of Vimalakirti. For Mahayana Buddhism samsara is essentially the same as nirvana, and so it is in our everyday world that the Dharma operates and shows itself. The ideal of Buddhism, beneficence as the practice of emptiness, is therefore to be realized in secular living itself. From this is born the idea of renouncing the life of the priest and of realizing Buddhist ideals in the existence of the layperson. Among the sutras based on this idea, the *Vimalakīrtinirdeśa* most clearly express the intuition of emptiness. In particular, the ninth chapter, which is entitled "Incorporation of the Teaching of Nonduality," is the high point of the work.

One day Vimalakirti fell ill. Shakyamuni tells his disciples to pay a visit to his sickbed, but they are in such awe of Vimalakirti—not only because of his enlightenment but also because of his eloquence—that no one dares to go to him. Eventually the bodhisattva Manjushri has to undertake the task. In the expectation of being able to attend the profound and holy conversation between Vimalakirti and Manjushri, thirty-two bodhisattvas and numerous saints go along too. There then ensues in Vimalakirti's castle a magnificent conversation about the Dharma between the sick host and his visitors. After some discussion of the Holy Path and the creatures that are to be led to salvation, Vimalakirti asks—in a changed voice—each one of the bodhisattvas what it really means to say that a bodhisattva embodies the holy teaching of the "nondual." Thereupon, each of the thirty-two bodhisattvas answers, one after the other, and a panorama of the purest and innermost spirit of Mahayana Buddhism unfolds.

One bodhisattva responds: "Arising and passing away are two things that are opposed. But since no being arises, none passes away either. To know that nothing arises is to embody the teaching of the nondual." Another says: "Impurity and purity are two things that are opposed. But when one contemplates impurity carefully, the delusion of purity vanishes as well. To tread the path on which all delusion is shattered is to embody the teaching of the nondual." A third then answers: "Life-and-death and nirvana are two things that are opposed. But when one sees the truth of life-and-death clearly, there is no life or death, no bondage, no salvation; nothing arises, nothing passes away: to realize this is to embody the teaching of the nondual." Further pairs of opposites are mentioned—desire and innocence, good and evil, happiness and misery, the profane and the sacred, the phenomenal and the empty, and so forth—the validity of which is then denied. When all thirty-two bodhisattvas have responded, Vimalakirti directs the same question to Manjushri. The latter replies: "What has been said is certainly true, but all of it is still dual. Not to speak, no words, not to say or express anything, not to point, not even any not-speaking. This is what embodying the nondual is." Manjushri then asks Vimalakirti himself to say something about the nondual. His response—not a word, absolute silence.

Manjushri's answer exemplifies the peak of Mahayana Buddhism and its intuition of emptiness. Everything that appears to have its own immutable essence is in fact only something that has become, and thus something perishable. Every being that is differentiated by means of categories is no real being, but is something that is merely realized through and as language. Differentiation by means of language tends to cover up the truth of the Dharma. Only when one lets go of language does one see the truth of all that has been formed, the truth of emptiness. Where everything is empty, there is no differentiation, and so no duality. When one lets go of all ideas, concepts, propositions—all language—there alone is the perfection of wisdom. The Mahayana view of language, or rather skepticism about language, is fully evident here, especially in the idea of *pāramitā*. Vimalakirti's silence expresses his agreement with Manjushri's answer—but not only that. He himself shows how one embodies the nondual, how the truth of the Dharma unfolds. In the face of this response Manjushri bursts out in admiration:

"Bravo, Vimalakirti, your silence resounds like a hundred peals of thunder!" Five thousand among the saints who were present were able to embody the "teaching of the nondual" and appropriate the truth that nothing arises. So it is reported in the *Vimalakīrtinirdeśa Sūtra*.

Nietzsche's mistrust of language as something that constructs a world separate from the world of actual becoming and covers up the essence of things is somewhat similar to the attitude of Mahayana Buddhism that centers around the idea of *prajñāpāramitā*. And yet Nietzsche had to employ the medium of language after all in order to communicate the idea of eternal recurrence, and he had to create a unique site of communication called *Thus Spoke Zarathustra* in order to communicate truth as a vital force. In this work not only things spoken but also things not spoken—and silence itself—help to project the uniqueness of the truth that is to be communicated. The highest teaching attained by Shakyamuni watered people's hearts just as a mountain spring overflows down to the valleys, and it manifests its ultimate form in the silence of Vimalakirti. Zarathustra, too, goes down to the world of human beings in order to communicate the idea of eternal recurrence, but he returns to the world of silence having understood the hopelessness of that kind of communication. But after going back and forth between speech and silence, he reverts after all to the world of language and speech. While retaining his profound mistrust of language, he nevertheless repeatedly returns to the joy of "speaking," of "expressing and communicating," the "fundamental human drive." This eternal return to expression and speech, in contrast to the oriental world of silence, may be understood as the destiny of the West.

Notes

1. EN—The story of the Buddha recounted in the preceding paragraph appears in Hermann Oldenberg's *Buddha*, 5th ed. (Stuttgart and Berlin, 1906), pp. 142–45—an early edition of which was in Nietzsche's library.

2. EN—*KSA* 11, 26[222]. A number of the notes from the summer and autumn of 1884 refer to Indian philosophy: see 26[193]–26[229].

3. If one were to understand Zarathustra as a bodhisattva figure, the old saint who appears in the second section of the Prologue would perhaps correspond to a Pratekya-Buddha.

4. EN—"On Truth and Lie in a Nonmoral Sense" in *Philosophy and Truth*, p. 81 (*KSA* 1, p. 877). Subsequent references to this translation (occasionally somewhat modified) will be made simply by the page number, followed by the page number of the original German in *KSA* 1.

5. EN—In some of the quotations from *Zarathustra* which follow I have departed somewhat from the Hollingdale translation in order to incline toward Professor Sonoda's Japanese renderings.

6. Karl Jaspers, *Vernunft und Existenz* (Bremen, 1949), lecture 3. (Available in English translation as *Reason and Existence*.)

Contributors

Joan Stambaugh of Hunter College at the City University of New York is the author of *Nietzsche's Thought of Eternal Return, The Problem of Time in Nietzsche, The Real Is Not the Rational, Impermanence Is Buddha-Nature: Dōgen's Understanding of Temporality,* and *Thoughts on Heidegger.*

Eberhard Scheiffele of Waseda University in Tokyo has taught *Germanistik* in Japan since 1972. He has published numerous essays on literary theory, philosophical hermeneutics, and eighteenth-, nineteenth- and twentieth-century German literature.

Johann Figl of the University of Vienna is the author of a book on Nietzsche's thought in the context of the philosophy of religion entitled *Dialektik der Gewalt* as well as a study of Nietzsche's hermeneutics: *Interpretation als philosophisches Prinzip: Nietzsches universale Theorie der Auslegung imspäten Nachlass.*

Michel Hulin of the Sorbonne is a comparative philosopher and the author of *Le principe de l'Ego dans la pensée indienne classique: la notion d'ahamkara, Le Mrgendragama: Sections de la Doctrine et du Yoga, La doctrine secrète de la Déesse Tripura, La face cachée du temps: Essai sur l'imaginaire de l'au delà, Sept récits initiatiques tirés du Yogavasistha,* and *Hegel et l'orient.*

Mervyn Sprung, emeritus from Brock University in Ontario, is the editor of and a contributor to *The Problem of Two Truths in Buddhism and Vedanta* and *The Question of Being: East-West Perspectives,* and the translator of *Lucid Exposition of the Middle Way: The Essential Chap-*

ters from the Prasannapada of Candrakirti. He is also the author of *The Magic of Unknowing.*

Glen Martin of Radford University in Virginia is the author of *From Nietzsche to Wittgenstein: The Problem of Truth and Nihilism in the Modern World,* as well articles in philosophical journals on the metaphysical and religious dimensions of these thinkers.

Chen Guying of Beijing University also teaches part of every year in the Department of East Asian Studies at U. C. Berkeley. He is the author of *Lao Tzu: Texts, Notes, and Comments* and *Beiju Zhexuejia Nicai* (The tragic philosopher Nietzsche), and has been a pioneer in the field of comparing Nietzsche's ideas with classical Daoist philosophy.

Roger T. Ames of the University of Hawaii edits the journal *Philosophy East and West.* He is the author of *The Art of Rulership* (a study of the political philosophy of the *Huai Nan Zi*), co-author of *Thinking Through Confucius,* and co-editor of *Nature in Asian Traditions of Thought: Essays in Environmental Philosophy.*

David A. Kelly of the Contemporary China Centre at Australian National University is the co-author of *Chinese Marxism in the Post-Mao Era,* and has published a number of articles on contemporary and modern Chinese intellecual and social history.

Ōkōchi Ryōgi of Kobé University has contributed a number of essays to *Nietzsche-Studien* and is the author of *Nīche to Bukkyō* (Nietzsche and Buddhism), *Jinen no fukken: Nīche no kagaku-hihan to Shinran no jinen hōni* (The restoration of nature: Nietzsche's critique of science and Shinran's idea of natural spontaneity). He is also one of the Japanese translators of the Critical Edition of Nietzsche's *Werke.*

Arifuku Kōgaku of Kyoto University specializes in both German philosophy and Zen Buddhist thought. He is the editor of *Rinrigaku towa nani ka* (What is ethics?), and the author of *Dōgen no sekai* (The world of Dōgen) and *Kanto no chōetsuronteki shutaisei no tetsugaku* (Kant's philosophy of transcendental subjectivity).

Sonoda Muneto of Osaka City University is the author of *Shinran und die Jodo-Shinshu: Das Menschenbild im neueren japanischen Buddhis-*

mus (Shinran and the Pure Land School: The view of humanity in recent Japanese Buddhism) as well as numerous articles in German and Japanese on Nietzsche and Shin Buddhism. He is also the most recent translator of *Thus Spoke Zarathustra* into Japanese.

Index

DATE DUE

GAYLORD   PRINTED IN U.S.A.